DON'T PANIC!

THE

UNAUTHORISED

DAD'S ARMY

HANDBOOK

HAYDEN GRIBBLE

ISBN 978-1-7393752-0-1

Printed and bound by Lightning Source, Milton Keynes, England

www.haydengribbleauthor.com

Dedicated to the memory of my Grandfathers -
Herbert Gribble and Kenneth Laskey.

Thanks for everything.

CHAPTERS

INTRODUCTION

It was Wednesday, November 7th December 2012. I was enjoying a gluttony of tennis at London's O2 Arena and had just bared witness to a close yet ultimately disappointing clash between two of the world's biggest stars, Novak Djokovic and Great Britain's very own champion, Andy Murray.

Irked by the Brit's defeat, I wandered through the crowds away from the arena to an all-you-can-eat restaurant hidden away in the stadium's bright and colourful walkways of shops and cafes. For me, this day out was a welcome break and a treat for the early research and work I had put into the book you are reading right now. After picking up some food, I went to sit down at a table in the centre of the room, just another member of the feeding frenzy during a break in play.

I sat back and thought to myself - not about the sporting highlight of the day so far - but of the work I had put into my first, proper book. I had reviewed just a handful of episodes, still in the monochrome early days of the show I was writing about, knowing full well that I still had the vast majority of 80 episodes to go.

I shook my head, snapping myself out of the panic I could feel washing over me, and I decided to check the news on my phone.

I had felt a little cut off from the world whilst I had been inside the formerly-known Millennium Dome in a bubble of sport, so I had a gander at the news. To my surprise, I sat, mouth open in shock and sadness as I read the headline that stared back at me in all its digital brightness...

'Clive Dunn, Dad's Army actor, dies aged 92'

The next thing I noticed was a little picture of an unopened envelope at the top of the display screen. I immediately scrolled down to reveal a text from my twelve-year-old sister, telling me the exact same news. I text her back and her reply, whilst being a little less punctual than the way that the BBC had put his passing in the article was more poignant to me than any words that a professional journalist had written.

'Yer, we just heard. Sad, innit. I loved him in it.'

The thing that got me about this short exchange was that this was from a girl who had never met this man and who was a whole 80 years younger than Dunn himself. But her exposure to *Dad's Army* through regular repeats that she must have caught every time I watched them over the years and my recent commission to write a book about the show itself, had meant that she had taken a part of the show to heart, and a character created and realised nearly 45 years previous to that day's outing to the ATP World Tour still had the brilliance, the genius and the endurance to be loved in this noisy, technological modern day.

Dad's Army is a show that still has the same magic that made fans of all ages fall in love with it back in the late 1960's and 1970's. It poked fun at a bygone time, whilst also celebrating the bravery, the resilience and the strong willed stiff-upper-lip spirit of dear old Blighty during its darkest hour.

To my young, wide eyes it made wartime Britain look fun, much in the way that I thought *Porridge* made going to prison look like a jolly boy's hotel for those who were just slightly naughtier than your average Joe.

It appeals to many people in many ways and unlike some modern-day sitcoms - out dated before they're time and crude in humour to get the jokes across - it never gets old and continues to build a fan base decades after many of the principal cast have passed away.

It has outlived many of those creative minds who made it such a success but they live on through the power of the show's endless popularity. And for me, it has rescued me on more than a few occasions. In the days when I need a boost I can forget about my tiresome, dreary days temping whilst I hope my writing gets me places I want to go and come home, relax and put a DVD in and lose myself in the adventures of the Walmington-on-Sea Home Guard.

There is something so wholesome, so rich in texture about *Dad's Army* that makes it just as popular today as it was when it first delighted millions.

The characters, no matter how pompous, laid back, hyperactive, back-stabbing, scheming, gentle, immature and rude they be (you can probably guess the characters by those descriptions) entertain and enthral for half an hour and completely remove you from the hustle of modern life.

It is a better de-stress agent than a massage and a hot bath. And just as comforting.

Like many people I missed the show when it was originally broadcast but I soon caught the *Dad's Army* bug during the carefree decade that was the 1990's. It was a popular show amongst my primary school demographic (yes, I really am that young, sorry!) To this day, there are a number of reasons why I think that this is the case.

We all love to see people behaving badly, so it was enthralling to see a bunch of old men act like boy scouts when their parent's backs are turned plus it was bloody funny to watch.

Still is too. Also - for me it lent weight to the stories I was told by my father's parents about the Second World War (my Grandfather had been a member of the Enfield Home Guard) and at times it was like peeking through a looking glass into a time that they had both lived in, so, so different to the times that I inhabited.

Who'd have thought that a train journey to Stratford East in 1967 could spark such a successful idea in the mind of actor Jimmy Perry? For a time, he had dreams of writing for television and, drawing on his own experiences of life in the Barnes and Watford Home Guard, decided upon a show that evoked a time in recent memory, but he felt had been forgotten by the public consciousness.

Indeed, this thinking was confirmed to him when he went to research the Home Guard at his local library, only to be met by a puzzled librarian, who was unaware of what the Home Guard was.

Perry's next stop on the research trail was the Imperial War Museum and after taking home pamphlets that explain how to make Molotov cocktails, he was transported back to his service as a 15-year-old. With his memory reinvigorated, Perry set to work on a synopsis for his project and initially struggled to find the balance and structure of his first script for a show he had intended to call *The Fighting Tigers.*

But the last piece of the puzzle was a about to fall into place, as that Sunday afternoon, Perry came across the Will Hay film, *Oh, Mr Porter!* The movie's three main characters were a diverse bunch - consisting of a pompous man, an old man and a boy.' Perry had his eureka moment - now how will he get the script noticed?

During the summer of that year, Perry took a two-month break from his acting duties at Watford Rep and took a call from his agent at the time - who by coincidence happened to be the wife of BBC Producer David Croft.

He had been offered a part in a sitcom called *Beggar My Neighbour* - which Croft had directed - and snapped at the chance. It was during rehearsals for the show, that Perry approached Croft with his script idea. The non-committal Croft promised to read it and by the following Monday put Perry out of his misery by declaring that he liked the idea.

Together, the pair worked on a second script and Croft took it to the Head of Light Entertainment at the BBC - Michael Mills.

It was Mills who came up with the idea of calling this wartime sitcom, *Dad's Army* - having expressed a dislike for the name *The Fighting Tigers.* And the rest - as they say - is history.

This book has been a labour of love for one of my all-time favourite programmes. It has taken over a year of research, hours upon hours of television viewing, more words than I thought I would ever write in my life and I take enormous pride in working on something that I hope you enjoy reading.

During the making of this book - I even became aware that my Grandmother on my Mother's side had been born on the actual day that Anthony Eden declared to the nation the formation of a civil defence called the Local Defence Volunteers. How's about that for spooky - maybe I was destined to write on the subject! I know that some people reading this will not agree with some of my reviews on certain episodes but of course everyone is entitled to an opinion so please, don't come looking for me if you think *Big Guns* was especially memorable (note to reader: It wasn't!) I hope you take as much pleasure from this book as I did in writing it.

So to end this passage, I would like to give my thanks to the following for nearly half-a-century of laughs and memorable moments - many of which are covered in this book. Arthur Lowe, John Le Mesurier, Clive Dunn, John Laurie, James Beck, Arnold Ridley, Ian Lavender, Bill Pertwee and the rest of the cast and crew, even the back row, I salute you.

Last but by no means least to Jimmy Perry and David Croft, your vision will last forever.

Hayden Gribble

October 2013

YOU HAVE BEEN WATCHING...

ARTHUR LOWE
CAPTAIN GEORGE MAINWARING

"You Stupid Boy!"

Date of Birth: 22nd September 1915 in Hayfield, Derbyshire, England
Date of Death: 15th April 1982 in Birmingham, England
Spouse: Joan Cooper (from 10th January 1948 to his death in 1982)
Children: Stephen Lowe (b. January 1953)
Memorable Roles: Charles Slomer in *This Sporting Life* (1963), Leonard Swindley in *Coronation Street* (1960-1965) and *Pardon the Expression* (1965-1967), Father Charles Clement Duddleswell in *Bless Me Father* (1979-1981)
How he got the part: Jimmy Perry had always wanted Lowe to play the part of the Captain but when he suggested his first choice for the role, the BBC Head of Comedy Michael Mills replied, 'Arthur Lowe? He doesn't work for us!'[1]

After Jon Pertwee dropped out of talks due to a disagreement in wages, Croft arranged for Lowe to meet with Perry and himself at BBC Television Centre. After a difficult meeting (as described below) Croft saw the actor's ability in taking on the part and Lowe signed his contract as soon as it was sent out on 21st February1968 for a fee of £210 per episode.

Perry on Lowe: 'It didn't get off to a good start. We'd whistled him up to the Centre so that we could talk over lunch in the canteen, and the first thing he said was: "I'm not sure, you know, about a situation-comedy. I hope it's not going to be one of those silly programmes. The sort of show I hate is *Hugh and I*." So I had to tell him the fact that I'd done about eighty *Hugh and Is*! He quickly backed out of that one. After all, it was work, and he wasn't over-employed at the time.'2

Did you Know? Although the marriage between Lowe and Mainwaring is now regarded as a match made in comedy heaven, he was not the original choice to play the self-appointed Captain of the Walmington-on-Sea Home Guard. The part was originally offered to comedy actor Jon Pertwee, a very well-known TV and Radio actor, who turned down the part then went on to play *Doctor Who.* Pertwee's cousin, Bill, would take up the role of Mainwaring's nemesis, Hodges. A golden statue of Lowe in character as Mainwaring sits proudly in Thetford, Norfolk after being unveiled by Perry and Croft in 2010.

JOHN LE MESURIER
SERGEANT ARTHUR WILSON

"Do you think that's wise, Sir?"

Date of Birth: 5th April 1912, Bedford, England
Date of Death: 15th November 1983, Ramsgate, Kent, England

Spouse: June Melville (1940-1949), Hattie Jacques (1949-1965), Joan Malin (1966 to his death in 1983)
Children: Robin (b. 1953) and Kim Le Mesurier (b. 1956)
Memorable Roles: Various roles in *Hancock's Half Hour* (1957-1960), Adrian Harris in *Traitor - Play for the Day* (1971), The Chamberlain in *Jabberwocky* (1977)
How he got the part: Originally, Jimmy Perry had a very different actor in mind for the part of Wilson - Robert Dorning, a portly man whose persona and appearance resembled that of Arthur Lowe. 'I'd seen him with Arthur in *Pardon the Expression* - he'd played Arthur's boss - and I'd thought to myself: "Wouldn't they make a good couple to play the leads [in Dad's Army]?" So I was very keen on getting them both and Dorning could certainly have been good as Wilson, but then of course, Michael Mills stuck his oar in...'[3] David Croft later revealed that Mills said: 'You must have John Le Mesurier! He suffers so well!'[4]
Perry on Le Mesurier: 'John's laid-back style and apparent lack of enthusiasm at times nearly drove me mad. It was only later that I realised he was a very shy man, strangely lacking in confidence. John was a consummate professional, always knew his lines and was never late. Sadly, it's only now looking back over the years I realise what a wonderful contribution he made to *Dad's Army.*'[5]
Did you Know? Le Mesurier won a BAFTA for Best Television Actor for his performance in the Dennis Potter play, *Traitor.* Not only was Le Mesurier renowned for his film, television and theatre work

but he also lent his voice to the children's animated series *Bod* in 1975 and was also the *McDougall's* flour advertisement campaign in the 1970s. In 1982, a year before his death, he was persuaded by his close friend, Clive Dunn to sing on a novelty single *"There Ain't Much Change from a Pound These Days"/"After All These Years"*, which had been written by Le Mesurier's stepson, David Malin. Bizarrely, he also penned his own death note, which was published in *The Times* newspaper on the 16th November 1983, reading; 'JOHN LE MESURIER Wishes it to be known that he conked out on November 15th. He sadly misses family and friends.'

CLIVE DUNN
LANCE CORPORAL JACK JONES

"Don't Panic!"

Date of Birth: 9th January 1920 (Full mane Clive Robert Benjamin Dunn), Covent Garden, London, England
Date of Death: 6th November 2012, Algarve, Portugal
Spouse: Patricia Kenyon (1951-1958), Priscilla Morgan (1959-2012 until his death)
Children: Polly and Jessica (with Morgan)
Memorable Roles: Henry Johnson in *Bootsie and Snudge* (1960-1963), Hodge in *Here Come the Double Deckers!* (1970-1971) and Charlie Quick in *Grandad* (1979-1984)

How he got the part: Dunn was offered the part of the elderly, eccentric Jones after Jack Haig, who was nine years Dunn's senior but was also a dab-hand at playing a character older than himself, had turned it down to concentrate on his own show, *Wacky Jacky*. Dunn was sceptical about the part and consulted with his friend, John Le Mesurier, whilst the BBC had another man in mind for the role in case Dunn turned the part down. Future *Only Fools and Horses* and *A Touch of Frost* actor David Jason was in line to take his place as Dunn was not playing ball. 'The order of events was as follows: I went to the BBC and read for the part at 11am; soon after, my agent received the message that I had the part; by 3p.m, I was out of work! Over the lunch period Bill Cotton had persuaded Clive to take the part, and hadn't informed the producer. The rest is history!'[6]

Croft on Dunn: 'Rehearsals for *Dad's Army* took place at first in various church halls and later in the BBC's rehearsal room complex in North Acton. The doors of the set were marked by moveable metal poles and the walls by white tape stuck to the floor. All the actors got on quite well with this arrangement except for Clive Dunn, who consistently went from Mainwaring's office to the church hall by crossing the white line. One day Jimmy Perry could stand it no more. "Do you realise," said Jimmy, "that you keep on walking through the office wall?" To which Clive replied witheringly: "Well, I won't be able to do it on set when the wall is actually there, will I?"'[7]

Did you Know? Clive Dunn's mother had once had an affair with David Croft's father when the two worked as professional entertainers. Dunn only accepted the role of Jones after speaking to his close friend John Le Mesurier and making a promise to each other that they would give the series a go as they both initially had reservations. At 48, he was one of the youngest members of the cast but played the oldest member of the platoon. He also released a novelty hit single called *Grandad*, which reached number 1 in the UK Charts on his 51st birthday. He was awarded and OBE when the series finished but this led to a rift with Arthur Lowe, whose conservative beliefs clashed with Dunn's socialist outlook, led him to declare that he would accept only a higher award from Her Majesty the Queen.

JOHN LAURIE
PRIVATE JAMES FRAZER

"We're Doomed! Doomed!"

Date of Birth: 25th March 1897 (as John Paton Laurie) Dumfries, Dumfriesshire, Scotland
Date of Death: 23rd June 1980, Chalfont St Peter, Buckinghamshire, England
Spouse: Florence Saunders 1924–26 (until her death), Oonah Todd-Naylor 1928–1980 (until his death)
Children: One Daughter

Memorable Roles: John, the crofter in *The 39 Steps* (1935), Jamy, Scottish Captain in the English Army in *Henry V* (1944) and Blind Pew in *Treasure Island* (1950)

How he got the part: Compared to his co-stars, the casting of the vastly experience Laurie was rather more straight forward. But Croft had immense faith that Laurie would be able to put flesh on the bones of what was at that time, a rather straight forward character. 'Frazer at the time, was described in the script as 'A Scotsman'. It can't have been very inspiring to such an experienced actor. Michael Mills said, "Make him into a fisherman." So Jimmy and I made him into a fisherman for that first episode. No use to us at all, as a fisherman never went out to sea in those days because it was the invasion coast. Later on, we started allowing him to make coffins in his workshop, and that developed into him becoming an undertaker - and then he became very useful indeed, a marvellous character. But we did find it difficult, at the start, to write for him, as this 'Scottish fisherman', and I doubt that John was too impressed either.'[8]

Perry on Laurie: 'John was a highly educated man and a serious Shakespearian scholar. He was also totally mad. He had complete disdain for "semi-literate Sassenachs" as he called me. Nevertheless, we got on amazingly well and became very close.'[9] Laurie was not impressed, but as he never refused work, he accepted his role.

Did you Know? Laurie appeared in several films with acting legend Laurence Olivier, including three cinematic adaptations of William Shakespeare plays *Henry V, Hamlet (1948)* and *Richard III (1950).*

He met his first wife at the Old Vic theatre in London and spent his early acting days working at the Royal Shakespeare Company. He fought during World War One but Laurie was badly haunted by his experiences, wincing at the memories of the conflict when reminded of his time in the trenches. By the time the war had ended, he joined the Royal Artillery Company before training as an actor. With the outbreak of World War Two, Laurie enrolled in the Home Guard something he would be doing again - under less serious circumstances - many years later. His final acting role was in a BBC Radio 2 series called *Tony's* in 1979.

JAMES BECK
PRIVATE JOE WALKER

"Sir, I've got an idea!"

Date of Birth: 21st February 1929, Islington, London, England (born as Stanley James Carroll Beck)
Date of Death: 6th August 1973, Roehampton, Wandsworth, London, England
Spouse: Kay Bullus (10th December 1959 to his death in 1973)
Children: Step Children from Kay's previous marriage, Christopher, Diana and David Bullus
Memorable Roles: James Ryder in The Blue Carbuncle (1968), Bert Jones in Romany Jones (1972-1973) and Brian in Groupie Girl (1970)

How he got the part: Beck had struggled to make a break in an established role and in 1963 had written to the BBC's Assistant head of artists' bookings, Bush Bailey, asking for an interview. Bailey organised a meeting with the actor and filed a good report on Beck but there was no parts upcoming that met his wishes. But by 1968, the role of the spiv, Walker came over the horizon. 'He was obviously a talented actor. He just came to me, in fact, in an audition. I had used him before, and fancied him very much for that particular part. There weren't any other real competitors for it - except Jimmy, of course (Perry had originally written the part with himself in mind for the role) and we'd already ruled him out - so casting Walker turned out to be one of the easiest ones of the lot.'10

Croft on Beck: 'We realised that all was not well with Jimmy Beck's health while on location filming for his last series. However, he soldiered on until we arrived at the studio on Sunday 22nd July 1973 for the recording of The Recruit to learn that he'd been taken to hospital. Jimmy Perry and I ran quickly through the script to see if the show could go on without Jimmy Beck's studio appearance. At that stage we hoped that Jimmy would return in time for the next series but he died about three weeks later. Jimmy's 'Walker' was a lovely character and we decided that he made a unique contribution to the programme and could not be replaced.'11

Did you Know? Before he became an actor, Beck studied at art college and was a keen artist, a passion he held for the rest of his life. Following national service in the army, Beck decided to take up acting as a profession and had relative success in early theatre roles in plays such as William Shakespeare's *The Merchant of Venice*. When he moved to London in the mid-1960s he found work in the form of one-off appearances in programmes such as *Coronation Street, Gideon's Way* and *The Troubleshooters.* During his time on *Dad's Army*, he appeared in a remake of the *Hancock's Half Hour* episode *The Economy Drive* with Dad's Army co-star, Arthur Lowe.

ARNOLD RIDLEY
PRIVATE CHARLES GODFREY

"Can I be excused?"

Date of Birth: 7th January 1896, Bath, Somerset, England (born as William Arnold Ridley)
Date of Death: 12th March 1984 Hillingdon, London, England
Spouse: Hilda Cooke (1926–1939), Isola Strong (1939), Althea Parker (1945 until his death in 1984)
Children: Nicolas Ridley
Memorable Roles: Mr Saunders in An Interrupted Journey (1949), Tom Cuffley in Green Grow The Rushes (1951) and Alderman Pratt in Carry On Girls (1973)

How he got the part: After a series of ventures that had brought success to Ridley's name, he still could not afford NOT to work. When he was seen by Croft for the role of Godfrey, he knew what qualities the pensioner could bring to the role. 'He'd been very good, very funny, and he was a lovely, gentle character. He looked right, sounded right. I was a bit worried about him because I think he was already 72 when I first interviewed him for the part...he turned out to be a very successful character.' 12

Croft on Ridley: 'Arnold was a distinguished actor in the theatre, had written successful plays and directed many films When he came to me he was in his seventies and I explained that I couldn't save him from being required to run about from time to time and did he think he could manage it? "Oh yes, I think so," he replied gently, and manage it he did for the next nine years.'13

Did you Know? Ridley was exposed to the horrors of both World Wars and was invalided out of the First conflict when he received several severe injuries during the Battle of the Somme in 1916.

His left hand was affected and his left leg was riddled with shrapnel, he was hit in the head by a German soldier's rifle butt, which led to a series of blackouts as an elder men and he was also bayoneted in the groin. He was medically discharged but rejoined the Army in 1939 but after seeing action in France, was discharged once again with the rank of Captain on the 1st June 1940.

He subsequently joined the Home Guard, like his colleague on the show, John Laurie. He was the author of *The Ghost Train*, after becoming inspired by an evening stranded at Marylebone Station, London in 1923. This led to a successful career as a playwright before he found fame as an actor in *Dad's Army*.

IAN LAVENDER
PRIVATE FRANK PIKE

"Whistle while you work, Hitler is a twerp!"

Date of Birth: 16th February 1946, Birmingham, England
Spouse: Suzanne Kerchiss (1967–76), Miki Hardy (1993–present)
Children: Sam and Daniel Lavender
Memorable Roles: Joe Baxter in Carry On Behind (1975), Michael Sparrow in Goodnight Sweetheart (1998) and Derek Harkinson in Eastenders (2001-2005)
How he got the part: David Croft was pointed in Lavender's direction by his wife. 'Ian was a client of Ann, my wife, who was an agent at that time. When *Dad's Army* was scheduled for production she insisted that I watch a TV drama in which Ian gave a sensitive and charming performance. She sent him to me and I thought him just right to play Pike and he got the part.'[14]

Lavender was taken to meet Croft and was not told that Ann was his wife as she did not want to ruin his chances of getting the part. She kept her relationship with Croft a secret and was shocked when he was told the truth and also given the part of the baby of the Home Guard.

Croft on Lavender: Being much younger than the rest of the cast, he was not a little daunted by their vast experience. He realised that he quickly found a character for Pike and fought for his survival. Accordingly, he appeared on the first day of filming with the now famous scarf and with his cap firmly on the centre of his head looking like a complete nerd. Lovely touches like sucking his thumb when asleep quickly followed until he'd built up a completely believable and true portrait of a late teenager earnestly playing at being a soldier. He was always a great pleasure to direct and write for.'15

Did you Know? The colours of Pike's scarf were not those of Aston Villa Football Club's playing strip by accident. Lavender is a lifelong supporter of the Midland's club and came upon the scarf when searching the BBC wardrobe. Following his stint in the popular BBC soap opera, *Eastenders,* Lavender toured the United Kingdom as the narrator in a production of *The Rocky Horror Picture Show.* When making an appearance on the quiz show Celebrity Mastermind, his past came back to haunt him when fellow contestant and friend, Rick Wakeman, shouted the catchphrase 'Don't tell him, Pike!' when he took to the chair and was asked to give his name by presenter John Humphreys.

BILL PERTWEE
CHIEF ARP WARDEN HODGES

"Put that light out!"

Date of Birth: 21st July 1926, Amersham, England (born William Desmond Anthony Pertwee)
Date of Death: 27th May 2013, Cornwall, England
Spouse: Jean Pertwee (1960), Marion Pertwee (1965 until her death in 2005)
Children: Jonathan James Pertwee (b. 1966)
Memorable Roles: Mr Crawford in *Bless This House* (1971), Lorry Driver in *Worzel Gummidge* (1979-1980) and PC Wilson in *You Rang M'Lord?* (1988-93)
How he got the part: Following a variety of smaller parts on television, Pertwee was offered a part in David Croft's *Hugh and I*, in which he only spoke a couple of lines, the producer kept him in mind when he went about looking for an actor to play the obnoxious ARP Warden Hodges. Pertwee was brought in for the pilot, in which again he only spoke a few lines, but his performance and repor with the cast led to even more involvement as time went on until he became an integral part of the cast by the third series.
Pertwee on the series: 'I'll always remember the early morning coach trip from the hotel to where we filmed the battle scenes. It was only three or four miles and the countryside was beautiful. The weather was always good. We had nothing but sunshine for our filming; in all the years we went there, we only had three days of rain and one day of snow.'16

Did you Know? Pertwee was born to an English father and a Brazilian mother. His brother James Raymond 'Jiggy' Pertwee was an RAF Aircraft pilot during the Second World War and was killed in an air crash following a bombing raid on Dortmund, Germany in 1941. He made a guest appearance in the children's television series *Worzel Gummidge* alongside his cousin, Jon Pertwee. In 2007 he was awarded an OBE in the Queen's Birthday Honours List for his services to charity. He was also bestowed an honour by the fans of the programme when he became the President of *The Dad's Army Appreciation Society*, a title he held until his death in 2013.

EDWARD SINCLAIR
THE VERGER/MR YEATMAN

"The vicar's not going to like this, you know!"

Date of Birth: 3rd February 1914, Oldham, Greater Manchester, England
Date of Death: 29th August 1977, Cheddar, Somerset, England
Spouse: Gladys Green (1940 until his death in 1977)
Children: 2 children
Memorable Roles: Sergeant Christian Nash in *The Bells* (1931), Nils in *Saraband for Dead Lovers* (1948) and the Postman in *No Sex Please, We're British* (1973)
Frank Williams on Sinclair: 'Teddy and I got on so well together. We became very close friends. In fact,

socially, Bill [Pertwee], Teddy and myself developed into something of a trio, just like, in the show, the warden, verger and vicar teaming up to provide Mainwaring and the Home Guard with a sense of conflict.'17

Sinclair's widow, Gladys on her husband's role in Dad's Army: 'It was only a small part at first but Teddy was delighted to be offered it. The role was wonderful for him, definitely the highlight of his career. Just as the series finished he'd started receiving offers to play panto, and if he'd lived long enough his career would have prospered thanks to *Dad's Army.*'18

Did you Know? Sinclair had a late than unexpected birth into the world of acting. He had always aspired to make it his profession but as a young man he found money hard to come by and was unable to finance a scholarship at drama school. Instead, he found work with amateur theatre companies until the outbreak of the Second World War, when he served in the Oxfordshire and Buckinghamshire Light Infantry. He deliberately put off an acting career until his family were financially secure, despite being born into the profession as his Father had himself been a stage actor until his death when Sinclair was just 14 years old.

FRANK WILLIAMS THE VICAR

"Quiet, Mr Yeatman"

Date of Birth: 2nd July 1931, Hampstead, London,

England
Date of Death: 26th June, London, England
Memorable Roles: Captain T R Pocket in *The Army Game* (1958-1961), Dr Freemo in *One Of Our Dinosaurs Is Missing* (1975) and Bishop Charles in *You Rang M'Lord?* (1990-1993)
How he got the part: 'I'd worked for Jimmy Perry before [in Watford Rep] and I'd also done a couple of episodes of Hugh and I for David Croft, but when I first came into Dad's Army I thought it was just going to be for one episode.'19
Perry on Williams: 'When I first thought of *Dad's Army*, even before the script was written, I knew we would need a vicar - and Frank's was the first name I wrote down. To me he was perfect casting as the Reverend Farthing, always slightly tetchy as he tried to come to terms with the platoon's invasion of his church hall.'20
Did you Know? As of 2014, Williams claims to still own the original pair of glasses he wore whilst appearing as Reverend Timothy Farthing in the series. In a not so radical departure from the role he is most famous for, Williams has served three terms between 1985 and 2000 as a member of the General Synod of the Church of England. When the Queen Mother passed away aged 101 in 2002, Williams walked in the funeral procession at her request as she was a huge fan of the show.

JANET DAVIES
MRS MAVIS PIKE
"Frank can't go out like that, he has got a chest!"

Date of Birth: 14th September 1927 in Wakefield, West Yorkshire, England
Date of Death: 22nd September, 1986 in Bromley, Kent, England
Spouse: Ian Gardiner (married in unknown year until her death in 1977)
Children: Andrew Davies
Appearances in Dad's Army: **S1**, *The Man and the Hour, Museum Piece, The Showing Up of Corporal Jones, Shooting Pains,* **S2**, *Operation Kilt, The Battle of Godfrey's Cottage, Sgt. Wilson's Little Secret, Under Fire,* **S3**, *The Armoured Might of Lance Corporal Jones, The Lion Has 'Phones, The Bullet Is Not for Firing, Something Nasty in the Vault, War Dance, Man Hunt,* **S4**, *The Big Parade, Boots, Boots, Boots, Sgt - Save My Boy!, Absent Friends, Mum's Army, A. Wilson (Manager)?* **S6,** *My British Buddy, The Honourable Man,* **S7**, *The Godiva Affair, Turkey Dinner,* **S8**, *When You've Got to Go, High Finance,* **CS**, *The Love of Three Oranges,* **S9**, *The Making of Private Pike, Knights of Madness, Never Too Old*
Memorable Roles: Various characters in six episodes of *Dixon of Dock Green* (1964-1972), Various characters in six episodes of *Z-Cars* (1962-1978) and Miss Jones in *Last of the Summer Wine* (1975)

Did you Know? Davies trained as a solicitor but after a while left and trained as a shorthand typist. She eventually secured a job as a secretary for two years at the BBC before moving into reparatory theatre in 1948. When she experienced quiet periods on the acting front, Davies made an income by exploiting her secretarial training at a variety of theatre agencies around the United Kingdom. Davies was extremely upset when she was not cast to play Mrs Pike - the role that made had made her famous – in the 1971 feature film of *Dad's Army* (see 'The Movie' chapter) and her appearances dwindled afterwards in the series eventually clocking up a credit in 30 episodes of the sitcom.

PAMELA CUNDELL
MRS MARCIA FOX

Date of Birth: March 1920 in Croydon, Surrey, England
Date of Death: 14 February 2015, Ipswich, England
Spouse: Bill Frazer (1981 until his death in 1987)
Children: None
Memorable Roles: Vi Box in *Big Deal* (1984-1986), Various Characters in four episodes of *Doctors* (2001-2009) and Nora Swann in *Eastenders* (2005-2006)
Apprearances in Dad's Army: S3, *The Armoured Might of Lance Corporal Jones, The Lion Has 'Phones,* **S4,** *The Big Parade, Mum's Army,* **S5**, *Getting the Bird,* **S6**, *My British Buddy, The Honourable Man,* **S7**, *Everybody's Trucking, The*

Godiva Affair, Turkey Dinner, **S8**, *When You've Got To Go,* **CS**, *The Love of Three Oranges,* **S9**, *The Making of Private Pike, Never Too Old.*
Did you Know? Born into the acting business, Cundell is the descendant of Henry Condell, who was a manager of the Lord Chamberlain's Men which was the acting company of William Shakespeare. Condell was also the first person to compile Shakespeare's work after his death in 1616. She trained at the Guildhall School of Music and Drama and spent her early years in the rep theatre and as a stand-up comic in summer shows before television came calling. Cundell made regular television appearances in the 1960s alongside such stars as Benny Hill and Frankie Howerd. She also appeared alongside her old *Dad's Army* colleague, Clive Dunn in his BBC show *Grandad* from 1979-1980.

SERIES ONE

ALL EPISODES MADE AND BROADCAST IN BLACK AND WHITE

MAIN CAST:

ARTHUR LOWE - CAPTAIN GEORGE MAINWARING
JOHN LE MESURIER - SERGEANT ARTHUR WILSON
CLIVE DUNN - LANCE CORPORAL JACK JONES
JOHN LAURIE - PRIVATE JAMES FRAZER
ARNOLD RIDLEY - PRIVATE CHARLES GODFREY
JAMES BECK - PRIVATE JOE WALKER
IAN LAVENDER - PRIVATE FRANK PIKE

FEATURING THE VOICES OF BUD FLANAGAN AND E. V. H. EMMETT

EPISODE ONE

THE MAN AND THE HOUR

RECORDED ON 15TH APRIL 1968
FIRST BROADCAST 31ST JULY 1968
VIEWING FIGURE: 7.2 MILLION

PLOT:

It is Tuesday 14th May 1940. Britain is at war and bank manager George Mainwaring organises the Walmington-on-Sea branch of the Local Defence Volunteers and appoints himself Captain and his chief clerk Arthur Wilson his Sergeant. That evening they enlist the townsfolk. Despite their only having makeshift weapons and virtually no practical skills, Mainwaring is not daunted, and rallies his troops with a cry of "Come on Adolf, we're ready for you!"

GUEST CAST:

Janet Davies - Mrs Mavis Pike
Caroline Dowdeswell - Janet King
John Ringham - Bracewell
Bill Pertwee - ARP Warden Hodges

REVIEW:

The Man and the Hour is an interesting and engaging start to *Dad's Army*'s long and successful run - with Arthur Lowe unquestionably the strongest player in the proceedings. Inevitably however, as it is a pilot, there are always going to be bits that work which will be developed upon, and bits that don't work which are going to be discarded (like the stereotypically posh Bracewell). The platoon have a long way to go before they become the finished article but overall, *Hour* is not a bad start at all though for the boys who will make Hitler think again.

MEMORABLE MOMENT:

When Godfrey brings his gun to the first line-up and Mainwaring converses with Wilson about how as superior officers they should have it. It's a funny scene, made all the more awkward by Mainwaring insisting that it should be Wilson, not him, who requests the weapon. When Godfrey refuses on the grounds that he does not see why he should give it up, Mainwaring threatens to have him shot for not carrying out an order. Walker pipes up, "That'll be a bit tricky since he's the only one with a gun!"

LINE:

Jones: Fuzzy-wuzzies, they were the boys. They'd come at you with a great long knife and zip you right open. They'd soon find out if you'd got any guts or not!

WATCH OUT FOR:

- **Two of the show's most popular catchphrases make their debuts: Mainwaring's iconic "You stupid boy!" and Corporal Jones's "They don't like it up 'em!"**
- **When signing up in the church hall, Frazer announces that he keeps a philatelist's shop, so either he is keeping his later job as an undertaker a secret or he made a drastic career move when the show went over to colour.**
- **The title sequence features a laughter track for the first and only time in the programme's history, and an audience member coughs twice (not so discreetly) over Bud Flanagan's vocals.**

BEHIND THE SCENES:

Once all location work had been carried out on the series, rehearsals for the studio sessions began on Monday 8th April at St Nicholas's Church Hall in Chiswick. Here the writers and actors put the finishing touches to both the script and the characters. Whilst it became apparent that the character of Bracewell would not work out in the long term due to too many similarities between him and Godfrey, others would be given the encouragement to develop further, such as Bill Pertwee's Hodges.

James Beck continued to work on making Walker a likeable rogue, basing his performance on a spiv he knew during the war, whilst Ian Lavender added his trademark Aston Villa scarf to his costume and used a combination of Brylcreem and colour spray to conceal his prematurely greying locks.

Writer Jimmy Perry was astounded at how laid-back John Le Mesurier was in his preparation for the role of Wilson: 'Talk about casual! The previous week, on the first day of filming at Thetford, John was sitting there very nonchalantly in the lounge of the hotel, and he said to me: "Oh, James, how do you want me to play this part?" Well, that was a laugh for a start!'[1] Perry told Le Mesurier to play the part the only way he could, *as* John Le Mesurier.

Following completion of the pilot, Controller of BBC1 Paul Fox was handed a viewing tape and he objected to the inclusion of real war footage of refugees fleeing the Nazis in Belgium and France in the episode's title and closing sequences.

Despite both David Croft's and BBC Head of Comedy Michael Mills' enthusiasm for these nuggets of real-life events at the beginning and end of the piece, the Controller had his way and both were edited out as he did not think it suitable to include these images of death and destruction in a light-hearted sitcom.

TRIVIA:

The episode's historical accuracy is tweaked for practical reasons: although the action takes places on the correct date (Tuesday 14th May 1940), the time that Secretary of State for War Anthony Eden announced over the wireless the formation of the Local Defence Volunteers was changed from the evening to the middle of the day.

E. V. H. Emmett, who narrated the newsreel following the title sequence and would do so for the rest of the first series, was the voice of *Gaumont British News* in the 1930s and 40s. He also lent his tones to the classic British film *Carry On Cleo* (1964).

SCORE: 7/10

EPISODE TWO

MUSEUM PIECE

RECORDED ON 22ND APRIL 1968
FIRST BROADCAST 7TH AUGUST 1968
VIEWING FIGURE: 6.8 MILLION

PLOT:

After the platoon's first full day on manoeuvres, Mainwaring is concerned by the men's obedience levels. He is also frustrated by the news that the uniforms and weapons will not arrive for another six weeks. However, a fortunate occurrence leads to the men marching on the Peabody Museum of Historical Army Weapons, but an unlikely person is set to stand in the way of their goal: Jones's elderly father...

GUEST CAST:

Janet Davies - Mrs Pike
Caroline Dowdeswell - Janet King
Eric Woodburn - Museum Caretaker
Leon Cortez - Milkman
Michael Osbourne - Boy Scout

REVIEW:

Despite some fun moments, a number of criticisms can be levelled at the piece. In these early days of the programme it seems possible that the writers had a slight lack of confidence in their characters, which led them to resort to more action-orientated content, which becomes tiresome and irritating. And although the story is presented well, some of the characters have yet to spring into life: Godfrey being one of the main examples of this, as Arnold Ridley is given very little to work with. However, *Museum Piece* is still a fun and engaging episode but not one that many fans would return to time after time.

MEMORABLE MOMENT:

The scene where Jones's father is defending the museum against the platoon and makes Mainwaring and his men look silly in the process is pure slapstick and has parallels with the hit 1990 movie *Home Alone*. Its unadulterated silliness and inventiveness, apart from when Jones Senior is quite willing to tip hot water on the men (which is a little dark for a family comedy), is fun to watch and the moment Mainwaring breaks the bottom rung of the scaling ladder is the first opportunity for Arthur Lowe to skew his hat and glasses to comedic effect.

LINE:

Caretaker: What do you want?
Frazer: ARP Warden. You've got a light showing.
Caretaker: No I have not.
Frazer: See for yourself!
Caretaker: I'm not opening the door in my nightshirt!
Frazer: I didn't know you had a door in your nightshirt.

WATCH OUT FOR:

- **In the scene in the bank, Bracewell is mentioned but he is not seen in the newsreel footage and does not make a further appearance after the pilot.**
- **Captain Mainwaring's inability to use the 24-hour clock is introduced as a running gag.**
- **At the very end of the episode when the Chinese gun begins to fire, the boom mike very**

clearly moves into view in preparation for Lowe to deliver his line from under the table.

BEHIND THE SCENES:

The scene when the horse disrupts the men's procession towards the museum was only the second to be shot for the series. According to Harold Snoad's filming schedule, the scene was shot on the first day of location filming in Thetford on Wednesday 3rd April 1968, preceded only by the scene in which present-day Mainwaring addresses his former platoon members at the 'I'm Backing Britain' campaign in *The Man and the Hour.*

Despite sharing no scenes with the actor, Caroline Dowdeswell recalled that she was rather astonished by how naughty Arnold Ridley could be in rehearsals: 'I was about 22 when I did *Dad's Army* and extremely naïve. I gravitated towards dear old Arnold Ridley as I already knew him via my agent, but was somewhat taken aback as the old boy used to tell the most risqué of jokes. I was rather shocked; it was as if the Pope swore!'2

TRIVIA:

As the platoon stampede towards the museum door with the fragile battering ram, wartime favourite *In the Mood* can be heard as the soundtrack for the scene. American bandleader Glenn Miller took the song to Number 1 in the US charts in 1940, the same year the episode is set in. It was recorded by Joe Loss and his Band for use in this episode.

SCORE: 6/10

EPISODE THREE
COMMAND DECISION
RECORDED ON 29TH APRIL 1968
FIRST BROADCAST 4TH AUGUST 1968
VIEWING FIGURE: 8.6 MILLION

PLOT:

Mainwaring cannot help but notice that there is a negative mood within the camp. Jones is also suffering as he admits that his morale has been shattered and that the lack of weapons at their disposal is getting to him. Soon after, a war veteran called Colonel Square announces his wish to lead the platoon and promises to give the men the rifles he has in his possession. Will Mainwaring do a deal that will see him relinquishing his captaincy when his men are at rock bottom?

GUEST CAST:

Janet Davies - Mrs Pike
Geoffrey Lumsden - Colonel Square
Charles Hill - Butler
Gordon Peters - Soldier

REVIEW:

Command Decision has a very different feel to the two

previous instalments. In fact, it is probably one of the most serious *Dad's Army* episodes of them all, due to the men's morale being at rock bottom. Although it does have its lighter, more jovial moments, Captain Mainwaring has to make a difficult decision for himself that may ultimately make life a lot better for the men. It is notable for depicting Mainwaring and his men being taken to breaking point. The acting from the main cast is right up to scratch, especially that of Clive Dunn, who is given an opportunity to show a more vulnerable side to the platoon's oldest recruit.

MEMORABLE MOMENT:

It would be easy to say the scene with the horses, but as a piece of character development and for its quiet charm, the scene in which Wilson reaches a compromise with Mainwaring over whether Pike is allowed to wear his muffler tops it. As he goes to take it off, Pike whispers 'Thank you' to the Sergeant for his fatherly concern – it is a touching moment.

LINE:

Square: Served for four years in the desert, 1915 to '19. Have you heard of El Aurens?
Mainwaring: I beg your pardon?
Square: El Aurens, man, El Aurens. What do you see in your mind's eye when I say the word 'El Aurens'?
Mainwaring: I'm not sure. What do you see in your mind's eye, Wilson?
Wilson: An ice cream, Sir?
Mainwaring: No-no that's Eldorado.

WATCH OUT FOR:

- The beginning of a long-standing gag in the shape of Mainwaring's name being mispronounced by those outside of the platoon.
- Arthur Lowe can be seen wearing heavy bandaging to his left hand in the first scene, but by the time the action moves to the bank the next day, it has disappeared.
- Corporal Jones is the subject of a complaint from a young lady after shining a torch on her legs whilst on patrol. As Harold Steptoe would say, 'You dirty old man!'
- Wilson becomes the first character to utter "Don't panic!" - the most recognisable catchphrase of the series, although ultimately not his own - beating Corporal Jones to the post by a couple of episodes.

BEHIND THE SCENES:

As Ian Lavender remembered, it was during a scene in this episode, filmed whilst on location in the grounds of Marsham Hall in Norfolk, that he came upon the voice for Pike:

> It was all a bit of a blur. The only thing I remember of the filming, quite honestly, was when I accidentally came up with Pike's voice.

> Most of the filming was mute - because it was going to be mixed in with stock newsreel footage - but one scene, featuring these circus horses going round and round, was done with sound. All I said was, 'Have you got the rifles, Mr Mainwaring?' And this *voice* came out: '*Have you got the rifles, Mr Mainwaring?*' Pure shock, I think. And so I more or less stuck with that voice for the next nine years.[3]

Also when filming that scene, three of the silent stars of *Dad's Army* showed off a talent that came in very handy indeed - horse riding. Colin Bean (who went on as Private Sponge to have a more important role in the show as time went on), Hugh Hastings and Richard Jacques were each paid an extra five pounds for their equestrian skills and in the process impressed the makers of the show, as Hastings recalled: 'During rehearsals I remember David Croft telling me I was riding too well! He wanted the platoon members to look as if they couldn't ride, so I spent the rest of the time attempting to look clumsy in the saddle - it was difficult.'[4] Hastings had been taught how to ride a horse as a boy in his native Australia.

The horses were supplied by Winship's Circus, a family business from Yorkshire, run by Geoff and Val Winship at the time of writing. They have been organising Medieval Jousting Tournaments since 1966 and were the first people to do so in the 20th Century.

TRIVIA:

The name given to the Local Defence Volunteers was changed at the insistence of British Prime Minister Winston Churchill as he found the title uninspiring. Despite a large number of government officials who did not want it to change as a million armbands with the initials 'LDV' had already been printed and dispatched, Churchill had his way and on 22nd July 1940, the LDV officially became known as the 'Home Guard', meaning the last part of this episode is set on that particular day.

SCORE: 6/10

EPISODE FOUR

THE ENEMY WITHIN THE GATES

RECORDED ON 6TH MAY 1968
FIRST BROADCAST ON 28TH AUGUST 1968
VIEWING FIGURE: 8.1 MILLION

PLOT:

An official from HQ Area Command arrives, asking Mainwaring questions about their weapons. The men are suspicious of the man who turns out to be Captain Winogrodzki from the Polish Free Forces. He informs

the platoon that lone parachutists are not to be shot down in case of mistaken identity, but if they do capture a parachutist and they are unharmed, the platoon can earn up to £10 per prisoner.
Later that evening, Jones, Walker and Pike shoot a swan by mistake before coming into contact with real Nazi parachutists...

GUEST CAST:

Caroline Dowdeswell as Janet King
Carl Jaffe as Captain Winogrodzki
Denys Peek as German pilot
Nigel Rideout as German pilot
Bill Pertwee as ARP Warden Hodges
David Davenport as Military Police Sergeant

REVIEW:

Four episodes in and *Dad's Army* finally begins to wake up and to look and feel like the show we know and love. Even though the familiar uniforms are some time off, the main ensemble are well-oiled cogs in the machine and, this time around, Clive Dunn and James Beck steal the show. The only part of the episode that feels slightly uneasy is the mistaken identity of the Polish-accented Captain, played by German actor Carl Jeffe. It is more than a little discriminating to suggest that a man should be incarcerated just because of his accent, but then this story element perhaps only highlights the state of insecurity that gripped the nation during the war. Despite this, *The Enemy Within the Gates* finally sees *Dad's Army* firing on all cylinders as both the characters and the overall tone of the series become more firmly established.

MEMORABLE MOMENT:

When Jones, Pike and Walker mistake a swan for a German parachutist and they ask to open fire, Jones tells them to wait until "he exposes himself." The proceedings eventually lead to them accidently capturing two German parachutists who initially mistake them for African soldiers due to Jones's cold steel. It is a great scene where all three actors excel, showing members of the platoon at their early bumbling best.

LINE:

Walker: I'd shoot fuzzy-wuzzies just the same as you. The poor blighters only had spears.

Jones: It wasn't just fuzzy-wuzzies. It was flies and dysentery and malaria and gippy tummy.

Walker: You should have packed it up, then.

Jones: We didn't pack it up 'cos we were soldiers, wasn't we? There's a field marshal's baton in every knapsack.

Walker: Sounds as if you'd have been better off with a bedpan.

WATCH OUT FOR:

- **Jones shouting "you cowardly bastards!" when he is on parade with Walker and Pike. It is surprising in its abruptness and one of only a handful of times an expletive is used in the series.**

BEHIND THE SCENES:

Actor Nigel Rideout was given an extra £10 for writing the German dialogue in the script. He had appeared in other famous television programmes of the 1960s such as *The Avengers* and *The Frost Report*, but spent most of his career in the theatre.

Arthur Lowe advised Ian Lavender on how to become more noticed in the show when there wasn't much for Pike to do. Lavender said: 'He was thoughtful. He'd help you. In fact, after the first series, Arthur came over to me, very discreetly, you know, and said: "I know you don't have a lot to do, so get yourself a funny costume and just come and stand next to me." So in those early episodes you can see shots of me standing next to Arthur, saying nothing and looking stupid!'[5]

The end credits were changed to reflect the narrative, with a brand new sequence being filmed to show that the main cast were slowly but surely acquiring their equipment. They were now shown wearing their berets and armed with the rifles they received at the end of the previous episode.

The Enemy Within the Gates had a Reaction Index (a score of audience appreciation internally recorded by the BBC) of 65 - a healthy if not outstanding score which equalled that of its predecessor - but was delayed transmission by a week due to news coverage of the Soviet Military invasion of Czechoslovakia.

TRIVIA:

When he is grilled by the platoon and asked who won the Boat Race between Cambridge and Oxford in 1935, Winogrodzki is correct. Cambridge did indeed win the Boat Race that year on April 6th for the 12th time in a row. It was the 87th meeting between the two rivals and Cambridge won by four-and-a-half lengths to claim their 46th win.

SCORE: 7.5/10

EPISODE FIVE

THE SHOWING UP OF CORPORAL JONES

RECORDED ON 13TH MAY 1968

FIRST BROADCAST ON 4TH SEPTEMBER 1968

VIEWING FIGURE: 8.8 MILLION

PLOT:

The platoon are overjoyed at their uniforms finally arriving, but trouble is just around the corner as Major Regan arrives to inspect the men and has reservations about Jones. Mainwaring is forced to tell Jones that he may have to leave due to his age. To keep his place in the ranks he must take part in an assault course, but after a punishing runthrough it looks like it will take a miracle to keep the old war veteran in the Home Guard...

GUEST CAST:

Janet Davies as Mrs Pike
Martin Wyldeck as Major Regan
Patrick Waddington as Brigadier
Edward Sinclair as Caretaker
Thérèse McMurray as Girl at the Window

REVIEW:

Simply put, *The Showing Up of Corporal Jones* is brilliant. It is silly and touching in all the right places, and although there are less one-liners than in previous episodes, the narrative is strong and the performances are stunning, most of all from Clive Dunn, who is both hilarious when he is messing up in front of Major Regan and melancholic when on the brink of losing the thing that keeps him going: fighting for his country. No wonder he went on to be such a beloved member of the platoon. As the first series neared its end, the show is undoubtedly getting stronger and stronger.

MEMORABLE MOMENT:

The scene in which Mainwaring tells Jones that he is overage and can only stay if he completes the assault course. It is both funny and moving, and it is lovely to see Arthur Lowe at his most gentle and understanding as Mainwaring, while Clive Dunn shows his character's determination in the face of adversity.

LINE:

Regan: Fine when you're fighting bags of straw but I want to see more guts! <*To Frazer*> You! Charge!
Frazer: Yeearrgghh!! Yer Bastard Nazi! <*Charges at the straw and bayonets it.*> I'm sorry Sir, I swore.
Regan: You thought you were doing that to a Nazi, didn't you?
Frazer: Oh no, Sir - just somebody I don't like very much <*looks at Regan*>.

WATCH OUT FOR:

- **Captain Mainwaring's surprising use of the word 'bastard' - the only time the character uses an expletive in the entire show.**
- **When Regan arrives in the Church Hall side office, only to find Mainwaring, Wilson and Pike in an awkward position and all wearing balaclavas with bunny ears.**
- **When John Laurie goes ballistic before attacking the sack of straw with his bayonet, an extra in the background cannot contain his amusement and sniggers on screen.**

- **The episode also includes the first, yet brief appearance of Edward Sinclair as the caretaker. Although he would later be known as the Verger and finally Mr Yeatman, his character was still in the early stages of development.**

BEHIND THE SCENES:

As Ian Lavender recalled, the introduction of the men's uniforms soon became a source of great discomfort for the cast: 'Our uniforms arrived in episode five. Everyone had been looking forward to receiving them, and when initially we were only issued armbands we were disappointed. It seemed ages before the full uniforms arrived, but they soon became the bane of our lives - they were so uncomfortable.'[6]

TRIVIA:

During the Second World War, the Home Guard's age requirements were officially between the ages of 17 and 65, meaning that, in real-life terms, Jones would indeed have been too old to sign up as a volunteer. However, it was common for men to lie about their age so that they could still defend the country from invasion. One volunteer, P.D. Willeringhaus, was awarded a 'Mention in Despatches' for brave conduct, despite being only 16 at the time.

SCORE: 9/10

EPISODE SIX

SHOOTING PAINS

RECORDED ON 20TH MAY 1968
FIRST BROADCAST ON 11TH SEPTEMBER 1968
VIEWING FIGURE - 9.7 MILLION

PLOT:

The men are told that they will have a session of target practice as ammunition is becoming more readily available. Despite their initial keenness, it turns out that they are all hopeless with a firearm. Mainwaring's post-mortem is interrupted by Regan, who declares that their role as guard of honour for the Prime Minister's visit will be stripped from the platoon after their performance on the range. Only a trick shooter from an entertainment stage show can restore Regan's confidence in them.

GUEST CAST:

Barbara Windsor as Laura La Plaz
Janet Davies as Mrs Pike
Caroline Dowdeswell as Janet King
Martin Wyldeck as Major Regan
Jimmy Perry as Charlie Cheeseman
Thérèse McMurray as Girl at the Window

Marksmanship by Geoff Winship

REVIEW:

Shooting Pains is the last episode of the first run and sets up the format for the show's future. For one thing, the physical comedy elements are present here more than in any of the previous five episodes, such as when Mainwaring is given a pistol and accidentally fires it in the office (enough to make one jump and laugh at both your own response and that of the characters on screen).

Moments like this are set to become far more frequent. All seven members of the regular cast have an equal share of the plot, and happily, for the first time since *The Man and the Hour*, an equal share of the script too. *Shooting Pains* is thoroughly entertaining and finishes the first series in sure-fire style, leaving the viewer begging for more. Everybody involved, whether in front of or behind the camera, is on top form. It is clear that *Dad's Army* could only go from strength to strength from here and, as we know, it did.

MEMORABLE MOMENT:

Forget Barbara Windsor firing a gun through her legs, Frazer saving the day or Jones being hoisted in the air on top of the target, the most memorable moment is the triumphant final scene when Mainwaring falls his men in for inspection by none other than...Winston Churchill. It is a brief yet wonderful moment that rounds the series off with a flourish and a nod to the Walmington-on-Sea platoon's progress over the course of the last six episodes. Even if the series had not been recommissioned, this would still have made a fulfilling and glorious ending.

LINE:

Mainwaring: To tell you the truth, Wilson, I was a bit ashamed of our shooting last week.
Wilson: <*glancing away and rubbing his ear lobe*> Oh, I don't know, sir, some of the men didn't do too badly.
Mainwaring: No, I still fail to understand how they can possibly mistake the tyres on the area commander's staff car for the target.
Wilson: All four of them?
Mainwaring: No, all five of them – they got the spare as well!

WATCH OUT FOR:

- **Writer and creator Jimmy Perry making a cameo appearance as entertainer Charlie Cheeseman, and a guest appearance from *Carry On* regular and national treasure Barbara Windsor as Laura La Plaz.**
- **Corporal Jones exclaims his catchphrase "Don't panic!" for the very first time.**
- **The moment Mainwaring and his men salute as guard of honour while a certain cigar-chomping, Homburg-hat-wearing iconic figure comes into shot...**

BEHIND THE SCENES:

The decision to take the cast to a real firing range came as a surprise to Thérèse McMurray, who commented: 'I remember being taken down to this army firing range and being a little scared when Harold Snoad told everyone to be careful where they walked as there could be live shells around. I kept thinking to myself: "What are the BBC thinking of!"'[7]

The show had passed its trial run and a second series was commissioned by the BBC, and the press, although varied at times, had started to see the potential in *Dad's Army* becoming a firm household favourite. BBC TV's Chief Publicity Officer Kevin Smith sent David Croft a collection of newspaper reviews just five days after *Shooting Pains* had been transmitted. Along with the clippings was a note from Smith, which read: 'More newspaper reviews for you. Just for the record there has been no comedy series in the last twelve months which has attracted anywhere near the number of reviews *Dad's Army* has. Nor has any comedy series received this kind of universal praise.'[8]

TRIVIA:

Private Pike, in one of the first instances where he displays his love of films, is influenced to shoot his gun on the range in a similar style to the way American actor Gary Cooper did in a film both he and Wilson saw. The film they are talking about, but do not mention, is the 1938 romantic-comedy western *The Cowboy and the Lady.*

SCORE: 8/10

With the series ending on a high it looked as though *Dad's Army* had the potential to become a mainstay on British television. Although some reviews at the time had been a little harsh, with The Daily Telegraph's Sean Day-Lewis praising Perry and Croft for their 'real gift of satire,' but then going on to say that the show had the 'tendency to go for laughs at all costs, even if they punctured the atmosphere.'[9]

Others had praised the programme and spotted the makings of a household favourite. Mary Malone of the Daily Mirror wrote, 'Who could resist the sight of little home guard commander, Mainwaring, harnessing his raggle-taggle fireside fighters into a force bent on the fight to a finish in true Dunkirk spirit? This make-do-and-improvise war effort is funny and human and nostalgic. This war I'll watch.'[10]

Dad's Army had slowly gathered momentum over its first series and by the end of the six episode run had aquired an average audience rating of 8.2 million. According to members of the BBC1 Viewing Panel - which gave feedback on material broadcasted by the BBC and was used as a method of gauging public opinion - *The Man and the Hour* was warmly received, with its bygone charm winning survey volunteers over: 'What memories it brought back! I really enjoyed it. We chuckled all the way through...its nostalgic appeal for the older generation goes without saying, but there were also comments to the effect that its entertainment value was not restricted to those who remembered the Home Guard, and that in many cases it made excellent family viewing.'[11]

However, not everybody on the panel were as high praising. 'Roughly one in three were more guarded in their opinions. Although some of them enjoyed the episode up to a point, even finding it "quite funny in parts", there was a feeling that the picture was rather exaggerated and the treatment "too farcical", with more than a hint of "taking the mickey out of the Home Guard" The following are two examples of this:

- "I enjoyed it, but wondered how those actually in the LDV would feel about this send-up. We can laugh now, but it was anything but laughable then." (Housewife/schoolgirl during the war)
- "Very true to life, but I didn't care for the lampooning of the LDV. Everything in the early days of the war had its funny side, but not buffoonery like this." (Book-keeper/former ATS)[12]

By the fifth episode, *The Showing Up of Corporal Jones,* the panel had warmed a little more to the show: 'This episode...was even more favourably received than the previous four. *Dad's Army* was clearly a popular show, and a number of regular viewers expressed their regrets that it was coming to an end and hoped for a further series.

'Viewers who could remember the war years obviously felt that it captured the spirit of wartime Britain, with endearingly recognizable characters "only slightly larger than life".

“The actors were highly praised, Arthur Lowe, Clive Dunn and John Le Mesurier having established themselves well in the leading parts, it was said, and the whole team giving convincing characterisations. There were a few complaints of such points as “forced acting”, “artificial sets”, and the contrast between film inserts and studio scenes being too noticeable, but the production as a whole was generally considered satisfactory.

‘Attention to detail and the inclusion of excerpts from wartime songs, it was remarked, added greatly to the atmosphere of authenticity.’[13]

Just over a month after the final episode had been broadcast, the team were back in the studio to commence filming on series two, one thing was clear: *Dad’s Army* had arrived.

SERIES TWO

ALL EPISODES MADE AND BROADCAST IN BLACK AND WHITE

Author's Note: At the time of writing, three episodes are missing from series two. I have tried to fill in the gaps with as much information about these installments as possible. As an audio-only recording exists of *A Stripe for Frazer* I was able to review the episode, but since *The Loneliness of the Long Distance Walker* and *Under Fire* are both missing entirely, I have not reviewed them. See the chapter 'Whatever Happened to the Missing Episodes of *Dad's Army*' for more information.

MAIN CAST:

ARTHUR LOWE - CAPTAIN GEORGE MAINWARING
JOHN LE MESURIER - SERGEANT ARTHUR WILSON
CLIVE DUNN - LANCE CORPORAL JACK JONES
JOHN LAURIE - PRIVATE JAMES FRAZER
ARNOLD RIDLEY - PRIVATE CHARLES GODFREY
JAMES BECK - PRIVATE JOE WALKER
IAN LAVENDER - PRIVATE FRANK PIKE

FEATURING THE VOICE OF BUD FLANAGAN

EPISODE SEVEN
OPERATION KILT

RECORDED ON 13TH OCTOBER 1968
FIRST BROADCAST ON 1ST MARCH 1969
VIEWING FIGURE: 13.9 MILLION

PLOT:

Mainwaring receives a letter from GHQ, detailing that all Home Guard units must carry out 15 minutes of physical training before parade. Captain Ogilvy of the Highland regiment interrupts the exercise to brief the men, telling them that his nine-man platoon will try to take over their headquarters at Manor Farm in a training mission and boasting that his men are real soldiers and much fitter than what Walmington-on-Sea has to offer. Determined to prove him wrong, the platoon hatch a plan...

GUEST CAST:

Janet Davies as Mrs Pike
James Copeland as Captain Ogilvy
Colin Daniels as Small Boy

REVIEW:

As the first episode of the second series, *Operation Kilt* has a difficult job on its hands. It must try to build on what has gone before, retaining the interest of those viewers who faithfully watched the first series, but also seek to be funnier and tighter than its predecessors, learning from what has worked before. Thankfully this episode fulfils this brief. The writing is so tight that the only extra padding on show is some of the cast members' beer bellies in the exercise scene.

While it is a chuckle to watch the men having a workout, this does take up a vast chunk of the episode and a little bit more time spent on the actual night of manoeuvres would have been preferable instead. Nit-picky perhaps, but it is hard to find a flaw in such a good episode. Repeated viewing does not diminish *Operation Kilt*'s power to entertain, and it stands as a shining example of *Dad's Army*'s monochrome days. For 25 years this episode was the stuff of myth and legend, seemingly lost forever. Recovered in 2001, it is now held in high regard by fans of the show.

MEMORABLE MOMENT:

Without a doubt, the scene with Walker and Frazer in the cow field while disguised as a member of the herd. It is laugh-out-loud hilarious. It isn't just the situation that makes the scene one of the funniest in the black-and-white era of the programme, it is the mannerisms of the pair as they waddle along in the crude outfit, especially the moment when we see a hand poke out of the 'cow' to open the gate. The conclusion of the sequence sees a big fierce bull look the way of the 'cow' and begin to run, slowly at first but then faster and faster towards his prey - it is a fantastic, stomach-hurting moment and my personal highlight.

LINE:

Jones: This is an order. Captain Mainwaring wants you to strip off.
Frazer: Strip off! For what?
Jones: You're gonna take some PT.

Frazer: (pointing at Godfrey) He can't strip off. It's only his clothes that's keeping him from falling apart.

WATCH OUT FOR:

- **Private Frazer has a tattoo on his left arm which reads 'Scotland forever.'**
- **Corporal Jones falls through a hole in the bottom of the cart while the platoon devise their plan to spy on the Highland regiment. But if Jones fell through such a hole, how does the hay stay on top of the cart?**

BEHIND THE SCENES:

Operation Kilt was recorded just under a month after the first series had finished transmission, and the crew had to come up with ways of making the budget stretch at the very start of the second run. The production team had originally intended to shoot the churchyard scenes at Honington School in Bury St Edmunds, Suffolk, but it was too expensive to transport the cast and crew to the location and so a set was built in the studio. Both David Croft and Jimmy Perry decided that this set should also be used for the line-up instead of the church hall, leaving space for only Mainwaring's office elsewhere in the studio. The churchyard set was redressed for the outdoor scenes in the final act and kept for later episodes.

Clive Dunn and James Copeland had body doubles for the scene when they are caught in the booby traps that Mainwaring and his men had made.

For the brief moment they are seen flying up in the air, Colin Bean (who played Private Sponge) and Richard Jacques stood in, remaining hidden behind straw until they were needed to achieve the illusion on screen. Jimmy Perry thought the episode was 'marvellous' and recalled the day when they shot the scene with Walker and Frazer dressed up as a cow. The sequence, which saw the actors replaced by stuntmen in case of any danger in the presence of the herd, was apparently enjoyed as much by the series' makers as the audience: 'In the same field there were 40 real cows. Suddenly they went crazy following the panto cow everywhere. We filmed it all, it was wonderfully funny.'[1]

TRIVIA:

This episode was considered lost forever after falling victim to the BBC's policy of wiping material they deemed of no further broadcast or commercial value. However, in June 2001, a 16mm telerecording of the show was discovered, along with *The Battle of Godfrey's Cottage*, having been kept in a garden shed since the 1970s. The films had been saved from a skip outside Elstree Studios and it is likely that these were copies made for the viewing purposes of filmmakers who were looking into the possibility of making a feature-length movie of the programme. After considerable restoration by BBC staff, the episode was repeated for the first time in over thirty years after its original broadcast.

SCORE: 8.5/10

EPISODE EIGHT:

THE BATTLE OF GODFREY'S COTTAGE

RECORDED ON 20TH OCTOBER 1968
FIRST BROADCAST ON 8TH MARCH 1969
VIEWING FIGURE: 11.3 MILLION

PLOT:

Captain Mainwaring briefs the men in the cramped Novelty Rock Emporium on their positions in case of invasion. He announces that the strongholds should be the Emporium and Private Godfrey's cottage, which will be used as the machine-gun post if the agreed alert of the church bells ringing signals the Nazis' advances. The next day in the Bank, Wilson and Pike are about to lock up and prepare for an evening's outing with the troops when they hear the church bells ringing. The Germans are coming!

GUEST CAST:

Janet Davies - Mrs Pike
Amy Dalby - Dolly
Nan Braunton - Cissy
Bill Pertwee - ARP Warden Hodges
Colin Bean - Private Sponge

REVIEW:

After a quarter of a century absent from the BBC Archives, lying forgotten in a garden shed, it is nothing short of a miracle that *The Battle of Godfrey's Cottage* survived to be viewed today. Luckier still, is the fact that it also turns out to be one of the best early episodes of *Dad's Army.* Here the relationships between the regular characters really begin to settle down, and the main cast clearly start to gel with each other, even if they are apart for the majority of the story. There is much to look out for in the episode, but in particular it allows us a brief glimpse into the private life of one of the platoon's quieter members. Godfrey, portrayed by the charming Arnold Ridley, is a sweet man, but it's hard to understand why he did not move out of the cottage he shares with his nightmarish sisters years ago as he seems rather hen-pecked and under the thumb. *The Battle of Godfrey's Cottage* still remains a strong episode, full of comedy hijinks, and while it may be lacking in some surprise and explanation of plot, we should be thankful that, unlike half of the other episodes from this series, it survives.

MEMORABLE MOMENT:

The underplayed yet touching scene when Mainwaring, Jones and Frazer admit to themselves that they alone would not be able to hold off the German invasion force, and that if this is indeed the moment they have been waiting for, it could mean the end of them. Beautifully acted, especially by Arthur Lowe, the sequence reminds us that behind the bumbling incompetence these men were heroes, willing to lay down their lives for the good of their country.

LINE:

Dolly: Would you like a cup of tea, Mr Jones?
Jones: Not just now Missus Godfrey, you see the Germans are coming.
Dolly: Yes, I know, so many people for tea. I think I'd better make some more.

WATCH OUT FOR:

- **Percy the Parrot calling his owners 'faggots'.**
- **In the first scene at the Emporium, Private Walker salutes Captain Mainwaring. In return, Mainwaring mistakenly calls him 'Corporal'.**
- **When putting the black board up over the window in Mainwaring's office, Ian Lavender manages to make the office wall wobble at the same time.**

BEHIND THE SCENES:

The Battle of Godfrey's Cottage, which was a particular favourite of David Croft, was written at a time when there was still a sense of uncertainty from the press that *Dad's Army* would be successful. The first series had been given a lukewarm reception by some and the pressure was on to impress both the viewing audience and those working on the show, although Perry and Croft had confidence that it would be a hit.

To make matters more difficult, during this episode's rehearsals, production manager Harold Snoad voiced his opinion that some of the cast were inept at learning their lines.

The actors, several of them veterans of stage and screen, were dumbfounded at the outburst, as Jimmy Perry remembers: 'There was a terrible silence, my blood froze, and the cast stared at Harold... they were a bunch of tough old pros, and it was the first time that anyone had had the courage to speak to them in that way. Would there be a terrible confrontation? They all stared at Harold in disbelief and then walked away muttering. It soon blew over.'[2]

TRIVIA:

The film that Sergeant Wilson is meant to be taking the Home Guard platoon to see at GHQ's request is *Next of Kin*, a 1942 propaganda film. Produced by Ealing Studios and commissioned by the British War Office, the film was an informative piece to promote the Government's message that 'careless talk costs lives.' It was still used by the British Military right up to the 1960s.

SCORE: 9/10

EPISODE NINE

THE LONELINESS OF THE LONG DISTANCE WALKER

RECORDED ON 27TH OCTOBER 1968

FIRST BROADCAST ON 15TH MARCH 1969
VIEWING FIGURE: 11.3 MILLION

THIS EPISODE IS CURRENTLY MISSING FROM THE BBC ARCHIVES

PLOT:

Private Walker is missing from parade, and the men begin to fret about how they will get their black-market supplies if he does not appear. When he does finally make it, he announces to Captain Mainwaring that he has been called up for his medical in ten days' time. Despite listing himself as a banana salesman and wholesale supplier of illuminated signs, it looks as though the platoon will be losing him to the war effort, and so Mainwaring and the men decide to take action. The following evening, Mainwaring and Wilson visit the Brigadier at the War Office in London to tell him of Walker's value and that he is indispensible to the Walmington-on-Sea Home Guard, but a crossed wire in communications results in the Brigadier thinking that Private Walker is actually a long-distance walker who is trying to get out of representing a walking tournament. Falsely, Mainwaring and Wilson believe he will help their cause and are about to begin their journey home, but an air raid forces them to sleep in the tube at Trafalgar Square Underground station, next to a polite blonde girl called Judy.

The following day, the pair arrive late to open the bank and Pike notices a blonde hair on the shoulder of his manager. Mainwaring, upon hearing that Wilson is on the Military Service Hardship Committee, which looks into individuals who have a case against being called up if they own a one-man business, decides that the Committee should hear Walker's case.

When the tribunal commences, Mainwaring does his best to support Walker, but Wilson is sitting on the other side of the desk and is adamant that he will remain impartial in the case. As the meeting ends, the Committee decide that Walker must present his books, but he cannot produce them as he does not keep any. After Mainwaring refuses to help him out in faking them, the rest of the platoon try out various methods to make him unfit for service, including getting him to jump barefooted off a ladder nearly 500 times in the hope of turning his feet flat, and making him eat soap to raise his heart rate. Walker is still passed A1. The Home Guard have lost him.

Walker reports at the infantry training barracks and is issued with a khaki uniform and treated to spam fritters for dinner. However, that night, the medics are called to his bed as he appears bloated and unwell. Back in the church hall some time later, Mainwaring is addressing his platoon when Walker arrives, announcing that he can rejoin the Home Guard as he is unfit to fight due to his allergy to corned beef.

GUEST CAST:

Anthony Sharp as Brigadier (War Office)
Diana King as Chairwoman

Patrick Waddington as Brigadier
Edward Evans as Mr Reed
Michael Knowles as Captain Cutts
Gilda Perry as Blonde
Larry Martyn as Soldier
Robert Lankesheer as Medical Officer
Colin Bean as Private Sponge

LINE:

Brigadier: Sit down, gentlemen. I can give you five minutes only. I'll just take down the details. What's this walker's name?
Mainwaring: I beg your pardon, sir?
Brigadier: The walker's name, man!
Mainwaring: Walker, sir.
Brigadier: I know that - I want his name.
Wilson: His name's Walker, sir.
Brigadier: Do you mean to say that you've got a walker named Walker?
Mainwaring: Yes, sir.
Brigadier: That's unusual - eh, Cutts?
Cutts: Oh, I don't know, sir. I knew a butcher named Butcher once.
Brigadier: Yes, perhaps you're right. Well - go on - what's his record?
Mainwaring: His record, sir?
Brigadier: He's got a record, hasn't he?
Mainwaring: <*Aside to Wilson*> Has he got a record, Wilson?
Wilson: I don't think he's ever been found out, sir.

BEHIND THE SCENES:

The episode was filmed at the same time as the *Christmas Night with the Stars* insert which was shown on Christmas Day in 1968, about three months before *The Loneliness of the Long Distance Walker* received its one and only transmission in the United Kingdom. It was also planned for broadcast on 20th January but the second series' transmission date was pushed back to be shown later in the year, and as a consequence, the episode was moved in the pecking orderto the middle of the series.

Patrick Waddington, who played the Brigadier who rings the church hall to ask Walker for his supplies and should not be confused with Anthony Sharp's Brigadier who works at the War Office in the episode, was a well-known stage actor who had toured with David Croft's mother in a musical called *Prudence* before the war.

Despite wanting to build a set for the tribunal scene, budget constraints meant that the church hall set would have to do, but the cast and crew did manage to get out on location to the Regent's Park Barracks and a tiny set was built at the side of the studio to represent the small room at the War Office.

TRIVIA:

The Lady Chairman of the Committee was played by actress Diana King, who went on to play Captain Peacock's wife in *Are You Being Served?* She had an extensive career and was a mainstay on both the small and big screen, but is remembered for her appearances in sitcoms throughout the 1960s and 1970s.

Her credits include *The Avengers, Dixon of Dock Green, Fawlty Towers, The Liver Birds, George and Mildred, Rising Damp* and *Some Mothers Do 'Ave 'Em.*

EPISODE TEN

SGT. WILSON'S LITTLE SECRET

RECORDED ON 4TH NOVEMBER 1968
FIRST BROADCAST ON 22ND MARCH 1969
VIEWING FIGURE: 13.6 MILLION

PLOT:

Wilson frets after overhearing part of a conversation between Mrs Pike and Frank that suggests she is pregnant. When he confides in Mainwaring, the Captain is adamant that he should do the honourable thing and marry her. Wilson admits that he has never gotten around to asking Mavis about marriage and is implored to ask her that night by Mainwaring. Will he go through with it before 'Little Arthur' arrives?

GUEST CAST:

Janet Davies as Mrs Pike
Graham Harboard as Little Arthur

REVIEW:

For years *Sgt. Wilson's Little Secret* was the only visual record we had of the second series of *Dad's Army*, and it turns out that it was actually rather representative. It is funny too, with some fantastic performances, several memorable scenes and, at its centre, a masterclass in suffering from John Le Mesurier, as Wilson is put through the emotional wringer for the very first time. We are finally allowed a peek into the Pikes' residence here, and can see the family set-up and just how Wilson fits into the fold, something that had only been hinted at in previous instalments. We also get the first, albeit off-screen, appearance of Mrs Mainwaring in this episode, revealing a more coy and somewhat timid side to Mainwaring's character when addressing his wife, while Wilson's delightful smile as he is witness to who really wears the trousers in the Mainwaring household is superb. There are good solid performances from the rest of the main cast, with the improvised disguise line-up a highlight of the piece. Sadly, the last few minutes spoil what would have otherwise been a very good episode.

MEMORABLE MOMENT:

When Mainwaring takes his military hat off and tells Wilson that he can confide in his Captain as it is obvious that something is bothering him. When Wilson announces that Mavis is pregnant, Mainwaring is shocked to the core. The second that the penny drops, Mainwaring changes tack completely, reverting back to being Wilson's superior. The whole scene is a demonstration in perfect comedy timing from Lowe and Le Mesurier.

LINE:

Mainwaring: Now what's all this about Mrs Pike?
Wilson: <*blurting it out*> She's going to have a baby, sir.
Mainwaring: Oh good, I expect her husband will be delighted and... but she's a widow isn't she?
Wilson: Yes.
Mainwaring: Then how can she have a baby? <*There is a silence - they both stare at each other.*> I thought you said you only went around there for meals!
Wilson: Well, I told you she had my ration card, sir.
Mainwaring: Yes and now she's got something else.

WATCH OUT FOR:

- **Mainwaring dressed in camouflage having his lecture interrupted by the hilarious ineptness of one Corporal Jones.**
- **In the line-up scene, Frazer calls Captain Mainwaring "Mr." This is not a mistake as he was scripted to say this, but it shows the lack of Frazer's trust in his Captain, undermining him by ignoring his rank.**

BEHIND THE SCENES:

During the making of this episode, Michael Mills, then Head of Comedy at the BBC, expressed the opinion that the viewers would begin to get tired of the now-famous 'line-up' scenes.

Apparently he shouted to Jimmy Perry in the bar of the BBC club one evening, "Don't do any more, the viewers will get bored with Arthur walking up and down inspecting the platoon. There's a limit to the amount of laughs you can get with the same joke, you know!"3

Of course, Perry and Croft were wise to ignore these instructions as the platoon inspections became part of *Dad's Army* folklore.

Mills himself had been a keen supporter of the show right from the word go when it was still entitled *The Flying Tigers* and it was he who changed the title to *Dad's Army*.

TRIVIA:

During the scene in which Mainwaring is told what is concerning Wilson, he worries about what people will think. Of course, even though there was a war on, Wilson could have been dismissed by his workplace for such conduct. In the book *Dad's Army: The Lost Episodes*, Jimmy Perry and David Croft cite the example of Lord Reith, a famously fastidious Head of the BBC, who sacked a radio producer because he was 'the innocent party of a divorce case.'4

SCORE: 6/10

EPISODE ELEVEN

A STRIPE FOR FRAZER

RECORDED ON 15TH NOVEMBER 1968

FIRST BROADCAST ON 29TH MARCH 1969
VIEWING FIGURE: 11.3 MILLION

ONLY THE AUDIO FOR THIS EPISODE SURVIVES IN THE BBC ARCHIVES

Author's Note: At the time of writing, this episode was not available for general release, but I was allowed an exclusive listen to the soundtrack for the purpose of writing this book. I thank the BBC and the BFI for making my 'viewing' possible and memorable.

PLOT:

Jones is late for platoon as Wilson struggles to get the men to keep in time and to grasp their rifles firmly. Mainwaring bursts in with a football rattle to surprise the men with a gas-attack drill. After ordering the men to fall out and practice putting on their gas masks, he notices that Walker has used his mask case to store four half bottles of whisky for the men, and Mainwaring's cigars, which Wilson notes down at his superior's request. As Mainwaring blows a whistle to signal the all-clear in their drill, a policeman rushes in, mistaking the sound as trouble and then mistakes thelecture for a real gas attack.

Captain Bailey arrives and announces that the Walmington-on-Sea Home Guard can promote one of their men to the rank of Corporal. After he leaves, Mainwaring and Wilson discuss who should be promoted, and Mainwaring proposes that they should create another Lance Corporal post first to see who has the best potential.

Wilson suggests Pike, but mostly as he would like to get back in Mrs Pike's good books after leaving her at the altar. Frazer is the only option. Wilson doubts the choice as he is insubordinate, but Mainwaring dispels his uncertainty by describing himself as a shrewd judge of character.

Mainwaring makes Frazer a Lance Corporal and breaks the news to Jones and Frazer that they will be in competition with each other for the promotion. Frazer has previous experience as he held an NCO rank, while Jones promises to temporarily stop his distribution of free meat to Mainwaring to make things fair, although he hints that he will stop completely if he loses.

Later in the church hall, Mainwaring gives a lecture on how to tackle a Nazi stormtrooper single handed and both Jones and Frazer compete for dominance, disrupting the lecture from the start, especially Frazer, who spouts glowing references for his Captain and shouts warnings to Walker for insolence. By the end of the lecture, Frazer is left in charge of the men and he leads them out of the hall. Mainwaring is impressed at how keen Frazer is to earn his stripe but Wilson is still very cautious.

The next evening, Mainwaring is astounded to find that Frazer has put several of the men on charge: Pike for deserting his post, Godfrey for cowardice in the face of the enemy and Walker for mutiny.

Jones arrives and complains as he has also been put "'on the fizzer "'for calling Frazer a word he can't repeat but is "what has been written on the paper."

Mainwaring confides in Wilson that he is reaching the end of his tether with this escapade.

At that moment, Colonel Square arrives on horseback and tells Mainwaring that he has been assigned by GHQ to instruct the platoon in guerrilla warfare under the commission 'Corporal-Colonel'.
When he sees the charge sheets, he remarks how in 1919 the platoon he was part of got through five thousand of them in a month as there was "nothing else about." He also reassures the pair that these charges would never stand up. As he departs to fall the men in, Mainwaring and Wilson seek to put a stop to the madness and call Frazer in, who complains that Square has been appointed on purpose to ruin his chances of promotion. He departs in a rage as Squaredeclares that Frazer is on charge for insolence. Frazer returns, boat hook in hand, and proceeds to try to batter his way into the side office.

GUEST CAST:

Geoffrey Lumsden - Corporal-Colonel Square
John Ringham - Captain Bailey
Gordon Peters - Policemen
Edward Sinclair - Caretaker

REVIEW:

It was always going to be a bit of a challenge to review an episode that only exists as an off-air audio recording. I worried that I may not be able to do it justice if I couldn't actually see the action, but in the event, I realised that I really didn't need to see the episode to appreciate how strong the performances were.

Here it is Frazer's turn in the spotlight, as the Scottish Private gets his big chance to step up and take on greater responsibility. However, it quickly becomes apparent that Mainwaring has made a grave error of judgment.

The script is tight and funny with some great one-liners, and John Laurie, in what is 'his episode' is quite rightly the star of the week.

Frazer lets the promise of power go to his head and becomes as overblown and over-the-top as Laurie can make him. It was to be another couple of years before Frazer's catchphrase "We're doomed, doomed!" would be uttered, but his brash Scottish manner still makes him stand out from the crowd in this second series, nowhere more so than in this episode when he alienates his chums in order to gain promotion.

At the episode's conclusion it is particularly enjoyable to hear just how angry and hurt he feels at Square's arrival. However, as with the previous episode, the central plot is not entirely cleared up by the time the credits roll, as Frazer's violent reaction poses the question of whether he will stay with the platoon after the indignity of being demoted. With only thirty minutes to tell their story, the writers appear to have run out of time for the second week running.

Wilson's lack of enthusiasm and trust in Mainwaring's decisions - from the outset here, he disagrees with his superior - makes for an interesting and subtle subplot. The rivalry between the pair is also emphasised when Mainwaring shows off his new officer's hat. Wilson fully expects to receive one too, but Mainwaring remarks that they are for officers only.

Mainwaring is clearly deeply threatened by Wilson's more upper-class status, and it is a theme that will continue to permeate the series, neatly reflecting the class-obsessed period in which the comedy is set.
Some of the interchanges between both characters are superb also (upon seeing the hat, Wilson remarks that it looks: "'...rather dinky."') Mainwaring replies, "'Suits me better than the forage cap, don't you think?"' and it gives Wilson an ideal moment to make a comment regarding his captain's appearance ("'Yes, Sir. Your face doesn't look nearly as round and moonlike."'
The physical limits the crew had when making the episode do not really come across on audio, but as there were only four scenes to spread out over the episode's duration, and with only the church hall set to play with, it took skillful writing and sterling performances to make the episode not feel static and un-engaging.
The sudden appearance of Edward Sinclair as the Verger is a somewhat wasted opportunity - he only spends a few short moments on screen, attempting to get on with the whitewashing before being shooed away by Mainwaring, who at this point is at the end of his tether due to a collision with a plank of wood. As the series progressed, the role of the Verger became more involving, but this walk-on skit does not really move the plot along and it almost feels like he could have been more involved in the script.

One way that the Verger could have been better realised on screen is to have him irritate Frazer instead of Mainwaring so it would give him an opportunity to have more of a share in dialogue and it would make more sense in the narrative as this story is all about the power Frazer acquires and how he goes too far with it. Wouldn't it have been funny to see him pick on those like the Verger who are not even members of the platoon! Ian Lavender doesn't fair much better as again he is terribly underused, with only one line of dialogue in the whole episode.

All in all *A Stripe for Frazer* is a good episode and slots nicely into the final sprint towards the end of this second series, but it is not as memorable as others. However it is unfortunate that it is missing and therefore forgotten, as Laurie is brilliant, and a couple of its set pieces featuring Walker and Mainwaring (described immediately below) are hilarious. The existing audio is an enticing window into a lost segment of *Dad's Army*.

MEMORABLE MOMENTS:

During Mainwaring's lecture on how to take on a Nazi stormtrooper, Jones, acting as the Nazi, launches himself at Walker, who instead of picking up one chair as his Captain advised, picks up a whole stack of them and gives Jones a shock for his troubles.

Mainwaring surprises the men with a gas-attack drill, which quickly descends into pandemonium as the men do their best to handle their rifles, hats and equipment and get their gas masks on as quickly as possible. In the confusion, Walker stands very still, unmoved by the chaos that surrounds him. Mainwaring is cross and as he inspects the open flap of his gas mask case, notices a bottle of whisky poking out...

LINE:

Mainwaring: ... You held NCO rank in the Navy, didn't you?
Frazer: Aye, I did that. Chief Petty Officer - before I was busted.
Mainwaring: Busted?
Frazer: Aye, I hit the officer of the watch.
Mainwaring: Did you?
Frazer: With a boat hook.
Mainwaring: Oh dear!
Frazer: The crooked end.
Mainwaring: Well, I'm sure you must have had a very good reason.
Frazer: Oh, I had that.
Mainwaring: <*To Wilson*> I thought so.
Frazer: I was drunk.
Mainwaring: Well, that's all in the past. There's not much danger of that happening again, is there Wilson?
Wilson: Not with a boat hook, sir.

LISTEN OUT FOR:

- There are reappearances for Geoffrey Lumsden as Square and John Ringham, who played Bracewell in the pilot and makes his first appearance as the recurring character Captain Bailey here.
- Captain Mainwaring obtains his officer's hat in this episode but, as pointed out by Bailey, should not wear it whilst in battle dress. Despite this 'red tape' as Mainwaring would put it, this is the look he would have for the rest of the series.
- The consequences of the events that followed *Sgt. Wilson's Little Secret* are eventually cleared up as it is revealed that Wilson left Mrs Pike stranded at the altar and the family are not presently on speaking terms. As Wilson explains: "'Oh yes, I'm speaking to them, they're not speaking to me.'"

BEHIND THE SCENES:

John Laurie once said to Jimmy Perry, 'You know, I have played every major Shakespearean role in the theatre and I'm considered the finest speaker of verse in the country, and I end up becoming famous doing this crap!'[5] Laurie's dry, cynical sense of humour marked him out from his fellow cast members, as did his rather damning and ungrateful take on the success of *Dad's Army*.

The episode also saw the return of actor Gordon Peters, who played a fireman in a cut scene from the pilot. Here he was given the role of the Policeman and finally made his first, belated, on-screen appearance on the show.

As this was the fifth show out of six to film, there was no budget left over for exterior scenes, giving Perry and Croft only the church hall set to work with and a small ensemble of guest stars. It was also the last time that Mainwaring addressed the platoon as 'chaps', as the writers felt that calling them 'men' was more in line with Mainwaring's character.

TRIVIA:

Although *A Stripe for Frazer* is currently listed as 'missing believed wiped', the off-air audio recording now held by the BFI was made by fan Ed Doolan when the show was originally broadcast. It was discovered in 2008 along with an audio copy of a *Dad's Army* sketch filmed for *Christmas with the Stars* in 1968, which is also missing.

SCORE: 7/10

EPISODE TWELVE

UNDER FIRE

RECORDED ON 27TH NOVEMBER 1968
FIRST BROADCAST ON 5TH APRIL 1969
VIEWING FIGURE: 11.6 MILLION

THIS EPISODE IS CURRENTLY MISSING FROM THE BBC ARCHIVES

PLOT:

Mainwaring and Wilson arrive at the church hall in their pyjamas, having endured a rough night away from their beds during an air raid. Corporal-Colonel Square arrives ready to help with the morning's exercise that has been planned for the platoon and is shocked at their attire.

Not long after, Captain Bailey also appears and informs Mainwaring that the docks along the coast took a heavy battering from enemy artillery in the night as the Germans are using a vast quantity of incendiary bombs, and so all Home Guard units are ordered to maximise their strength to full capacity in regards to the amount of men they can muster to take them on. Mainwaring plans to use spotters on the church tower and to use the rest of the men in the field as a mobile unit.

Later that evening, Frazer and Godfrey are posted at the church tower to oversee the town when they see a light flashing on Mortimer Street, near the site where a bomb dropped the previous evening. After they inform Mainwaring, who announces that he plans to phone the police, Square manages to convince the Captain that he has the authority to act and does not need the help of the local constabulary. Mainwaring takes Square's advice and decides that it is the men's responsibility to investigate the matter.

When Mainwaring and the platoon arrive at Mortimer Street, they decide that the light must have been coming from the top flat. They discover that the culprit for the shining is a man called Murphy, who immediately rouses their suspicion when he displays an Austrian accent and says he was born in Vienna. Murphy is adamant that he is a naturalised civilian, having lived in England for 25 years, but the men do not buy his story and think he is a spy. When they meet the another two occupants, Mrs. Keen and Mrs. Witt, they too join the platoon's suspicions of Murphy being a spy and claim that he was trying to signal the Nazi's the previous night. They arrest him and take him back to the church hall, but are troubled by yet more incendiary bombs and the responsibility of dealing with a fire as well when one of the bombs crashes through the church hall roof as Walmington-on-Sea comes under heavy bombardment. The scene in the church hall becomes one of panic as the men try desperately to put the fire out, with Mainwaring taking the full blast of a fire extinguisher to his face by accident. .

The men prove to be terrible in a crisis and chaos ensues, as they flap the fire to fan away the flames but it is all to no avail. The lack of order is restored as Mrs Pike arrives and calmly puts the fire out with a sand bag. Amongst the panic, Hodges is drawn to the church hall by the fire and is outraged at the way in which Murphy is being kept by Mainwaring's men. He proceeds to drop a bombshell of his very own by telling them that Murphy is in fact married to his aunt and it therefore his uncle and not a Nazi after all.

GUEST CAST:

Geoffrey Lumsden as Corporal-Colonel Square
Janet Davies as Mrs Pike
John Ringham as Captain Bailey
Queenie Watts as Mrs Keen
Gladys Dawson as Mrs Witt
Ernst Ulman as Sigmund Murphy
Bill Pertwee as ARP Warden Hodges
June Peterson as Woman

LINE:

Mainwaring: Frazer, you have been responsible for the stirrup pump, is it in working order?
Frazer: Yes, sir. I'll bring it round after parade.
Mainwaring: Bring it round? Why isn't it here?
Frazer: I was using it for the Dig for Victory campaign in my garden. My apples had the blight.
Mainwaring: This is a vital piece of military equipment. It must not leave our headquarters. I take it you didn't borrow the water as well?
Frazer: No, sir. Only the bucket.

BEHIND THE SCENES:

Under Fire was the final episode of *Dad's Army* to be recorded in black and white. Soon after the episode was in the can, the series was re-commissioned and in future would be made using the BBC's new colour facilities. The episode was moved back in the schedules along with the whole series from the 3rd February to its eventual transmission date and has the rare distinction of being one of the few black-and-white episodes to

have been given a repeated viewing - on the 29th August 1969, two weeks before the first episode of series three - making its absence from the archives all the more irritating.
According to pictures taken on the set, Hodges is shown wearing a black helmet. This was the last time he wore the prop, as from the beginning of series three he would be seen wearing his trademark white helmet, having been made Chief Warden and becoming a further nuisance to Captain Mainwaring.

TRIVIA:

The episode sees another early appearance of Geoffrey Lumsden as Corporal-Colonel Square and on his uniform the character was given Colonel's stripes and Corporal's pips to represent his new rank. This rank was indeed given to the veterans of the First World War, who similar to Square, were awarded a lower rank for the Home Guard to the one that they obtained during their service in The Great War thirty years previously.

The return of *Dad's Army* had been well received by viewers and the press. The average viewing figure for the series was an impressive 12.2 million - an increase of 4 million over the figure that the first run had obtained.

The show was becoming a hit, especially with members of the BBC1 viewing panel, who gave the following feedback on the series opener, *Operation Kilt*:

The panel's findings discovered that there was 'a generally warm welcome for the return of the show.'

The series opener was also praised as a good start to the second series, with the report declaring: 'if this was a sample of what was to come, they were in for a real treat, viewers often observed.'

The panel also found time to praise Dad's Army's authentic roots and that:'part of its appeal lay in its nostalgia, its reflection of wartime Britain and the early days of the Home Guard being only a little exaggerated.'

The report also found that the characterisation of the regulars had developed as: 'each member having become a real personality it was said and, in spite of the slapstick, there was always the feeling that such situations might just have occurred.'

However, the same panel also reported that some had, 'considered it dated, "corny" and "idiotic," with one member writing a particularly scathing review:

'...It was all rather silly and childish, they thought, and too far-fetched to be really funny. For the most part, however, reporting viewers responded cordially to both the script and the performance.'

Another member of the panel was impressed by the accurate portrayal of Joe Walker, commenting, "as an old Home Guard sergeant myself, I can vouch that we had a James Beck in every platoon."

Under Fire was also covered by the panel and as the audience report showed thatover two-thirds of the panel had found themselves laughing:

"immoderately and out loud" at the character's antics and that: "although larger than life," the regulars evoked an ethos that was: "so true to the spirit of the Home Guard." The scene in which the platoon tries to put the fire out: "resulted in a hilarious half-hour's viewing which achieved its comic effect without recourse to either malice or vulgarity" many declared, and therefore "made excellent family viewing." The appeal of the show to younger members of the panel was also mentioned as: "it was not only those who remembered the war who enjoyed *Dad's Army*, several reporting viewers said that their youngsters "wouldn't miss it for anything!"
However there were still some criticisms regarding the slapstick nature of some of the platoon's escapades.

The same report confirmed that:

"For a few the joke was apparently beginning to wear a bit thin," but despite this on the whole, the minority (which was recorded to be around about one in ten panel members) that expressed their disappointment: "were viewers who usually enjoyed the series but found this episode rather below standard." The episode was also criticised for its: "slapstick and childish fooling about" with buckets of water in the fire-fighting sequence which, a number had felt, spoilt the more:

"natural humour of the characters," Some also added that they were also disappointed by the "overacting of artists whose performances up to now had contributed so much to the success of the series."
However, these criticisms did not dampen the overall enjoyment of the series. The vast majority of the sample mentioned that the show's: ,"main appeal lay in its gentle humour, stemming from accurate observation of human nature in general and personal traits of a mixed bunch of men in particular."

Despite being the only series of *Dad's Army* affected by the BBC's junking policy, there is much in the remaining three episodes that displays the growing confidence and stability of the series.
The show was also a hit with the press, as exemplified by Stanley Reynolds of *The Guardian*, who wrote on March 10th 1969: 'At a time when television is going through a craze for comedy series, *Dad's Army* stands out. It is the equal of *Steptoe and Son* or *Till Death Us Do Part*. Like those superior comedies, *Dad's Army* is rooted in seriousness... This puts the comedy on a much higher plane than the jolly knockabout where the characters are obviously having a whale of a time, and the viewer is somehow supposed to get carried away by it all.'
Jimmy Perry and David Croft had arguably hit on a winning formula that they would now by-and-large stick with for the next eight years. With a spring in its step, *Dad's Army* boldly marched onto the next, extended run and into the glorious world of colour...

SERIES THREE

MAIN CAST:

ARTHUR LOWE - CAPTAIN GEORGE MAINWARING
JOHN LE MESURIER - SERGEANT ARTHUR WILSON
CLIVE DUNN - LANCE CORPORAL JACK JONES
JOHN LAURIE - PRIVATE JAMES FRAZER
ARNOLD RIDLEY - PRIVATE CHARLES GODFREY
JAMES BECK - PRIVATE JOE WALKER
IAN LAVENDER - PRIVATE FRANK PIKE

EPISODE THIRTEEN

THE ARMOURED MIGHT OF LANCE CORPORAL JONES

RECORDED ON 25TH MAY 1969
FIRST BROADCAST 11TH SEPTEMBER 1969
VIEWING FIGURE: 10.5 MILLION

PLOT:

Mainwaring gives the men a lecture on the gases that the enemy is likely to use in the event of an attack, and tells them that they need to step up their relationship with the ARP during an exercise intended to simulate an invasion. Later, Walker enquires about the availability of Jones's delivery van but Jones tells him it is out of action as he cannot get any petrol. Walker then announces his plan: to loan the van to Captain Mainwaring as platoon transport. But after the van's conversion to gas, things start to go wrong at the exercise.

GUEST CAST:

Janet Davies as Mrs Pike
Bill Pertwee as ARP Warden Hodges
Frank Williams as Vicar
Queenie Watts as Mrs Peters
Pamela Cundell as Mrs Fox
Jean St. Clair as Miss Meadows
Olive Mercer as Mrs Casson
Nigel Hawthorne as Angry man
Harold Bennett as Old man
Dick Haydon as Raymond

REVIEW:

In a burst of colour, *Dad's Army* was back with a bang, with arguably the best episode yet. Not only is *The Armoured Might of Lance Corporal Jones* brilliantly scripted, but at its heart is a magnificent performance by Clive Dunn, who is given plenty of opportunity to show off the hallmarks that made Corporal Jones such a well-loved character. In just under thirty minutes, Dunn, only 49 at the time of recording, also gives a master class in acting older than your age. However, Jones does not get to hog the limelight alone, sharing it here with Private Walker. The repartee between the characters is bang on form, especially in the cold-room scene in which they have a lot of screen time together and display obvious chemistry. The fleshing out of their respective characters is excellent. Unfortunately the final scene drags a little, showing the platoon to be idiotic rather than simply bumbling as they try to fit the 'patient' on the stretcher through a car window. Having said that, the guns-through-the-portholes-in the-van skit is still funny, even if it has become overused throughout the years. Still, what a great start to series three we have!

MEMORABLE MOMENT:

Tempting as it is to plump for the first appearance of the butcher's van and its defence mechanisms, it has to be the moment Jones and Walker converse in the freezer at the butchers and start to change as the frost bites around their faces. It is the clever yet simple application of editing and make-up that make this scene so funny and it culminates in Walker, showing delight in his colleague agreeing to lend him the van, snapping off the ends of Jones's moustache as he tries to playfully twiddle them. Brilliant.

LINE:

Mainwaring: The result? Instant decapitation, doesn't know what's happened.

Walker: Not until he nods his head!

WATCH OUT FOR:

- The debut appearance of the Vicar played by Frank Williams. We also see Corporal Jones's van for the first time, a vehicle that was set to return time and again in the series.
- **Mrs Fox tells Jones that she went away for the weekend with her 'hubby'. Later on in the run, she is widowed but nothing further is said about her marital status.**
- **Despite being promoted to Chief Warden, Hodges is still wearing his black helmet from the previous two series.**
- **Mainwaring finally gets the time correct when using the 24-hour clock and corrects Hodges in the same moment.**

BEHIND THE SCENES:

The working title for this episode was *The Armoured Might of Jack Jones.*

The fact that this was the show's first colour outing would have gone completely unnoticed by the viewing public, as BBC1 did not switch over to a colour service until 15th November the same year, meaning that the first episode to be transmitted in colour would actually be *Branded,* the eleventh episode of this series. Even then colour televisions were very rare, with most households continuing to watch *Dad's Army* in black-and-white for many years to come.

A new face to the programme was Pamela Cundell, appearing as Jones's future love interest, Mrs Fox. She remembers, 'I'm sure I was offered the part of Mrs Fox because of my wink! I was playing a fortune-teller in a BBC programme and at the end of a scene winked at the camera. David Croft was in the audience, spotted the wink and liked it. So when I appeared in *Dad's Army*, one of the first things I had to do was wink at Jonesey. Mrs Fox was a woman in a queue to start with but she developed as the series progressed. She was a wonderful character.'[1]

TRIVIA:

The part of the elderly man was played by Harold Bennett, who would go on to appear as a semi-regular, 'Mr Blewitt'. He is of course best known as Young Mr Grace over 46 episodes of *Are You Being Served?* (1972-81).

The part of the angry man was played by well-known stage and screen actor Nigel Hawthorne, who is best remembered as Sir Humphrey Appleby in *Yes, Minister* (1980-84) and its sequel *Yes, Prime Minister* (1986-88), for which he won four BAFTA awards, and for the title role in *The Madness of King George*, for which he was nominated for a Best Actor Oscar.

SCORE: 9/10

EPISODE FOURTEEN

BATTLE SCHOOL

RECORDED ON 1ST JUNE 1969

FIRST BROADCAST ON 18TH SEPTEMBER 1969
VIEWING FIGURE: 11.4 MILLION

PLOT:

The men make their way to a guerrilla warfare training camp where they meet the unconventional Captain Rodrigues, who served in Spain during the Civil War. Rodrigues describes himself as an informal person who delights in Nazi killings. After a disastrous day in which they are supposed to capture the HQ, Mainwaring goes missing.

GUEST CAST:

Alan Tilvern as Captain Rodrigues
Alan Haines as Major Smith
Colin Bean as Private Sponge

REVIEW:

Battle School is a well-rounded and strongly written instalment featuring some very enjoyable physical comedy. However, at times it is somewhat spoiled by some poor special effects and continuity problems, that at certain points seriously detract from the narrative. Some of the problems relate to the BBC's early experimentation with Colour Separation Overlay (CSO, a technique whereby sequences were filmed in front of a green or blue screen and later blended in with another pre-filmed background.

Here, when the platoon are on the train, the scenery rushing past does not tally with the speed at which they are meant to be going. Specifically, unless Private Godfrey was an early prototype for the Six Million Dollar Man with bionic legs, his hopping off the train for a second and then rushing back to catch it again while it is travelling full pelt is less than believable. The best part of the episode, in which the men are put through their paces on the battlefield, features a blatant continuity error. Walker is meant to have broken away from the others to search for food in a nearby barn, but he keeps appearing back with the platoon and taking part in the exercise. Perhaps there was a lack of suitable location footage and the editor had no choice but to use what he had, or maybe the script had to be changed for unforeseen reasons? Whatever the explanation, it makes for distracting viewing.

MEMORABLE MOMENT:

Arthur Lowe flexes his physical comedy muscles many times in this episode, and his pratfalls make the exercise scenes in particular very entertaining. The slapstick doesn't dull by repetition either as Mainwaring falls in water twice as well as down a concealed hole, bangs his head on the underside of a table and even falls victim to an unwanted fag end in his food. Lowe ensures that the sight of his small, pot-bellied frame, flinging himself into the murky waters is a joy to behold, and not just by us - Wilson's smirk when Mainwaring falls feet first into a lake looks so natural that it is perhaps more John Le Mesurier than his character.

LINE:

Jones: I just wanted you to know I've still got faith in you.

Mainwaring: Thank you, Corporal.

Jones: ... even if no one else has.

WATCH OUT FOR:

- **When the platoon is marching to the battle school, they whistle the programme's theme tune to keep up morale on their journey.**

BEHIND THE SCENES:

The opening scene will be familiar to fans of the 1953 British comedy film *The Titfield Thunderbolt* as footage of the train (a 14xx Great Western Tank Engine) is recycled for the programme's use. When the platoon are seen departing the train at the station, a different train was used. The sequence was filmed at Wendling Railway Station near Dereham in Norfolk, which had been closed for a year by the time the *Dad's Army* team arrived on location.

It was whilst filming the *Battle School* location scenes that the actors were individually recorded walking past the trees for the famous end credit sequence. This sequence would remain in place until the final episode *Never Too Old* was transmitted in 1977.

A number of narrative elements from this episode were later used in the 1971 feature film, namely the platoon attending a training school, their missing both supper and breakfast affecting the men's morale, and Godfrey's use of the poem *The Owl and the Pussycat* to distract him from wanting to be 'excused'.

TRIVIA:

Character actor Alan Tilvern, who plays Rodrigues here, later featured as R. K. Maroon in the 1988 feature film *Who Framed Roger Rabbit?*

There are some striking comparisons between the battle camp in this episode and a real one located in Osterley Park, London during the Second World War which was also used to train Home Guard volunteers in unconventional methods of guerrilla warfare, and was even run by a veteran from the Spanish Civil War.

SCORE: 5/10

EPISODE FIFTEEN

THE LION HAS 'PHONES

RECORDED ON 8TH JUNE 1969

FIRST BROADCAST ON 25TH SEPTEMBER 1969

VIEWING FIGURE: 11.3 MILLION

PLOT:

Mainwaring gives the troops a lecture on communications and tells them that the main areas that the Nazis are likely to attempt to destroy in order to put the town out of action are the gas station, railway bridge, telephone exchange and reservoir. He decides that two men will be posted at each of the points and orders that if they find themselves under attack they are to run to the nearest telephone box to call him in the church hall. Later that evening, Frazer and Walker are out on patrol and witness a plane crash into the reservoir...

GUEST CAST:

Janet Davies as Mrs Pike
Bill Pertwee as ARP Warden Hodges
Avril Angers as Telephone Operator
Timothy Carlton as Lieutenant Hope-Bruce
Stanley McGeagh as Sergeant Waller
Pamela Cundell, Olive Mercer, Bernadette Milnes as Ladies in the queue
Gilda Perry as Doreen
Linda James as Betty
Richard Jacques as Mr Cheesewright
Colin Daniels and Carson Green as Boys

REVIEW:

The Lion Has 'Phones is an improvement on the previous helping and sees the men right at the heart of protecting their community for the first time, although in the event we don't really get to see enough of that. Ian Lavender's portrayal of Pike is wonderful here. In the previous two series the character has had very little to do and this episode is the first time he is given enough dialogue to showcase just how good he can be. It is very easy to forget that Lavender was playing a character younger than his own age (he was 23 when he recorded this episode, six years older than Pike) as he is spot on as the molly-coddled 'stupid boy'. He is yet to aggravate Mainwaring as much as he would later on in the run, but here you can see their double act start to work. The scene with Pike and Mainwaring in the phone box is particularly brilliant and instantly quotable. Praise must also go to Clive Dunn as Jones, especially for the scene in which Jones's ineptness leads to a farcical piece of miscommunication between the box office lady and the telephone operator. The dialogue sparkles and the conviction is very amusing. The episode is built on communication and how a lack of it or a misunderstanding can lead to problems for all involved. It is a theme that could perhaps have been explored a little more, but it does prompt some great moments of comedy. There are a couple of elements that just slow the pace too much, particularly the scene in the church hall. Storylines are just as important in a comedy show as in drama, and *Dad's Army*'s biggest problem at this point is still its inability to wrap up a plot satisfactorily. Obviously budget played a part here as scenes in the studio were far more cheaply realised than those on location, but it is a shame nonetheless.

LINE:

Mainwaring: Now, as you know, very few of us can survive for long without water to drink.
Frazer: I've been managing for years.

WATCH OUT FOR:

- When Mainwaring exclaims "Bloody cheek!" Wilson claims to have never heard him swear before. This is inaccurate as in the series one episode *The Showing Up of Corporal Jones* he hears Mainwaring say a much ruder word.
- Pike wears a white scarf instead of his iconic Aston Villa one when he joins the platoon at the reservoir.
- Wilson gets a chance to try out Jones's catchphrase as he tells Lieutenant Hope Bruce that the Germans "Don't like it up 'em."

BEHIND THE SCENES:

The episode's original title was *Sorry, Wrong Number*, and was changed to the rather clumsy *The Lion Has 'Phones* at a late stage. When the episode was remade for the *Dad's Army* radio series, broadcast on 6th May 1974, the original title was used instead.

Richard Jacques, who played Mr Cheeseman, later said about his time on the show, 'Working on *Dad's Army* was a very happy period for me. The 'stars' were very kind and considerate, as were all the crew. My favourite memory was of dear old Arnold Ridley, at our lunch break when we were filming in the middle of a forest, sitting on a tree stump, eating his lunch, and looking for all the world like a little rosy gnome.'2

TRIVIA:

The episode's title is a nod towards a 1939 propaganda film called *The Lion has Wings*, which persuaded the government to see the value in war propaganda and encouraged them to use the medium of film as a way of

disseminating information to the public.
Meanwhile, the popular 1941 film *One of Our Aircraft Is Missing* features in both the script and in poster form on a wall in the cinema box office.

SCORE: 6/10

EPISODE SIXTEEN

THE BULLET IS NOT FOR FIRING

RECORDED ON 22ND JUNE 1969

FIRST BROADCAST ON 2ND OCTOBER 1969

VIEWING FIGURE: 11.8 MILLION

PLOT:

Mainwaring and Wilson greet the men back from patrol who admit that they have used up all their ammunition in one evening after being on patrol all night. Mainwaring is shocked by the news as except for Godfrey the men only have five rounds left each. Mainwaring tells Wilson that he will have to report the matter to HQ and tells the men to boil their weapons before they have their tea. The men are unhappy with the decision, and despite Wilson's pleas to let the situation go, Mainwaring organises an enquiry.

GUEST CAST:

Janet Davies as Mrs Pike
Frank Williams as the Vicar
Edward Sinclair as the Verger
Harold Bennett as Mr Blewitt
May Warden as Mrs Dowding
Michael Knowles as Captain Cutts
Tim Barrett as Captain Pringle
Fred Tomlinson as Choir member
Kate Forge as Choir member
Eolith McNab as Choir member
Andrew Daye as Choir member
Arthur Lewis as Choir member

REVIEW:

In an episode about Captain Mainwaring's desire to do things by the book, Jimmy Perry and David Croft allow the character's adverse reaction to an incident as a plot device to drive the narrative along. It also explores how his outright refusal to let the event slide leads to an ultimately unnecessary enquiry, a deed that could potentially have landed the platoon in hot water. The main theme that runs throughout *The Bullet is not for Firing* is Mainwaring's stubbornness in the face of adversity and statements of fact from members of his platoon. The voice of reason this episode is Wilson, who is on top form as Mainwaring's counter point in the piece. When his suggestions on how to obtain more ammunition falls on deaf ears, he admits defeat...but not before delivering another verbal blow to his superior's arrogance. As Mainwaring goes to cheer the men up, Wilson advices him against it as he is the catalyst for their demeanour. As soon as the court of enquiry commences it soon descends into farce, with attendees for the Vicar's choir meeting and members of Mainwaring's own platoon sabotaging proceedings with brilliant comic timing. It is clear that Mainwaring has lost control of the situation - especially as the two officers from Area Command are clearly disinterested by the whole affair. The episode culminates with Jones literally bringing the roof down when demonstrating what he did as the suspected enemy plane flew overhead, leaving us with a great visual gag to take away from a very memorable episode. With the cast in fine form and some of the snappiest dialogue delivered so far this series, *The Bullet is not for Firing* is one of the strongest episodes so far in *Dad's Army*'s run.

MEMORABLE MOMENT:

A subtle yet laugh-out loud moment when Mainwaring walks out of the side office into the church hall to be smothered by the Union Flag by Walker and Pike - further evidence that Arthur Lowe didn't need dialogue to be funny. His look here is as hilarious as any one-liner.

LINE:

<Choir singing in the background>

Jones: I was just about to give the order...I was just gonna...

Mainwaring: What's the matter, Corporal?

Jones: I think I'm going, sir. I hear angel's voices.

Mainwaring: Those aren't angels. It's the choir in the office!
Jones: Well, if that's what it's like to go, I like it, I like it.

WATCH OUT FOR:

- **The old lady resting her head on Mainwaring's shoulder as he tussles with the Vicar in the side room over the choir noise.**
- **Harold Bennett's first credited appearance as semi-regular Mr. Blewitt contradicts his earlier performance in *The Armoured Might of Corporal Jones* as he says that he has had his leg up in bed for 16 months.**
- **Walker has rather skilfully recycled his empty cartridges into lighters.**

BEHIND THE SCENES:

Edward Sinclair makes his first appearance as the Verger, despite previous appearances in a handful of episodes as 'the Caretaker' for which he had not yet donned his familiar costume. We must assume that this is his official debut as the character we recognise for the rest of the series' run.

Frank Williams (playing the Vicar here in one of his earliest appearances in the series) remembered watching the scene in which Wilson is told that a Court of Enquiry has been ordered, and marvelling at the actor's performance. 'The scene in this episode where John Le Mesurier walks around Mainwaring's desk saying: "Oh dear, Oh dear" all the time is brilliant. I used to watch it every day in rehearsals because the timing was just perfect.'3

TRIVIA:

Michael Knowles, who makes his second appearance as Captain Cutts, went on to find fame in *It Ain't Half Hot Mum* as another upper-class-twit Captain Jonathan Ashwood. As a member of Perry and Croft's unofficial repertory company he also went on to a similar role in *You Rang M'Lord.* He also co-wrote the radio sequel of *Dad's Army,* entitled *It Sticks Out Half A Mile* and also contributed in adapting the programme from television to radio with Harold Snoad.

SCORE: 8/10

EPISODE SEVENTEEN

SOMETHING NASTY IN THE VAULT

RECORDED ON 15TH JUNE 1969

FIRST BROADCAST ON 9TH OCTOBER 1969

VIEWING FIGURE: 11.1 MILLION

PLOT:

An unexploded bomb is discovered in the bank's strong room after an air raid. Both Mainwaring and Wilson try to move the object but are then trapped with the bomb in their arms and they both admit they are frightened by the situation. A while later, the platoon are the first to arrive on the scene. They think of ways of calming the situation and keeping morale up. Will the platoon come up with a way of saving their Captain and Sergeant's lives?

GUEST CAST:

Bill Pertwee as ARP Warden Hodges
Janet Davies as Mrs Pike
Robert Dorning as Mr West, the Bank Inspector
Norman Mitchell as Captain Rogers

REVIEW:

The superlatives that can be used to describe *Something Nasty in the Vault* would not do it justice. The script is near flawless - masterfully Perry and Croft produce their best thirty minutes up to this point in the series life and it delightfully manages to stay minimalistic in its premise. The script is all about the relationship between two men, polar opposites in class, opinion and temperament. Mainwaring and Wilson, trapped together in a perilous situation is a nice idea as we get to see a slight bond form between them. They are forced together, burdened by their predicament yet neither shirks or panics. It is testament to the acting abilities of both Arthur Lowe and John Le Mesurier to portray both the panic and the humour brilliantly. Their performances are the epitome of British stiff upper lip. The moment where they both admit that they are both scared is brief but poignant and neither undermines the other for the comment. For the first time in the show, the situation is deadly and serious. The situation also seems to bring out a less pompous and more humorous side of Mainwaring, who almost thrives on the pressure. Of course, when they are relieved of the bomb and go back to their respective normal, everyday lives again, we know the Wilson will once again become distant and that this will infuriate the po-faced, serious and self-important Mainwaring but for these rare minutes they are equal, stuck in a desperately grave moment that could see them, and the bank, perish. There is next to nothing to fault with *Something Nasty in the Vault* and over forty years on it still remains a fantastic representation of *Dad's Army* at its best.

MEMORABLE MOMENT:

Trapped in the bank's vault holding onto a German bomb that could go off at any second, Wilson admits that he is a little frightened by proceedings. Mainwaring, instead of dismissing the claim and telling his Chief Clerk to keep a stiff upper lip, attempts to keep his spirits up with a joke about an Australian soldier to boost his colleague's spirits (see Line) It is quite out of character and also shows the bravery of Mainwaring under pressure and no matter how shirked he is by the bomb that threatens to blow both him and Wilson out of existence, he will not let his morale wilt.

LINE:

Wilson: You know. Sir, I don't think I can stand very much more of this.

Mainwaring: Oh, come on, Wilson. Cheer up. There is a destiny that shapes our ends, rough-hew them as we will. I'm reminded of the tale of the Australian soldier. He arrived up at the front and was met by a British officer who said, "Ah, my man! Have you come here to die?" He said, "No, sir. I came yester-dye."

WATCH OUT FOR:

- **The moment Mainwaring is kind enough to scratch Wilson's nose and the look off delight that the Sergeant has on his face after the itch has gone.**
- **The reaction of the platoon, when Jones goes to salute Captain Rogers and nearly sets the bomb off by clicking his feet on the ground.**
- **The men's refusal to leave Mainwaring and Wilson in danger and their determination, including Frazer's, to get them out of the situation.**

BEHIND THE SCENES:

The entirety of the very first scene was cut prior to transmission, and had it been shown, it would have included Mainwaring and Wilson having a shave in the bank office after being on patrol all evening and the calendar on Mainwaring's desk saying '14th May 1941', dating this episode a year to the day since the Home Guard formed in its earlier guise as the Local Defence Volunteers. This would also mean that *Something Nasty in the Vault is* set a whole year after the events of the very first episode *The Man and the Hour.*

John Le Mesurier was a keen admirer of the piece and went on to label it as one of his favourite editions in the series' run. His wife, Joan Le Mesurier, confirmed this and revealed how much he enjoyed working with the man who played Wilson's nemesis: 'This was John's favourite episode. There are some lovely moments between him and Arthur, particularly when they're sitting holding the bomb. He had a wonderful rapport with Arthur Lowe, and loved the little moments in the episode where he was alone with him.'4

Jimmy Perry and David Croft decided to change the title at the scripting stage of production to *Don't Let Go.*

TRIVIA:

The bomb that lands in the bank strong room is correctly identified as a Sprengbombe Cylindrich 250 (SC250) bomb, which was frequently used by Nazi Germany to blitz the United Kingdom throughout

World War II. It was commonly used by the Junkers JU-87 Stuka dive-bomber, although it could be used by any German bomber and was feared as being one of the most destructive weapons used against the British during the campaign.

SCORE: 10/10

EPISODE EIGHTEEN

ROOM AT THE BOTTOM

RECORDED ON 29TH JUNE 1969
FIRST BROADCAST ON 16TH OCTOBER 1969
VIEWING FIGURE: 12.4 MILLION

PLOT:

Captain Bailey arrives at the church hall side office to find Wilson alone. He informs the Sergeant that Mainwaring has to be demoted as he is not really a Captain as he has not obtained the ranks. This leaves Mainwaring dejected and the men without their true leader so they write to GHQ to get him reinstated. Will their letters be accepted, or will a member of the platoon throw a spanner in the works when he decides to put himself forward for the captaincy?

GUEST CAST:

Edward Sinclair as the Verger
John Ringham as Captain Bailey
Anthony Sagar as Drill Sergeant Gregory

Colin Bean as Private Sponge

REVIEW:

Now fully re-mastered to a better quality than its original transmission, *Room at the Bottom* is gleaming from start to finish and although its premise isn't one of high comedic value, it tells a slightly melancholic and sympathetic story of Mainwaring becoming stripped of more than his command, but his pride too. At the centre of the action is a towering performance from Arthur Lowe, who is fantastic yet again as Captain Mainwaring. In a plot slightly reminiscent of series one's *Command Decision. Room at the Bottom* is another early example of the character's struggle to maintain supremacy over his men, and more importantly to him, over Wilson. The Sergeant obviously delights in the thought of his superior succumbing to his inadequacies and dare to dream that just this once he will have supremacy over his working-class boss. In conclusion, *Room at the Bottom* is another brilliant episode and with the third series now at the halfway mark it is a further reminder that the writing, the acting, the jokes and the set-up that the men of Walmington-on-Sea were going from strength-to-strength.

MEMORABLE MOMENT:

When Mainwaring falls in with the men he used to command there is an element of pathos and you feel sorry for the man, no matter how pompous and big-headed he has been in the past, nobody is better suited to lead Walmington-on-Sea's defence against Hitler. When Drill Sergeant Gregory drills the men it is great to see him being so brutal as the real leader shows himself, not as Wilson who is timid in his approach, but the short and stumpy man standing proudly in the ranks.

LINE:

Pike: I wanna go in the navy... but me mum says I'm too delicate.
Gregory: Oh dear. I am sorry. What's wrong with you, lad?
Pike: Me mum says I've got a chest.
Gregory: Oh really? (shouting) You'd look bloody funny without one, wouldn't you?!

WATCH OUT FOR:

- **Mainwaring wears the makeshift shoulder protector that Walker designed back in series two's *Sgt. Wilson's Little Secret* to hide his lack of pips on his uniform.**
- **During the opening scene, a soldier is on parade outside the side office and is seen to march up and down throughout the segment.**

RESTORATION:

For nearly forty years this episode only existed in the BBC Archives as a 16mm black and white telerecording on film, although it had been recorded on videotape and in colour. The master recording was wiped sometime after its repeat viewing on 9th May 1970. As domestic home video recorders were almost unheard of at this time the only existing colour copy of the episode, was lost forever.
However, in 2007 a Colour Recovery Working Group was established by James Insell, a preservation specialist at the BBC Archive and a member of the group called Richard Russell, developed a technique to recover the colour pictures and restore programmes to their former glory.
They discovered that on certain black and white programmes there is a faint break out of colour information coming onto the screen and found that if the programme had been recorded from the original PAL videotapes at the BBC and had kept the sub-barrier colour in the black and white recording, then they could identify the colour information in the 'chroma dots' that only appear in this instance.
Using computer software, the raw colour can be recovered and after the film was re-mastered in both picture and sound, *Room at the Bottom* was restored to its original state and transmitted in all its Technicolor glory on 13th December 2008 on BBC Two. This recovered copy is now stored at the BBC Archives as the master tape for future repeated viewings.

TRIVIA:

The Verger tells Mainwaring that the German battleship *Bismarck* has been sunk, dating this episode on the 27th May 1941. The *Bismarck*, along with the heavy cruiser *Prinz Eugen* of the German Kreigsmarine, engaged in conflict with the Royal Navy's battleship *HMS Prince of Wales* and the battle cruiser *HMS Hood* at the Battle of the Denmark Strait on the 24th May. The battle was considered a successful one tactically by the Nazi Germans but at a cost as the Bismarck succumbed to its damage, critically in the forward fuel tanks, and it went down after a further attack three days later.

SCORE: 9/10

EPISODE NINETEEN

BIG GUNS

RECORDED ON 6TH MAY 1969

FIRST BROADCAST ON 23RD OCTOBER 1969

VIEWING FIGURE: 13.2 MILLION

PLOT:

The men clamber around and are ecstatic at the delivery of an old naval gun. The only trouble is: nobody seems to know how it works, but Mainwaring tells Wilson not to worry as Frazer was in the Navy and can tell them how to use it. Frazer has to break the news to Mainwaring that he does not know how to use the gun, although he was a Chief Petty Officer during the last conflict. But when he proves unsuccessful with the weapon, how will the men get it going before an inspection from HQ?

GUEST CAST:

Edward Sinclair as the Verger
Edward Evans as Mr Rees, the Town Clerk
Don Estelle as the Pickford's Man
Roy Denton as Mr Bennett

REVIEW:

The biggest problem with *Big Guns* is its lack of plot. It does so little to entice the viewer in as the premise of the platoon receiving a heavy duty gun is not that exciting, unless we get to see it in action. The first scene lasts about half the episode and involves mainly monotonous, uninteresting dialogue – which feels forced by a cast who are struggling to find any nuggets of comedy gold in a barren script. The direction is lacking panache and although the second act is a slight improvement - the men playing with their model of the town - is much better and more inventive.

The closing scene is an embarrassment as the men make a complete mess of the presentation of the gun. It all descends into an unfunny and silly climax where the men of the Home Guard fall about under a camouflage net for the final five minutes. There is just no co-ordination on screen and when the credits roll the episode whimpers to a disappointing end. In conclusion, *Big Guns* is the weakest edition of *Dad's Army* to date and one that is instantly forgettable, possibly due to its scheduling between two very popular episodes but mostly down to its overdrawn, uninteresting and tepid realisation.

MEMORABLE MOMENT:

There aren't many in this episode, but the best bit is when Mainwaring sets up the TWET in the side office and the men make a model on the town. It isn't until the toy soldiers are introduced to act as the men that the platoon argue over who should be who and Wilson's sarcastic remark about him guessing that he would be the Indian toy shows that when toys are around, men of any age will always regress back to childhood.

LINE:

Mainwaring: Seven hundred yards. Angle of inclination: 2.5 degrees.
Jones: Mr Godfrey, have you got the inclination?
Godfrey: No, I'm perfectly all right at the moment.

WATCH OUT FOR:

- **The Verger waiting in the background for nearly ten minutes to deliver his big moment.**
- **Frazer reveals that he was not a fighting man during the last World War and actually served as a cook during the conflict.**
- **Wilson is revealed to be the captain of Walmington-on-Sea's cricket team.**

BEHIND THE SCENES:

The character of the town clerk was changed before the show was filmed as in the original script, Mr. Rees would have actually been called Mr. Pendleton and a be-speckled Yorkshireman who also would have been short in stature. The part could have been played by Don Estelle, who went on to find recognition in the Perry and Croft sitcom *It Ain't Half Hot Mum* but he went on to make his *Dad's Army* bow as the Man from Pickford's instead.

Perry and Croft decided to write more and more of the cast's mannerisms and ticks into their own characters and this lead to parallels being drawn between the ensemble and their on-screen creation. Arthur Lowe was well-known to be rather picky and self-pompous and it was his love for a well-known brand of cake that showed the extremes he could go to just to satisfy his needs.

'He was a man of habits. He liked his food and, particularly, Mr Kipling cakes. He rang me once, just before we were going filming, and said: "I've got the scripts." Instead of talking to me about them, he wanted to ask about the new assistant floor manager. He said: "Have you told the boy about Mr Kipling cakes? I don't want any trouble, see that there is always Mr Kipling cakes for tea. Last season, they had to go to a local baker to get the cakes and they weren't a match."'5

TRIVIA:

Frazer mocks the call that the platoon are looking for to fire the gun by wailing, 'hands away!' which annoys Mainwaring and he tells him that this is a field gun not Ben Gunn. Ben Gunn was a fictional character in the Robert Louis Stevenson classic adventure *Treasure Island.* Gunn was a member of Captain Flint's crew who was left half-insane after being marooned on the island for three years and is capable of finding the treasure due to the time he spent on the island.

SCORE: 2/10

EPISODE TWENTY

THE DAY THE BALLOON WENT UP

RECORDED ON 23TH OCTOBER 1969

FIRST BROADCAST ON 30TH OCTOBER 1969

VIEWING FIGURE: 12.5 MILLION

PLOT:

Whilst trying to discover which member of the platoon has written a rude word on the church harmonium, the men are startled by a stray balloon, with the verger dangling from it. Later, the group transport the balloon the fields with Jones' van but they must still hold onto it whilst Mainwaring marches out in front. But soon, the Captain is left clinging on to his life when the balloon gets away!

GUEST CAST:

Bill Pertwee as ARP Warden Hodges
Frank Williams as the Vicar
Edward Sinclair as the Verger
Nan Braunton as Cissy Godfrey
Jennifer Browne as W.A.A.F. Sergeant
Andrew Carr as Operations Room Officer
Thérèse McMurray as Girl in the Haystack
Kenneth Watson as RAF Officer
Vicki Lane as Girl on the Tandem
Harold Bennett as Mr Blewitt
Jack Haig as Gardener

REVIEW:

It is easy to love *The Day the Balloon Went Up* due to its unashamedly slapstick and farcical premise but also as it is one of the finest paced scripts that Perry and Croft ever came up with. It runs along with impeccable timing and the spaces between the big action moments (such as Mainwaring being dragged off the ground by the balloon) and smaller, more dialogue driven moments (the case of the rude word on the harmonium) results in a balance that is expertly delivered on screen by the cast. Unlike the previous edition, which felt as fast as a freshly painted wall drying in a windless arctic cave, both Perry and Croft recovered after that blip and rediscovered a knack for great dialogue, which they must have momentarily misplaced for *Big Guns.* It is also nice to see Frank Williams and Edward Sinclair take more of a centre stage as they are given plenty to do in the script and become more than just secondary characters for the first time. The Vicar's exchange with Miss Godfrey, when she proclaims that she thought the stranded Verger was actually, 'an angel from on high' coming to visit her, she is assured that this is a natural response by the reassuring Vicar, only to be confirmed that it was definitely not an angel when she replies, 'And then he cried out, "Help, I'm caught in this ruddy string."' On the downside, the character of Pike is still struggling to find its full form as Ian Lavender continues to act like a secondary character. In conclusion, *The Day the Balloon Went Up is* an instant classic. It is well regarded by long-term fans of the series as a fine example of Dad's Army at its peak.

MEMORABLE MOMENT:

Mainwaring's not so joyous ride on the balloon is brilliant and whilst it is expected that this form of farce could occur at any moment, if you haven't seen it before, you would not expect the member of the platoon that would be caught on the end of the rope to be the Captain himself. What ensues is an extremely funny segment that is well rehearsed, brilliantly shot (apart from the CSO that is) and it even has time for some fabulous one-liners from the men.

LINE:

(Someone has written a naughty word on the back of the harmonium).

Mainwaring: Now, Corporal Jones, do you see that word?

Jones: Yes, sir.
Mainwaring: Have you done that?
Jones: Do you mean recently, sir?

WATCH OUT FOR:

- **When the men fall in for parade, Godfrey has forgone his left boot for a slipper and cane as he is experiencing trouble with gout.**
- **Jones' meat van makes its second appearance in the show and the men's memorable shooting drill from its roof 'Up-two-three, BANG!-two-three!' also gets another airing.**
- **The Verger is referred to as Mr Yeatman for the first time but is still credited by his job title.**
- **The look on the Verger's face as he is pulled up past the church window by the untethered balloon.**

BEHIND THE SCENES:

Like another episode from the third series, *Battle School*, the production team chose to use more footage from the 1953 British comedy film, *The Titfield Thunderbolt* for the moment that Mainwaring is dangling under a railway bridge that the balloon has drifted into and puts the Captain's life at risk as a train enters the bridge about to collide with him.

The cast and crew once again set off to Thetford, Suffolk to film all the location footage of the series in a part of the county that frequently produced something the crew called, 'Croft's Weather' as no matter what time of year they filmed, barring the first day's shooting on the first series when it snowed, the weather was always glorious. The scenes with the platoon keeping hold of the balloon and then chasing it when Mainwaring is in his predicament were filmed Croxton Heath at the Ministry of Defence owned Stanford Training area in near Thetford.
The episode was not just a memorable one for the fans as the cast also thoroughly enjoyed making it hugely. Frank Williams said: 'I have fond memories of *The Day the Balloon Went Up* and remember marching across a field holding onto the barrage balloon with strict instructions not to wind the cord around our hands because if the balloon did escape, we'd have been pulled up with it. David [Croft] said: "If you can't hold the cord, why don't you put your hands together as if you're in prayer." It was a funny moment.'6

TRIVIA:

When inspecting the men Mainwaring remarks that Godfrey is wearing his hat straight on his head instead of to the side and it makes him look like George Formby. Formby was massive star in the United Kingdom in the 1930's and 1940's and was well-loved as a musician, comedy actor and singer-songwriter. Accompanied by his banjo or ukulele he cut an iconic image throughout wartime and beyond and he went on to star in over 20 feature films. He died of a heart attack on 6th March 1961, aged 56.

SCORE: 9/10

EPISODE TWENTY ONE

WAR DANCE

RECORDED ON 30TH OCTOBER 1969
FIRST BROADCAST ON 6TH NOVEMBER 1969
VIEWING FIGURE: 12.6 MILLION

PLOT:

Pike's workload has disappointed Mainwaring recently and Wilson believes that he is walking out with an ATS girl, Violet Gibbons, whose Mother used to serve Mainwaring as a cleaning lady. The news shocks Mainwaring and he announces that she could ruin the boy's position at the bank. He asks Wilson to have a word with him, as he is the closest thing to a father Pike has. But on the night of the dance, the platoon tries their best to stop Pike from announcing his engagement at the party and dropping a bombshell of a lifetime on his Mother.

GUEST CAST:

Edward Sinclair as the Verger
Frank Williams as the Vicar
Janet Davies as Mrs Pike

Nan Braunton as Cissy Godfrey
Olive Mercer as Mrs Yeatman
Sally Douglas as Blodwen
Dora Graham as Dora
Doris Graham as Doris
Hugh Hastings as Private Hastings, the Pianist
Eleanor Smale as Mrs Prosser

REVIEW:

After appearing like a secondary character for the majority of the show's run up until this point, Private Frank Pike is the central focal point of *War Dance,* which does not disappoint as a tale of adolescent, young love. It is an episode that sees a tone shift totally different to anything the writers had scripted previously. With the young man suffered from what could be called, 'first love sickness,' Pike is obviously head over heels for the wrong girl but his naive and impulsive desire to marry Violet at such a young age is something we can all identify with as we have all raced into relationships and fallen too hard, too soon at some point in our lives. The tone of the piece is set right from the word go as Pike sings to himself in the bank office. He has a look of youthful innocence and happiness on his face that soon disperses in the presence of Mainwaring and Wilson. The former's inclination that Pike would be bringing an 'old, boy scout friend' to the dance clearly indicates that he does not consider the young man to be old enough to be bringing girls to nights out just yet. The bank manager's statement that he has not been satisfied with his work recently inclines a view that there is a distraction in Pike's life, and it's obvious where it is coming from. So, with young love the theme, *War Dance* is a very different episode to the ones that occupy it in series three. It's not be an episode that shoots to mind as a classic but it is an important milestone in the evolution of Frank Pike and one that sees him grow as a character and become more of a key figure in the front row of the Walmington-on-Sea Home Guard.

MEMORABLE MOMENT:

The moment where the men sit in the side office, some nursing their hangovers, other nursing knocks they have picked up both emotionally and physically. It is a great moment of bonding between the main characters and when the naive Pike opens up to the older, more cynical members of the platoon such as Mainwaring and Wilson, he is spoken to on the same level as them. It is as if both the social lubrication of alcohol and the mutual experience of heartache have given him a new bond to share between them.

LINE:

Walker: This is Doris and Dora. They're twins.
Jones: Blimey, I thought I was seeing double. Here, which is which?
Walker: I don't know. One kicks and the other one bites so what's the odds?

WATCH OUT FOR:

- **Walker and his two companions for the evening are alluded to have been up to something very unholy in the church crypt.**
- **Mrs. Mainwaring is heavily referenced by her husband and despite remaining off screen; her mark can be seen very clearly. Literally.**
- **Godfrey's attire at the dance is mesmerizing and not dissimilar to that worn by Bela Lugosi in the 1931 horror classic, *Dracula*.**

BEHIND THE SCENES:

This episode is unique in that none of the main characters appear in their army uniforms apart from in the usual footage shown in the end credits. It is also another in a tantalising sequence of episodes where the viewer on first watch believes they will finally see the elusive Mrs. Elizabeth Mainwaring, but once again she is only mentioned in name and does not appear.

As David Croft said: 'We never saw Mrs Mainwaring, she was much more potent as a character, at the end of a telephone. You heard her approaching occasionally or saw her bulge in the top bunk. Just when you think there's a possibility of seeing her, something happens - its good comedy.'7

Ian Lavender admitted that he battled with both Croft and Perry on one occasion to save Pike from looking too young and naive. 'The only time I had a disagreement with David and Jimmy was when they tried making him do things like suck his thumb...I said I'd suck my thumb when I've fallen asleep but I'm not going to walk around sucking my thumb, that's stupid.'8

TRIVIA:

To stop Pike from announcing his engagement to Violet, Jones does his best to entertain the party with his impressions of famous actors from radio and screen in the early 1940s. Among these impersonations is a rough approximation of Arthur Askey, a well known English comedian and actor who featured heavily on the nation's airwaves from 1938 when he rose to stardom in the BBC's first regular comedy series, Band Waggon. His illustrious career came to end in 1982, a year after he received a CBE, when he passed away aged 82 following amputation to both his legs, which had been infected with gangrene due to poor circulation.

SCORE: 8/10

EPISODE TWENTY TWO

MENACE FROM THE DEEP

RECORDED ON 7TH NOVEMBER 1969
FIRST BROADCAST ON 13TH NOVEMBER 1969
VIEWING FIGURE: 13.3 MILLION

PLOT:

The Home Guard are put in charge of patrolling the pier whilst the armed forces are away for a couple of weeks. However their hopes of having a fun time are dashed when Pike fails to tie the boat to the pier and they are trapped, with no food or water either. To make matters worse, Hodges also ends up trapped on the pier with the men and when a mine shows up bobbing towards them, an unlikely hero steps up...

GUEST CAST:

Bill Pertwee as ARP Warden Hodges
Stuart Sherwin as 2nd ARP Warden
Bill Treacher as 1st Sailor
Larry Martyn as 2nd Sailor

REVIEW:

It is not surprising that *Menace from the Deep* is so highly regarded and thought by many to be one of the greatest *Dad's Army* episodes and its reputation is well deserved. The decision to set the narrative in a place the platoon cannot escape from is new at this point in the series. With a trapped and secluded platoon with no amenities to speak of, it is a fresh situation that soon falls into farce and is strongly reminiscent of poorly-planned boy-scout trips. The story is really brought to life by an enthusiastic cast who again appear to be at the top of their game with one of the funniest scripts to date. However, the opening ramble from Mainwaring to his troops is meandering and boring but this is quickly forgiven when the action switches to the deserted pier. Here the story really comes alive and we are gifted with some wonderful moments of dialogue from the regulars. When Walker goes to relieve Godfrey from his post as night-watchmen, he tells Mainwaring that he has shot him, but the Captain can only reply with the word 'good' as he fiddles with the crane machine when the men are starving. When the boat and food go missing, it is a little sad to see how disappointed the men are in Pike but you can understand their frustrations at his incompetence. Their mood is also soured by the appearance of Hodges, with Bill Pertwee stealing his scenes with some brilliant drunk acting. His drunken antics later on in the night are fall on the floor funny but his lack of clothing after nearly drowning in the sea leaves a lasting image that is less than desirable. With so many strong performances, killer lines and a resolution that sees Hodges as the hero for a change, *Menace from the Deep* is *Dad's Army* riding high on a tide of consistency in what was definitely the best series so far. Just one small nitpick though. How the hell did the men get off the Pier at the end!?

MEMORABLE MOMENT:

With the platoon all sound asleep and making the best of a difficult night, they are awoken by a drunk Hodges, who in a moment that probably traumatised many viewers, proceeds to attack Mainwaring wearing nothing but his Y-fronts, which resemble little else than a saggy nappy. Though Bill Pertwee is acting his heart out and doing very well as the inebriated warden, he is rather upstaged by the lack of what he is wearing.

LINE:

Mainwaring: Now you were in the Navy Frazer, you understand the Morse code, how do you spell 'help'?
Frazer: Just a minute... (thinks for a second) ...H.E.L.P.

WATCH OUT FOR:

- **The men's increasingly frustration as they attempt to salvage chocolate bars from an arcade claw and crane vending machine are upstaged by Frazer's brilliant reactions.**
- **Wilson has a stomping, childish fit of anger when Mainwaring announces that he intends to sleep in the one hammock on the pier.**
- **Hodges is revealed to be the best bowler in the town's cricket side, and proves it at the end of the episode.**

BEHIND THE SCENES:

In what soon became a recurring gag, ARP Warden Hodges gets into deep water and is soaked as the children's paddling boat sinks on his way towards the Pier. Hodge's costume is also changed to his signature white helmet for the first time and a Chief Warden's uniform but he briefly returns to his suit and tie combo in the next episode.

Menace from the Deep can also lay claim to being the episode where the cast's catchphrases are used more frequently than any other. Mainwaring utters 'you stupid boy!' twice, Hodges uses his 'put that light out!' line four times whilst Jones speaks two of his catchphrases, 'Don't Panic!' is uttered three times, while his other 'Permission to speak, Sir' and its variation, 'permission to wake you up, Sir' is used four times. He also declares that 'I'd like to volunteer' at least three time also, meaning that there are 16 occasions when a catchphrase is used in nearly thirty minutes.

The episode required extensive location footage of the platoon on the Pier and their journey to it by boat. These scenes were filmed at the beginning, like that of the rest of the series, before the show was videotaped for its interior scenes in front of a live studio audience at BBC Television Centre. These shots were filmed on Britannia Pier in Lowestoft, Suffolk, which doubles as Walmington Pier.

TRIVIA:

Many times in the show's history it is mentioned that Pike wears his Aston Villa scarf to protect him from Croup. Mainwaring asks Wilson that Croup is something that only chickens get...and Pike, but that is not strictly true. Croup (also known as laryngotracheobronchitis) is a respiratory condition that can be triggered by a viral condition of the upper airway, such as the neck. The symptoms include a barking cough and hoarseness and can today be treated with an oral steroid that can be taken once to cure it. It is a condition that affects 15% of children but more commonly between the ages of six months and the 5-6 years.

SCORE: 10/10

EPISODE TWENTY THREE

BRANDED

RECORDED ON 14TH NOVEMBER 1969
FIRST BROADCAST ON 20TH NOVEMBER 1969
VIEWING FIGURE: 11.1 MILLION

PLOT:

Mainwaring receives an alarming letter from Godfrey where he informs the captain of his resignation from the platoon as soon as possible. Godfrey proceeds to tell Mainwaring and Wilson that he made his mind up after a recent incident in which he found a mouse in his kitchen, but found himself unwilling and incapable of killing it, so he has come to the conclusion that if he can't kill a mouse, how can he be expected to kill a German?

GUEST CAST:

Bill Pertwee as ARP Warden Hodges
Nan Braunton as Miss Godfrey
Stuart Sherwin as Bill (2nd ARP Warden)
Roger Avon as Doctor

REVIEW:

Branded is a fantastic episode that gets the audience thinking about the futilities of war and how the moral compass of the time was skewed by the conflict that ensued across Europe. Instead of being a more spectacular, grandiose instalment, *Branded* is a deliberately quieter, more reflective and calculating story about one man's decision to turn away from the lingering possibility that he could be asked to fight and kill another human being in the not so distant future. What better way to channel this thought-provoking tale than through the most gentle and pleasant member of the Home Guard, Godfrey. This is truly Arnold Ridley's story, written with subtle understanding by Perry and Croft, who explore the old man's inner conflict in a tentative way and in return give Ridley his finest thirty minutes in *Dad's Army.* He goes full circle in a script where the jokes are secondary to the subject matter when he is ostracised by his Home Guard comrades when they find out he was conscientious objector during the First World War but a moment of bravery sees the faith in him restored and then by an act of heroism that saves Mainwaring's life. The characterisation of the gentle pensioner is spot on and poignant as he makes his fellow platoon members reflect in the final scene on what it really takes to be brave and stand up for what is right. One of the only sympathisers that Godfrey has to call on within the platoon is Wilson, who is again played with effortless ease by Le Mesurier. *Branded* may not be the funniest episode of *Dad's Army* ever but it more than makes up for it by having an adult and moralistic story at the heart of it with a naturalistic and poignant performance from Ridley at the centre.

MEMORABLE MOMENT:

The touching scene when Godfrey admits that he could not kill the mouse and therefore questions his role in the Home Guard as he may be called upon to kill a man in battle one day, is a master class in acting and reaction, the latter falls firmly at the feet of Arthur Lowe, but his brilliant counter against Arnold Ridley does not overshadow the elder actor's brilliance at getting across the full delicacy of Charles Godfrey and just how difficult the dilemma he faces is for him to deal with.

LINE:

Wilson: We're going to miss him.
Mainwaring: What do you mean, "We're going to miss him"? He can't just leave like that.
Wilson: I don't think you've anything to stop him. He's given you two weeks' notice.
Mainwaring: This is war, Wilson, not Sainsbury's.

WATCH OUT FOR:

- **The men's reaction to Godfrey's appearance when they are on an evening patrol.**
- **Mainwaring comes through the hut backwards and ends up crawling on all fours, pushing Jones out the way he had came with his forehead.**
- **Hodges hilarious antics when disrupting Mainwaring's speech to the platoon.**

BEHIND THE SCENES:

Both Jimmy Perry and David Croft spoke admiringly about their verdict on the episode, with the former even going on to label it as his favourite of the 80 they wrote together. Both knew that they subject matter would inspire empathy from the audience for Godfrey and Perry said, 'I was in the war and don't have much time for conscientious objectors. This was a lovely episode and we included all the old sayings about, "What's a matter with you, don't you want to fight?" and "You're not normal." It worked very well, and the tag was that Godfrey had won a Military Medal.'9

David Croft also commented on the difficulty that Godfrey faced from his friends in the episode. 'Being a conscientious objector was a difficult thing to be. There was no sympathy for them, they were scrutinised very closely.'10

When Arnold Ridley died in March 1984, *Branded* was repeated just a few days later as a tribute to the late actor. It was also the very first episode to be broadcast in colour, despite the whole series being made in colour; the third series had been going out in black and white as the vast majorities of home in the United Kingdom were still watching on black and white television sets.

TRIVIA:

The Military Medal was established on 25th March 1916, three months before the Battle of the Somme that Godfrey was involved in and his bravery during the conflict saw him awarded with the accolade. It was awarded for bravery on land and was eventually discontinued in 1993 and replaced by the Military Cross. The medal was given out to those below a commissioned rank and on the silver medal's reverse were inscribed the words 'FOR BRAVERY IN THE FIELD.'

SCORE: 8/10

EPISODE TWENTY FOUR

MAN HUNT

RECORDED ON 21ST NOVEMBER 1969
FIRST BROADCAST ON 27TH NOVEMBER 1969
VIEWING FIGURE: 11.8 MILLION

PLOT:

During a parade, Mainwaring tells the men that the war has been in progress for 18 months and he has received a memo from GHQ to tell them that empty parachutes are being dropped to confuse the men. Jones asks how they can distinguish a British and German parachute; he is told that British ones are white, while the Germans are off-white, almost cream like. Walker admits that he has recently made women's knickers out of a parachute he found but he can't remember what colour they were...

GUEST CAST:

Bill Pertwee as ARP Warden Hodges

Janet Davies as Mrs Pike
Patrick Tull as Suspect
Robert Moore as Large Man
Leon Cortez as Small Man
Olive Mercer as Fierce Lady
Miranda Hampton as Sexy Lady
Robert Aldous as German Pilot
Bran as Himself

REVIEW:

Man Hunt is a stuttering edition of *Dad's Army.* Its story does not lead to an overly interesting script and every time that the dialogue builds to an expected crescendo of action and hilarity, the momentum gets lost. It still maintains some funny interchanges between the regulars but there is lack of clout in some of the performances, especially Arthur Lowe, who seems a little slow and rambling in periods, just like the episode itself. However, that is not to say it is a bad instalment. There are some great moments with Jones drilling the platoon and the unlikely threesome of Mainwaring, Wilson and Walker knocking on people's doors asking the ladies what colours their private garments are in a moment that comes close to a *Carry On* skit. But it is surprising that when Hodges demands to know what is going on that the police do not get involved as three men asking to see you're knickers is questionable, especially when the people knocking on the door are respectable citizens of the town with reputations to uphold. The production as a whole is good and whilst there aren't so many memorable moments to talk about, the cast deliver a strong performance on the whole, ensuring that even one of the weakest episodes in the run is not spoilt entirely. The extended period that James Beck and Arthur Lowe spend on screen together is the first time they have engaged at length as characters and it is nice to hear that Mainwaring regards the spiff as a friend, no matter how different their backgrounds. I sympathise with the writers because there is a good story here but ultimately it isn't as funny as it set out to be. But then again, sub-standard *Dad's Army* is still good to watch and way better than many comedies I can think of.

MEMORABLE MOMENT:

Mainwaring, Wilson and Walker have to knock on the doors of all his clients who brought the knickers he made out of the parachute to confirm if it was a British or German parachute that he found two weeks previously. Although their job is an unpleasant and slightly uncomfortable one, Wilson knocks on the door of a young lady, who clearly likes her men mature and does not hesitate in flashing her particulars for him. That Wilson sure is a ladies' man!

LINE:

Mainwaring: Jones?
Jones: Yes, Sir?
Mainwaring: Tell him to come out with his hands up.
Jones: Oi, Comen ze out, with handy hock!

WATCH OUT FOR:

- **Arthur Lowe's pronunciation of the word, 'cream.'**
- **Mainwaring announces that the war has been raging for 18 months, meaning the episode is set somewhere in June 1941.**
- **There is a slight gap in the scenery as the men run down the church hall staircase and knock Mrs Pike over.**

BEHIND THE SCENES:

At the end of the studio shoot, an extra scene was filmed and dressed as the cast and crew prepared to film their second appearance in *Christmas Night with the Stars* in a short called *Resisting the Aggressor Through the Ages* which saw the platoon acting out as famous men from the past and how Britain fought them to keep the Country's independence.

Location work was carried out at West Tofts T-Junction at the Stanford Training Ground owned by the Ministry of Defence near Thetford, a frequent stomping ground for the cast and crew.

The final scene was made almost on the spot, as Robert Aldous explains: 'I was employed to play a German pilot in *Christmas Night with the Stars* in 1969, which was recorded with this episode. Jimmy and David didn't feel the end of *Man Hunt* tied up very well, so asked whether I'd rush on at the end, again as a pilot, and say one line. I wasn't to tell the rest of the cast, just to come on at the technical rehearsal. When I did it the rest of the cast stared as if I was bonkers. It was an interesting episode to work on because normally when you rehearse a TV show, people that aren't required sit and read newspapers. But on *Dad's Army* people moved between sets watching each other because the comedy was so inventive, and no one wanted to missanything.'[11]

TRIVIA:

Captain Mainwaring admits that he struggles to remember who gave the 'Wake Up England' speech, Winston Churchill or Gillie Potter. Potter, whose real name was Hugh Peel, was born in 1888 and was a well known radio star of the day. He died in 1955.

SCORE: 6/10

EPISODE TWENTY FIVE

NO SPRING FOR FRAZER

RECORDED ON 28TH NOVEMBER 1969
FIRST BROADCAST ON 4TH DECEMBER 1969
VIEWING FIGURE: 13.6 MILLION

PLOT:

Whilst on parade, Mainwaring asks Jones, Frazer and Pike to come into the side office so he can inspect their armoury. He discovers that Frazer has lost the butterfly spring that goes in the Lewis gun, rendering the weapon useless without it. When they depart to the recreation hall for a lecture, the men make a detour to Frazer's coffin workshop. Scot then realises that he has accidentally put it in a coffin that has already been sent off for storage at HE Drury's, the funeral directors in Walmington-on-Sea!

GUEST CAST:

Edward Sinclair as the Verger
Frank Williams as the Vicar
Harold Bennett as Mr Blewitt
Joan Cooper as Miss Baker
Ronnie Brandon as Mr Drury

REVIEW:

Yes, *Dad's Army* really did base a plot around the grizzly contemplation a grave robbery. But despite this morbid notion, *No Spring for Frazer* is another highlight of the third series. Its faux pas storyline and well-crafted storyline makes for another highly re-watchable thirty minutes of comedy and must surely rank as one of the all time greats. The biggest aspect as to why this is one of the best episodes that Perry and Croft ever wrote is the central performance of the mercurial yet lovable John Laurie. Form this episode on he starts to deliver a slightly different edge to the platoon's most surly and gloomy member, who in this episode begins to undergo a transformation more fitting with his character. Up until this point, Frazer was the keeper of a Philately shop and here were see a sizeable shift in his own personal development that lead to a career change more fitting to the temperament and dark foreboding that Frazer exhibited from time to time. The reveal that his is a funeral director would come later, but here we see a new side of Frazer through his hobbies. The dialogue is once again as good as it gets this series, with memorable lines such as Wilson being encouraged to be less mindful of his manners when ordering the men around, ('Would you kindly step this way please?' Mainwaring: 'Oh Wilson, bark it out, bark it out!' Wilson: 'WOULD YOU KINDLY STEP THIS WAY PLEASE!!!') There are also some fantastic scenes with the platoon at the bumbling best. *No Spring for Frazer* is one of the all-time classics of *Dad's Army* and deserves to be mentioned in the same breath as *Asleep in the Deep* and *The Deadly Attachment* as one of the very best examples of Perry and Croft's writing partnership. It is a fundamental cornerstone of what is one of the strongest series the show ever produced.

MEMORABLE MOMENT:

Although to me the notion of grave robbing should only be confined to Mary Shelley's *Frankenstein* and episodes of *Cracker*, the grizzly subject matter is made funny by members of the platoon giving the poor old Verger a fright when the dirt he puts into the ground to fill in the grave is thrown back at him by Jones is a brilliant moment of physical comedy and one that puts the morally horrific task firmly out of your head as you watch him whimper away in fright.

LINE:

Mr. Blewitt: He come home 'ere, he put the shopping down on the table and unwrapped that very piece of meat you just served him with.
Jones: You never know do you?
Mr. Blewitt: No, you never do. And do you know what the very last words he said?
Jones: No. What were they?
Mr. Blewitt: He stood there, where Mr. Frazer's standing now with the meat in his hand. Look at that, he says, all bloody bone!

WATCH OUT FOR:

- **John Laurie's Scottish accent makes the line, 'It's screwed down!' laugh out loud funny.**
- **Corporal Jones' reaction to Miss Baker's presumption that he has kicked the bucket.**
- **A great visual gag of Mainwaring breaking an out of shot window pane by throwing a prop over his shoulder.**

BEHIND THE SCENES:

There are a number of editing problems with the episode that try as you might, sometimes detract from the pictures on screen including video cuts as people are in the middle of talking. This can be highlighted when Miss Baker is talking to Frazer, there is a cut and she begins talking again.
Arthur Lowe's wife, Joan Cooper makes her debut on the programme. She would appear in many guises over the course of the series and appeared in four episodes.

It was her husband who won her the party on the programme and they even get to share a scene at the funeral directors.

Hugh Cecil revealed how the weather when on location regularly benefitted the cast and crew, but not on this occasion. 'We were blessed with splendid weather for most of our days on location. But I remember one scene that had to be halted because of bad light. We resumed the next day and David Croft said to Arthur Lowe: "This is better, isn't it?" Arthur looked at him and replied: "I suppose God sent you an apology as well." A perfectly timed reply.'12

TRIVIA:

In one scene, Mainwaring and Pike argue over a movie that the youngster has seen and who had starred in it. The movie Pike refers to is the 1930 version of *Raffles* starring Ronald Colman. It was produced by Samuel Goldwyn and was a remake of a 1925 film by the same name by Universal Studios and was remade itself nine years later with David Niven in the title role.

SCORE: 10/10

EPISODE TWENTY SIX

SONS OF THE SEA

RECORDED ON 5TH DECEMBER 1969

FIRST BROADCAST ON 11TH DECEMBER 1969

VIEWING FIGURE: 13.3 MILLION

PLOT:

In the bank, Mr Maxwell, a solicitor, sits in Mainwaring's office telling him about the death of a Mr Johnson. The former client to the bank has no relatives and the only possessions he had left when he passed away were the clothes he was wearing and a boat named The Naughty Jane. Mainwaring plans to use the boat on river patrols and wants to drill the men. A panic ensues when the men realise that they are indeed in the channel, they panic about getting home safely and not being caught by Nazis...

GUEST CAST:

Michael Bilton as Mr. Maxwell
John Leeson as 1st Soldier
Jonathan Holt as 2nd Soldier
Ralph Ball as Man on Station
Desmond Cullum-Jones as Private Desmond

REVIEW:

Concluding the upward trajectory of quality episodes that make the third series of *Dad's Army* so rich in comedic value, *Sons of the Sea* is a fun and jolly jaunt that sees the members of the Walmington-on-Sea Home Guard in choppy waters, and the enticing anticipation that Mainwaring and his men might face the Germans behind enemy lines. The episode's central narrative is catapulted into life by the actions of Captain Mainwaring, played with efficient, authoritative precision by Arthur Lowe. It is Mainwaring's fault that the men end up getting lost in the Channel (due to his need to take full command even when there are more able men to row a boat than he in his platoon) but you can't begrudge Mainwaring for his improvisation and his knack of using whatever equipment or idea that comes his way to help thwart Hitler's army. Arguably, this is the best storyline of the series as it is the first to truly land Mainwaring et al in hot water. From a serious perspective it has great potential to become more of a dramatic piece but the brilliant end reins it back into the realms of comedy and even in the most serious moments, it still has time to make us laugh.

MEMORABLE MOMENT:

As the men await the moment to disembark on a train they believe has delivered them to the Nazis, Mainwaring announces that it is every man for himself. He thinks again when he goes to shake the hand of Godfrey and tells the old man he will look after him and get him home safely. It shows just how far the pair had come since the Godfrey's controversial announcement that he was a conscientious objector during the last war and his redemption after saving the life of his Captain at the end of *Branded.*

LINE:

Jones: 'No, you've got to have the sun, we used to find our way by that in the Sudan, you know, got a lot of sun out there, except at night, of course, we didn't get a lot of sun then...'

WATCH OUT FOR:

- **Frazer's sulking at losing the command of the boat as the men make their ultimately perilous maiden voyage.**
- **This is the only appearance of member of the platoon called 'Desmond' who, despite being in most of the shots that make up the episode, does not get a credit at the end and only utters one word, 'Goodbye.'**

BEHIND THE SCENES:

Writer Jimmy Perry has stated in the past that this is one of his favourite episodes and that the production struggled to cope with the technical demands of the day, which explains the rather crude use of CSO compared to today's standards.

John Leeson, who would go on to be well remembered as the voice of K-9, the robotic dog in *Doctor Who* made an early television appearance as the first soldier and had to suffer for his art. 'I played a soldier in Sons of the Sea and remember confusion between the costume and make-up. The make-up department had insisted on a short army haircut, much to my wife's horror. But when I got to the studio I discovered my uniform included a Balaclava helmet - you couldn't see any hair at all!'13

TRIVIA:

When Godfrey is late to the drill, Mainwaring admits he is not worried by his time keeping as he was playing bowls and that was good enough for Drake. Mainwaring is referring to Sir Francis Drake (c. 1540 - 1596) who was busy playing bowls when the Armada was sighted close by on 29th July 1588 and Drake insisted in finishing his game of bowls before engaging.

SCORE: 8/10

Despite good will towards the series, rumours began to circulate in the press that the BBC were reluctant to commission more episodes. So, with *Sons of the Sea* wrapping up a highly successful run, viewers had begun to think that they had witnessed the end of the show. However, these rumours were just pure speculation and as a new decade dawned, it was clear that both the BBC and the audience wanted more.

One of the first to sing his praises was Paul Fox, the Controller of BBC1 who had originally wanted the line-up sequences written out of the show during the making of the first series. In a letter addressed to David Croft on the 13th January 1970, he wrote: 'I am sorry it has taken me so long to write a note of thanks to you for "*Dad's Army*". You made enormous success of it and like millions of others, I am only sorry it has to come to an end. Temporarily, I hope.

He then went on to declare that he was glad that he had been proved wrong regarding the title for the series and the footage of the men marching at the end of each episode: 'Looking back to that first programme, I am glad to say you were right 100%. Thanks for your persistence - and despite that title change! - the show became a great hit.

He concluded: 'To you - and all who've been associated with this splendid series - many congratulations and grateful thanks.'

The Audience Research report shared in Fox's enthusiasm for the third series. When the panel was asked to give their opinions on *The Armoured Might of Corporal Jones*, the report declared that: 'According to the majority of the sample audience this edition of *Dad's Army* had been all they had expected - a hilarious romp, deliciously amusing and delightfully nostalgic.' There were also comments regarding: 'the chaos resulting from the well meaning efforts of "our heroes" of the Home Guard,' which managed to bring: 'vividly to mind some of the lighter moments of the last war.' For instance, the scene between Jones and his punters in the butchers shop, was singled out for praise, with one panel member concluding: "I did laugh at the scene in the butcher's shop. This was so very true during rationing, people trying to get a bit more than their share."

By the time the series was over and *Sons of the Sea* was put before the panel, it was clear that this had indeed been a very successful run for *Dad's Army*:

'This had been one of the most amusing series they had seen for a long time,' the panel suggested and for some they remarked that: 'their only regret was that it had come to an end - for good, according to the current press reports.' Of course, these rumours turned out to be false but at the time, *Sons of the Sea* was considered: 'The platoon's final adventure...rounded off the series quite hilariously, as far as most reporting viewers were concerned.'

The Reaction Index for *Sons of the Sea* was an incredibly high score of 77. To put this score into consideration, those that were deemed 'poor' are normally scored at 60 or under whilst shows that are considered 'excellent' normally score an appreciation figure of 85 and over. This score is measured out of 100 and its purpose is to gauge the audience appreciation of the show that they are watching (this score was collected by the British Audience Research Board up until 2002).

The third series of *Dad's Army* was nothing short of a triumph. With series three double the length of its two predecessors, it was clear that *Dad's Army* had well and truly established itself as one of the BBC's treasures and with the run's audience figures hovering between the 11-13 million mark consistently as the series progressed, the audience thought so as well, despite being down by 0.1 million on the last season, which had an average of 12.2 million viewers. The show also began to attract accolades from the television industry. Something Nasty in the Vault was awarded a BAFTA for Best Light Entertainment Production and Direction in 1970.

Episodes such as *Something Nasty in the Vault, The Day the Balloon Went Up,* and *Menace of the Deep* would go down as classics among fans. And as the 1960's gave way to the 1970's, the show was taken into the next decade, looking to continue on its fine run of form...

SERIES FOUR

MAIN CAST:

ARTHUR LOWE - CAPTAIN GEORGE MAINWARING
JOHN LE MESURIER - SERGEANT ARTHUR WILSON
CLIVE DUNN - LANCE CORPORAL JACK JONES
JOHN LAURIE - PRIVATE JAMES FRAZER
ARNOLD RIDLEY - PRIVATE CHARLES GODFREY
JAMES BECK - PRIVATE JOE WALKER
IAN LAVENDER - PRIVATE FRANK PIKE

FEATURING THE VOICE OF BUD FLANNIGAN

EPISODE TWENTY SEVEN

THE BIG PARADE

RECORDED ON 17TH JULY 1970
FIRST BROADCAST ON 25TH SEPTEMBER 1970
VIEWING FIGURE: 14 MILLION

PLOT:

Whilst at the pictures, Mainwaring is inspired as he watches the newsreel and decides that the platoon should find themselves a regimental mascot in time for the big parade that takes place on Sunday. It will include all the civil defence units to mark the start of Spitfire Fund Week. The next day, Number 1 section, led by Jones is sent to Private Sponge's farm to catch the potential mascot but they struggle to tame a ram. Before long, the main attention is attracted towards Pike, who in his efforts has become stuck in a bog...

GUEST CAST:

Bill Pertwee as ARP Warden Hodges
Edward Sinclair as the Verger
Janet Davies as Mrs Pike
Pamela Cundell as Mrs Fox
Colin Bean as Private Sponge

REVIEW:

This is a great start to the fourth series as we get to see the men struggle to rescue Pike in a famous and thoroughly entertaining episode for the men from Walmington-on-Sea. What plays to *The Big Parade*'s advantages is the spine of a good solid, half an hour story that opens the run with a confident air and one where the cast and crew are obviously enjoying every minute. After setting the plot up with extended exposition, we get to the action halfway through as we are treated to the fields of Sponge's farm and it is here where the episode really wakes up. I feel, despite the average age of the cast, it is the physical aspect of *Dad's Army* that really gets the chuckles. The sight of middle to elderly aged men acting like schoolchildren is rather magical and planting Pike in the bog is clearly the highlight of *The Big Parade.* Not to take anything away from the beautifully crafted script but really, it's the platoon's pursuit of the ram that makes the show memorable. *The Big Parade* is a fine opener for the fourth series. It continues the impressive run of form after the long run last time out and the cast look as though they are rejuvenated after a small break. Even though I wouldn't put it in my top ten, *The Big Parade* is still a class act.

MEMORABLE MOMENT:

The platoons efforts to rescue Pike from the bog is the standout moment from the piece as, predictably, their attempts are blighted by poor hindsight and Wilson being indisposed by catching himself in a rather delicate place on a barbed wire fence. Ian lavender really suffers on screen here as the running plot deviceof Private Pike either getting wet or in a dangerous predicament for the use of comedic and storytelling effect is exploited for the first time.

LINE:

Mainwaring: I shall be marching with a ram.
Hodges: Your personal life has got nothing to do with me.

WATCH OUT FOR:

- **The men whistle the Laurel and Hardy theme to Hodges as he leaves the church hall.**
- **After failing to obtain the ram from Sponge's farm, Walker brings in a smaller, less intimidating ram with fake horns.**

BEHIND THE SCENES:

The episode title was lifted from a classic 1925 silent film of the same name but bears very little in resemblance to the narrative of the silver screen edition. The platoon whistling the *Laurel and Hardy* theme tune when Hodges appears was used sparingly in the series from here on in.

The writers decided to give some more background to a couple of the secondary characters in the show. Private Sponge as played by Colin Bean, who by this point is fast establishing himself as the star member of the back row, is revealed to be a farmer and most of the second act commences on his farm and the Verger, who arguably has been evolving in nearly every appearance since his debut, is seen as the Leader of the Walmington Sea Scouts.

Ian Lavender remembered making the episode, '*The Big Parade* was a very uncomfortable episode because I spent most of my time stuck in a bog. A hole was filled with water, and then topped with earth and cork. I stood on a set of steps and gradually stepped down so it looked as if I was sinking deeper into the bog.

'It was deemed a waste of time to get out for tea breaks, so drinks - deliberately laced with liquor for warmth - were handed out on a tray nailed to a long piece of wood. Other than getting out for lunch, I was in the bog all day in my wet suit.'1

TRIVIA:

When we join the men in the cinema at the start of the episode they are watching *The Spy Is Black* a 1939 film starring Conrad Veidt. Veidt, shown on screen during the opening scene, was a German actor who obtained British citizenship in 1933. Mainwaring clearly does not like him, as he alludes to with the dialogue by appearing to be prejudice about his German background.

SCORE: 8/10

EPISODE TWENTY EIGHT

DON'T FORGET THE DIVER

RECORDED ON 24TH JULY 1970

FIRST BROADCAST ON 2ND OCTOBER 1970

VIEWING FIGURE: 12.3 MILLION

PLOT:

Mainwaring informs the platoon that there is a big exercise coming up that will involve all of the Home Guard units. He tells them that Captain Square and the Eastgate platoon will stake out at a windmill and Mainwaring's platoon will have to lay pretend high explosives in Square's base without getting themselves captured. As the men discuss their plans, the Verger, unnoticed by the Home Guard, acts as a spy and listens out for any information that he can pass onto to Eastgate and Colonel Square...

GUEST CAST:

Bill Pertwee as ARP Warden Hodges
Edward Sinclair as the Verger
Frank Williams as the Vicar
Geoffrey Lumsden as Captain Square
Robert Raglan as HG Sergeant
Colin Bean as Private Sponge
Don Estelle as Gerald, the 2nd ARP Warden
Verne Morgan as Landlord

REVIEW:

Don't Forget the Diver! is great from start to end. It carries on much in the same vein as the previous episode, in which we see the men put their practical uses to work and the production shifts to expansive, luscious green fields on location, instead of the familiar stuff church hall set. As much as I like the church hall and the line-up sequences that commence inside of them, sometimes too many of these scenes can deflate the scene and slow the pace down. I compare them to my living room, there is something wholesome and comforting about them but then again, you wouldn't want to live in that room forever. When the story shifts to the mission in hand, the pragmatic and ultimately successful effort made by the men is very entertaining and although it is only the edited cuts to Jones' progress that really makes me chuckle and Square believing that the men have turned into sheep just because they are wearing their tin hats. How moronic must Square be? Once again the use of location work really helps the episode to breath as an elaborate, almost scout-like in its conception, course of action may seem silly in some places, but is instantly likeable. If I had to split hairs it would be the fact that the men would believe a military man like Square would think that the men had turned into sheep is clutching at straws a little bit but the physical comedian that was Clive Jones is on fine form, especially when he is supposedly hanging onto the windmill as it rotates its blades. That's no way to treat an old age pensioner!

MEMORABLE MOMENT:

Giving the chance, Clive Dunn would always jump at the opportunity to show off his physical skills in the realm of comedy. Here, he pulls off an utterly ludicrous and barking mad set piece when Jonesy attaches himself to windmill and it starts to revolve, leaving the old age pensioner, stuck like a fly on a spider web, going around with it. It's a remarkable moment and filmed expertly, lending the scene the credibility it deserves, no matter how preposterous the sight is. The scene is a fine way to end a fine episode.

LINE:

Mainwaring: You're getting on my nerves creeping around the place with that miserable look on your face.
Verger: This happens to be my normal expression. You can't be a Verger with a funny face, you know.
Jones: You seem to have managed alright.

WATCH OUT FOR:

- **The debut of the long, imaginative and wild stories as told by Frazer.**
- **Square keeps up his mispronunciation of Mainwaring from his first appearance when he is heard on the receiving end of the phone to the verger.**
- **The men elaborate and surreal distractions aimed at the Eastgate platoon.**

BEHIND THE SCENES:

The sequence featuring the windmill was filmed in Drinkstone, Suffolk whilst the scene involving Wilson and Walker marching the rifles up and down the field was filmed in another scenic part of the county called Bardwell.
The title of the episode is a hark back to the wartime catchphrase of Tommy Handley, who starred in the BBC Radio comedy show It's That Man Again!, which ran from 1939 to 1949 . Handley regularly uttered the line 'Don't forget the diver sir; do not forget the diver' to a character that was called Deepend Dan.

Robert Raglan makes his first appearance as Captain Square's Sergeant but would later return in a semi-regular role as the 'Colonel'.
Guest star Don Estelle recalled his relationship with Captain Mainwaring himself, 'Arthur Lowe was wonderful, always calling me his protégé. He had a great style, particularly all the pausing he did. If he couldn't remember his lines he'd do a lot of mumbling, a pattern of behaviour which gave him time to collect himself and recall his next line. But it looked so theatrical and was very funny - he would milk a scene tremendously.'2

TRIVIA:

The final scene was written in homage to the 1939 film *Oh, Mr Porter!* which starred Will Hay. That is not the only link between the two as the film was based loosely on the play *The Ghost Train* written by none other than Godfrey actor Arnold Ridley. Jimmy Perry also admitted that the characters of Mainwaring, Jones and Pike were inspired by his recollection of watching the film when he was younger.

SCORE: 7/10

EPISODE TWENTY NINE

BOOTS, BOOTS, BOOTS

RECORDED ON 31ST JULY 1970

FIRST BROADCAST ON 9TH OCTOBER 1970

VIEWING FIGURE: 13.2 MILLION

PLOT:

On parade one evening, Mainwaring decides to implement the three F's to the platoon - these are fast feet, functional feet and fit feet - and decides to check everybody's feet. He declares that the men will have to look after them more and they need to be healthier so forms a fitness routine that includes the frequency of long, difficult marches. Pike has an idea that he shares with Wilson, while Walker, Jones, Frazer and Godfrey also have the same thought but only share it with themselves on how to sabotage a planned 20-mile march.

GUEST CAST:

Bill Pertwee as ARP Warden Hodges
Janet Davies as Mrs Pike
Erik Chitty as Mr Sedgewick

REVIEW:

Boot, Boots, Boots is marvellous, planting itself firmly as one of this author's all-time favourite. Mainwaring is arguably at his most fastidious here, forcing the men, of which most of them are OAPs as we all know, to route march mile after mile, to the point that the drills are enough to keep Pike up in the dark of the night and plant the seeds of a small mutiny within the ranks with plans to sabotage Mainwaring's own two plates of meat. The double farce in the shape of the two groups of the men having the same idea to change their Captain's boots with a smaller size is a funny plot twist, culminating in a memorable reveal at the end when the shoe shop owner brings the correct pair in anyway. The touch on Wilson and Pike's true relationship is also a fine addition to the script and both Le Mesurier and Lavender are in perfect sync when acting out the mannerisms of the pulling of the ear lobe, a regular trait that 'Uncle Arthur' possesses. It is striking just how convincing Bill Pertwee's reaction to the puddle scene was and it's hard to see whether they filmed his reaction but it looks so authentic and makes you wonder as to whether Arthur Lowe was warned at how deep the puddle was prior to the filming of the sequence. Still, *Boots, Boots, Boots* is another gem. Even Mrs Pike isn't as grating as her earlier appearances. I hope this doesn't mean I have developed a soft spot for her!

MEMORABLE MOMENT:

Seeing the boys playing a barefoot football match with the old fashioned pig's bladder balls is hilarious and poor old Godfrey as the goalkeeper is a small yet inspired piece of writing. The whole montage scene with the men taking part in various drills that are expected to harden the souls of their feet is fun, culminating in Hodges warning the men not to wander too far on the sea front as there is a massive puddle coming up. Of course, Mainwaring falls in, cutting to Bill Pertwee failing to contain his laughter.

LINE:

Mainwaring: I never realised what big feet you had, Walker.

Walker: You know what they say, "Big feet, big ..."
Mainwaring: Big what?
Walker: Just an expression
Mainwaring: (To Wilson) What is he talking about?
(An embarrassed looking Wilson whispers in his ear.)
Really? His nose looks absolutely normal to me.

WATCH OUT FOR:

- **Walker's ingenious method of concealing his smart shoes under his boots.**
- **The moment Mainwaring wanders unwittingly into a big puddle on the sea front.**
- **The surprise Mainwaring gets when he spots what both Frazer and Pike have on the soles of their feet...**

BEHIND THE SCENES:

The location footage, showing the men playing football was shot at Buckenham Tofts, Stanford Training area near Thetford, where it doubled for the Walmington pitch. Winterton Beach in Norfolk doubled for Walmington Beach when the men are marching. During the football match the piece of music played is called *I Came, I Saw, I Conga'd* a music hall tune written by Weldon and regularly sung on the football terraces from the 1950s to the 1970s. The version heard in the episode was performed by Nat Gonella and the Georgians with vocals from Stella Moya.

Despite Mainwaring working the men hard in this episode, Ian Lavender recalls that he could see similarities in the character and the actor playing him. '...I was also very fond of Arthur Lowe. We were all like our characters and he was like Mainwaring - a pompous little man. What you didn't know, until he let you in on it, was that he knew he was a pompous little man. And quite often he'd burst his own bubble. Yes, he was pompous but a lot of the time he was playing along with it.'3

TRIVIA:

The title is inspired from a song of the same name, which is played throughout the episode repeatedly as incidental music. The music was written by J McCall and the words were written by Rudyard Kipling. Kipling was born in 1865 and in a long and successful writing career, wrote *The Jungle Book, The Man Who Would Be King, Just So Stories and If.* He was awarded the Nobel Prize for Literature in 1907.

SCORE: 8/10

EPISODE THIRTY

SGT. - SAVE MY BOY!

RECORDED ON 27TH JUNE 1970
FIRST BROADCAST ON 16TH OCTOBER 1970
VIEWING FIGURE: 14.5 MILLION

PLOT:

Following the events at Dunkirk, the orphans who occupied the Harris Orphan's Holiday Home have left and it is no longer in use. Since the site is deserted, the platoon is using the chalet as a patrol hut. When the men are there one evening, Mrs Pike arrives to give Pike a tin of biscuits he forgot to take with him. Meanwhile outside, Frazer, who is on patrol, hears a cry for help, which turns out to be Pike, who is tangled in barbed wire and trapped in the middle of a minefield!

GUEST CAST:

Bill Pertwee as ARP Warden Hodges
Janet Davies as Mrs Pike
Michael Knowles as Engineer Officer

REVIEW:

If it was a stinker then it would stick out like a sore thumb, but due to its less showy nature when compared to *Don't Forget the Diver* there is a quiet charm about *Sgt - Save my Boy!* The title suggests a daring rescue, a continuation of the more action focused scripts we have had lately and a possible intrusion into the family life of the Pikes. Alas, there is none of this really. Instead, we just get Pike falling into trouble yet again and Wilson, as alluded to in the title, not actually doing very much. The episode does give Arnold Ridley his first chance to steal a bit of the limelight since the Godfrey-centric episode *Branded.* Here, he unwittingly saves Pike, wandering into the minefield on a safe path he has found but the others have failed to find. It lends to a moment between two characters that have barely spent time together alone on screen and it allows both of them to shine before the rest of the ensemble snatch the episode back from them.

Finally, for the second time in four episodes, poor Private Pike is in hot water yet again. It seems a strange choice to have the same platoon member stuck in a life threatening situation yet again. Why not Godfrey? Was it to give Ian Lavender, who was underused in the first two and a half series of the show, more screen time? However you look at it, the young bank clerk is fast becoming the Penelope Pitstop of the Home Guard, needing a rescue from a band of gruff looking men like the damsel in distress from *Wacky Races*.

MEMORABLE MOMENT:

Despite what looks like a cramp, claustrophobic set for the beach line, the camera work and editing is exemplary when conveying a much bigger and expansive location. The journey the men make to the trapped Pike looks as long and dangerous as it was intended, with false alarms on finding mines aplenty. When they finally get to the teenager, who is entangled in barbed wire, they find that they have been beaten by the supposedly least able body in the platoon, Godfrey.

LINE:

Jones: Permission to shout a short message of encouragement to Private Pike, sir?

Mainwaring: Yes, go ahead.

Jones: (Shouting) Cheer up, Pikey, and don't you move a muscle or you'll be blown to Kingdom Come!

WATCH OUT FOR:

- **Godfrey frequently appears to be nodding off in the opening scene.**
- **The exchange between Mainwaring and Wilson when the latter throws his hat at his superior.**
- **When the men are marking the route to Pike with flags, Jones hands Mainwaring a small Nazi flag.**

BEHIND THE SCENES:

Writer Jimmy Perry admitted that the character of Frank Pike was written as a reflection of his times as a young man at the outbreak of World War Two and had always wanted to have a younger member involved as a main character in the platoon.

'In a way, Ian Lavender was playing a young person similar to me in the Home Guard. But what we really wanted was a soppy boy. When you have a lot of old men, it's funny to have a young person amongst them; it makes for a lot of humour.'4

TRIVIA:

Janet Davies continues her semi-regular appearance as Mrs Pike, Wilson's not-so-secret lover and mother to Frank Pike in the role that gave her the part that she is best remembered for. However, the actress also appeared in other staples of the BBC's repertoire in the 1960s and 1970s, including *Z-Cars, Dixon of Dock Green, Last of the Summer Wine* and *The Fall and Rise of Reginald Perrin.*

SCORE: 6/10

EPISODE THIRTY ONE
DON'T FENCE ME IN
RECORDED ON 10TH JULY 1970
FIRST BROADCAST ON 23RD OCTOBER 1970
VIEWING FIGURE: 16.4 MILLION

PLOT:

Mainwaring is contacted by the Colonel and informed that the Walmington-on-Sea Home Guard will be taken off active duty for two weeks as they are given a mission to relieve the regular guards at a nearby Italian POW camp. Mainwaring sees it as a chance for his platoon to prove themselves. But when they see how Walker liaisons with the prisoners, Mainwaring and the rest begin to have their suspicions of Walker being a fifth columnist.

GUEST CAST:

Edward Evans as General Monteverdi
John Ringham as Captain Bailey
Larry Martyn as Italian POW

REVIEW:

Despite giving James Beck arguably the most he has had to do all series so far I dislike the writer's storyline of making Walker do such a silly and selfish thing as to let the prisoners out to mend his radios. The conviction does not sit well with the idea, and an opportunity is lost to explore beyond the confines of Walmington-on-Sea. This episode seems to be the straw that broke the camel's back, so to speak. Perry and Croft's golden streak is at an end with a challenging yet somewhat mispitched effort that does not match up to its brothers and sisters in the fourth series and it brings into question the true allegiance of a main, well loved member of the Home Guard. James Beck does well as Walker at a tipping point for the character. From here on in, his integrity could be questioned every time he does something suspicious and the trust that the platoon have in him, no matter how thin on the ground it was to start with, could be further stretched. His excuses do not quite add up in my book. It isn't a very good idea to let prisoners out, especially on home soil and I can't quite fathom why he does it. Unless he is a humanitarian and believes they should not be locked up? Still, *The Great Escape* it is not, and despite being an average offering in a season that shines, there are many points that keep it interesting and not the just top class comedy.

MEMORABLE MOMENT:

With only twenty of the sixty prisoners in the camp, Jones comes up with an idea inspired by his experiences of the pantomimes he saw as a boy but Pike likens it more to *Ali Baba and the Forty Thieves.* As Captain Bailey arrives and counts the POW in, Jones gets the men to run through the camp in one direction and then straight out again to come back through again to give the impression that there is a full quota. Unfortunately the game is up when smoke emits from Walker's cigarette in the escape tunnel...

LINE:

Mainwaring: The point is, if Hitler kicks off over the next two weekends, we shan't be here to stop him... We'll be playing nursemaid to a lot of comic-opera soldiers.

WATCH OUT FOR:

- **Mainwaring is a little too wide for the escape tunnel and gets stuck, leading to the men having to push and pull him out.**
- **Jones has to resort to using his cold steel to scare the prisoners into attention.**
- **Frazer captures the apparently treacherous Walker and is quite willing to 'string up' his friend.**

BEHIND THE SCENES:

The location footage of the Home Guard at the Italian POW camp was shot at Trope Camp, situated at the cast and crew's regular stomping ground, Stanford Training near Thetford. The grounds were used frequently by the production unit.

Edward Evans, who appeared in the episode as General Monteverdi, was an old acquaintance of writer Jimmy Perry and was surprised to be cast after years without contact, but he had played a similar part to the one that he had seen him play nearly twenty years earlier. As he recalled, 'I'd worked with Jimmy Perry at Watford Rep during the 1950s. I hadn't spoken to him for years when he called out of the blue, saying: "You know that mad Italian waiter you played at Watford, well you'll be just right for a part I've written called General Monteverdi." He asked whether I was interested and I told him whenever money is concerned, I'm interested. It was a very funny part and I enjoyed playing him.'5

TRIVIA:

When Mainwaring is stuck in the tunnel, Wilson remarks that the situation reminds him of *Winnie-the-Pooh*, the well-loved children's character and book, written by A.A Milne and published in 1926. There is an incident in the second chapter of the first novel called *In Which Pooh Goes Visiting and Gets Into a Tight Place* that Wilson is referring to. The book was so successful it spawned *The House at Pooh Corner* in 1928 and a character that has endured for nearly 90 years.

SCORE: 5/10

EPISODE THIRTY TWO

ABSENT FRIENDS

RECORDED 7TH AUGUST 1970

FIRST BROADCAST ON 30TH OCTOBER 1970
VIEWING FIGURE: 13.9 MILLION

PLOT:

Mainwaring unexpectedly arrives for parade while his men are taking part in a darts tournament against the ARP wardens at the local pub. With just Mainwaring, Wilson and Jones attending parade, Mainwaring is infuriated. He receives an emergency call from GHQ. There is an armed IRA suspect that has been discovered in Ivy Crescent and the police have called upon the Home Guard to help in capturing the man...

GUEST CAST:

Bill Pertwee as ARP Warden Hodges
Janet Davies as Mrs Pike
Edward Sinclair as Verger
J. G. Devlin as Regan
Arthur English as Policeman
Patrick Connor as Shamus
Verne Morgan as Landlord
Michael Lomax as 2nd ARP Warden

REVIEW:

After the disappointing no score draw of an episode we got with *Don't Fence Me In* it is refreshing to have an edition that challenges the command Mainwaring has on his men. *Absent Friends* shows that loyalty is rather thin on the ground in Walmington-on-Sea and that darts is the big distraction in a great show that throws up a tricky situation for Wilson, more bullying from his wife for Mainwaring and the men copping off for the evening with consequences that are almost dangerous to the few who did attend. For the first time, we see that Mavis is not as faithful to Wilson as we have been led to believe. It turns out that when he is on parade, she sneaks out to the local pub for a drink or two with Hodges, the enemy within the gates for the Home Guard. His reaction to seeing Wilson arrive is one of fear and horror but when he is reassured that the Sergeant will do nothing to harm him, he decides to install his false sense of superiority, only to be send scampering away at the very end of the piece, leaving Wilson to take Mavis back. The IRA sub-plot is one that I am uncomfortable with. Not only are the names of the accused, Shamus and Patrick, incredibly stereotypical yet again but also the inclusion of the terrorist group is a slightly dodgy one in hindsight. No wonder it took over 40 years for the episode to be repeated. All in all, *Absent Friends* is very enjoyable. It has a steady, engaging pace and surprises the viewer with Wilson's actions at the very end. I liked seeing Wilson stand up and be a man, keeping a cool head while those around him were nursing theirs. When he walks back into the room having dealt with the IRA threat single handed, he is a new man. Watch out Hodges, come near Mavis again and this is what could happen!

MEMORABLE MOMENT:

Having to endure the sight of his secret lover courting the platoon's number one enemy besides Hitler, Wilson lets all his pent up rage out on the three IRA members who have broken into the church hall to rescue one of their own from the Home Guard. In one moment of off-screen bravado, Wilson redeems himself in the eyes of Mavis and scares off the coward Hodges and earns a new sense of respect from the men who failed to step up to the mark and were beaten up in the process.

LINE:

Hodges: Joe, you've got to help me. Tell him the drink came from you?
Walker: What for?
Hodges: If he finds we're going out, he'll kill me.
Frazer: Yon Sergeant? He couldn't punch a hole in a new-laid egg.

WATCH OUT FOR:

- **There appears to be no metal distinguishing the numbers on the dartboard, possibly as some metals were requisitioned for the war effort.**
- **Mainwaring endures a torrid time speaking to his wife on the phone throughout the first act as she bullies him into obtaining oxtail from Jones.**
- **The appearance of Arthur English as the policeman. He went on to appear in *Are You Being Served?* as maintenance man, Mr Harman.**

BEHIND THE SCENES:

The writers explored the difficulties between Arthur Wilson and Mavis Pike's relationship in this episode, even hinting at another man who had taken Private Pike's Mum's fancy, ARP Warden Hodges. Both Jimmy Perry and David Croft wanted to hint at the past and present that the couple shared and at the possible true paternity of Pike himself.

David Croft recalled, 'The Mavis Pike - Arthur Wilson relationship added a lovely element to the series. The fact that we never knew if they were partners, or just friends, and whether Pike was Wilson's son was a nice little mystery which was left resolved, although in my estimation he was always Wilson's son.'6

TRIVIA:

This episode had only been repeated once in the same year of its original broadcast until the 19th May 2012, nearly 42 years later as the subject matter and sub-plot involving the IRA was seen as being a sensitive subject in the years in between.

SCORE: 8/10

EPISODE THIRTY THREE

PUT THAT LIGHT OUT!

RECORDED ON 30TH OCTOBER 1970
FIRST BROADCAST ON 6TH NOVEMBER 1970
VIEWING FIGURE: 13 MILLION

PLOT:

When giving a lecture to the men, Mainwaring announces that he has been given permission for an observation post to be set up in the lighthouse at Walmington-on-Sea. On patrol, Jones decides to take matters into his own hands and he accidentally turns the generator on and illuminates the coastline at the same time the air raid sirens go off. As the Germans come across the channel, it's a race against time to put the light out!

GUEST CAST:

Bill Pertwee as ARP Warden Hodges
Stuart Sherwin as Mr Alberts, 2nd ARP Warden
Gordon Peters as Lighthouse Keeper
Avril Angers as Freda, the Telephone Operator

REVIEW:

Here we get the first real clunker of the fourth series as an episode built around a well-used catchphrase fails to illuminate the screen with a glow of comedy gold. More screen time for Bill Pertwee makes it better than it could have been but the friction between the men and the ARP Warden is beginning to grate a little. To paraphrase a quote from *The Naked Gun* for a moment, 'Can't they all just get along!' The first half is of the episode is unbelievably slow and it never picks up, even in the panic of the lighthouse sparking into action unexpectedly. It is a good idea to split the main characters up for the episode however, and I think the separate interactions expand the unit's dynamic. We have Mainwaring and Wilson in the church hall, Jones and his men in the lighthouse causing the problems, apart from Walker who has been excused to do some dodgy dealings after guaranteeing Mainwaring his black market whiskey. The episode is lacking in laughs and the audience clearly thinks so too. Where in past episodes there have been huge ruptures of delight on the soundtrack, this week in some places it is as though the audience is made up of door mice! They reflect that the humour is not up to scratch as it has been so often in this run and for that it is a shame as a couple of set pieces go begging. In conclusion, *Put that Light Out!* really is not as strong as it should be and is apparently lost on the audience too. In some places there is barely a titter, apart from a couple of slapstick moments. An opportunity wasted then.

MEMORABLE MOMENT:

Walker joins Mainwaring and Wilson on the scene and realising that there is little they can do to reach the lighthouse and Jones' men; they decide to take out the generator, which is rigged up near the Jolly Roger Ice Cream Parlour, where they are situated. With the lighthouse ablaze and the air raid siren wailing, time is running out to put the lighthouse out of action before the invasion fleet arrives. Mainwaring borrows Walker's tin hat to short fuse the generator and the plan it blows up in his face...literally.

LINE:

Pike: I wish Uncle Arthur was with us, don't you?
Jones: No, I wish we was with him.

WATCH OUT FOR:

- **In the scene when Jones' men enter the lighthouse, the studio light is reflecting in clear sight on the window behind him.**
- **As Frazer goes to fetch Godfrey, he puts his pipe, which has just light, back in his pocket before settling down to tell a story about a haunted lighthouse, let's hope it didn't light!**
- **Godfrey nearly loses his life when Mainwaring aims the lewis gun at the light but luckily the light goes out just in time.**

BEHIND THE SCENES:

Production Assistant Harold Snoad had the idea that was used as a base for this episode. Looking back, he said: 'The basic idea came to me one day when it suddenly occurred to me that there could be fun gained from the use of the Warden's slogan ("Put That Light Out!") if applied to a much larger light. I spent ac lot of my youth living at Eastbourne and fairly frequently saw Beachy Head lighthouse. I remember associating the two ideas and realising the possibilities.

'I put the idea of the platoon using the lighthouse - and the problem that would arise if they accidentally switched on the huge beam lighting up Walmington just as an air raid starts - to Jimmy and David who were very keen. Obviously none of us were that conversant with the basic workings and layout of a lighthouse, so I contacted the authorities at Trinity House and gained permission for Jimmy and myself to visit the one at Beachy Head. A date was duly arranged for the recce and as access can only be gained by boat I also fixed this up with a local company. I remember driving down to Eastbourne with my wife early on the agreed date and finding the boatman on the beach declaring that, unfortunately, the sea was particularly rough that day and the trip wouldn't be possible. We met Jimmy off the train and I had to break this news to him.

'We (and the designer, Paul Joel) eventually did some other research instead - without actually visiting a lighthouse - and managed to gain enough information to make it work.'7

TRIVIA:

In the scene when Mainwaring has a blackened face, Hodges calls him 'Hutch.' This is due to what the Warden believes is a similarity to Leslie 'Hutch' Hutchinson who lived from 1900 to 1969 and was a talented black pianist who toured the country's finest wine bars and restaurants and was well known for his collaborations with Noel Coward and Cole Porter during the 1930s and 1940s.

SCORE: 4/10

EPISODE THIRTY FOUR

THE TWO AND A HALF FEATHERS

RECORDED ON 6TH NOVEMBER 1970
FIRST TRANSMITTED ON 13TH NOVEMBER 1970
VIEWING FIGURE: 15.6 MILLION

PLOT:

Frazer introduces a new recruit to the men called George Clarke who he has met at the local pub earlier in the week. Upon the question of his Military background, Clarke tells the men that he was in the Warwickshire regiment, the same one that Jones was in. Clarke instantly shows distain for the old man upon meeting him again. Soon, Clarke begins to spread rumours about Jones and the pair's history. Jones takes his colleagues back in time to explain the reasoning behind the feud...

GUEST CAST:

Bill Pertwee as ARP Warden Hodges and Dervish warrior
John Cater as Private Clarke
Wendy Richard as Edith
Queenie Watts as Edna
Gilda Perry as Doreen
Linda James as Betty
Parnell McGarry as Elizabeth
John Ash as Raymond

REVIEW:

This is easily the best episode of the series so far and head and shoulders above the rest. More is revealed to us about Jack Jones' time in the desert and how as closely guarded secret and the reappearance of a man he has not seen in years nearly ruins his reputation in the Home Guard. The conduct of arguable every fan's favourite character in Jones is brought into question when an old pal from his former regiment comes back to haunt him. John Cater is great a Private Clarke and in striving to stain the name of the man he believed left him to die in the desert but the stand out performance if of course given to us by Clive Dunn, who is at the peak of his powers here as Jones. We see a different, more vulnerable side to Jonesey than we have done before this and to see him tested is great and a smart piece of writing. We actually get the back story first, so the scenario and what we need to know is given to us straight up early on, such as Clarke being a former friend of the butcher and that he has labelled him a coward when he has always come across as arguably the most experienced of the entire platoon in battle so they all look up to him in a way and are crushed when they hear this rumour. I think it is sensible to have Jones tell his side of the story over the flashback so the remaining mystique is not ruined to early or too late. The whole production is faultless with even the sands of Norfolk doubling well for the deserts of the Sudan. Everyone is once again on top form here, proving that this truly was the golden age of *Dad's Army.*

MEMORABLE MOMENT:

What can be more memorable than a flashback to Jones' past in the Sudan? We have heard many a story about his time in the military but here we actually get to see it, and also see our favourite characters appear as very different personas to the ones we know and love. The stand out performance, apart from Clive Dunn who plays a younger version of Jones, is Arthur Lowe's shift as the tourete suffer of the year candidate Sergeant Ironside, who'd have thought putting raspberry sounds over naughty words would be so funny?

LINE:

Mainwaring: Do you know Mr Clarke well?
Frazer: Aye, sir, I do that.
Mainwaring: And you've known him for some time?
Frazer: Oh aye, sir, I have that.
Mainwaring: And you'd say that he is a man of integrity?
Frazer: And very generous, sir. He stood me several drinks in the bar at The Anchor last Thursday.
Mainwaring: When did you first meet him?
Frazer: In the bar at The Anchor last Thursday.

WATCH OUT FOR:

- **A much younger-looking Jones, who shows he has always had his enthusiasm and urge for 'permission to speak.'**
- **Hodges displays the same fear of fire as his dervish warrior alter ego.**

- **Impressive location footage that doubles superbly for the deserts of the Sudan.**

BEHIND THE SCENES:

For the flashback scene, the cast and crew relocated to a disused quarry in Leziante in Kings Lynn called British Ind Sands Ltd. For this scene, the main cast played differing characters for the first time in the show's history. These new parts represented a character from Jones' memory, with only Clive Dunn, who did not require his ageing make-up, appearing as the person they regularly play on screen.

Arthur Lowe played the rude and blasphemous Sergeant Ironside, John Le Mesurier was Colonel Smythe, who appeared to be the 'Uncle' of the Second Lieutenant played by Ian Lavender, whilst James Beck assumed the role of Private Green and Arnold Ridley as an old Fakir. John Laurie and Bill Pertwee played the two dervish warriors.

This spoof of *The Four Feathers* is linked by the appearance of Laurie in both as he played the Khalifa in the original film. The footage of the dervish warriors opening fire on Jones' platoon are also taken from the feature.

The medals that Dunn wears as Jones when he is preparing to leave for his reunion were meticulously researched by the writers and were the actual medals that were awarded to soldiers during the relevant conflicts. They were seen as being so valuable that after a take, the crew had to keep them safe in a vault in case of damage or theft.

TRIVIA:

The episode is based on the 1939 film, *The Four Feathers* which starred Ralph Richardson, John Clements, C. Aubrey Smith and a young John Laurie. It was based on the 1902 novel of the same name and deals with themes of betrayal, cowardice and set during the suppression of the Arabi Pasha in 1882. It was filmed in the Sudan and nominated for an Academy Award for Best Cinematography.

SCORE: 10/10

EPISODE THIRTY FIVE

MUM'S ARMY

RECORDED ON 13TH NOVEMBER 1970
FIRST BROADCAST ON 20TH NOVEMBER 1970
VIEWING FIGURE: 16.4 MILLION

PLOT:

Mainwaring announces that he has been approached by the women of Walmington-on-Sea to help the men with the war effort. The next evening, the men bring along who they believe would be good candidates and Mainwaring interviews them in the side office. The last applicant is a Mrs Fiona Gray, who Mainwaring takes an instant liking to. But soon, tongues start to wag and the relationship between the two blossoms into something more than professional.

GUEST CAST:

Carmen Silvera as Mrs Gray
Janet Davies as Mrs Pike
Wendy Richard as Edith Parish
Pamela Cundell as Mrs Fox
Julia Barbury as Miss Ironside
Rosemary Faith as Ivy Samways
Melita Manger as Waitress
David Gilchrist as Serviceman
Jack Le White as Porter

REVIEW:

Mum's Army is without doubt one of the best. It takes the show into new territory and shows that even middle age, hardened men, willing to defend their country no matter what, can be stripped bare by the introduction of females to the platoon. In what is arguably one of Perry and Croft's most rounded scripts, we get funny moments, scenes that vividly memorable and a breathtaking performance from the show's leading man and the woman who sets his pulse racing. Carmen Silvera's performance as Mrs Gray is up there with one of the best guest star appearances by anybody in the show's long and illustrious history. Her on screen chemistry with Mainwaring sparkles and I love how uptight and cautious he is in scenes with her when men of his platoon are around. Since he has a reputation to uphold, it would have been a scandal in those days if these two had ever got together. But in the end, Mainwaring's one chance for happiness is taken away from him. I love the end of this episode; it's so poignant as we witness our favourite Captain have his only chance of escaping his unhappy marriage and displaying his true feelings. When he tells Fiona that he can 'damn the bloody bank' for all he cares. You really sympathise with him, for all his pompousness, middle class frustrations and inferiority complex, here we see Mainwaring naked metaphorically and his emotions have taken hold. He even whispers 'I love you' to her as the train departs. It is such a powerful end to such a memorable episode.

MEMORABLE MOMENT:

The touching, and surprisingly heartbreaking end, in which Mainwaring, despite of his reputation in the town and his status as Captain of the Home Guard, is quite prepared to leave his reclusive wife and destroy his good name just to have Fiona in his life. It is a strong performance from both Arthur Lowe and Carmen Silvera and the look on reaction on Mainwaring's face as Mrs Gray's train leaves the station is immensely sad.

LINE:

Edith: Blimey what a way to win a war!
Godfrey: The captain knows best you know you ought to listen to what he's saying.
Mainwaring: Godfrey, look to your front, stop staring at the ladies.
Walker: Yeah, quite right, he's woman mad he is, woman mad!

WATCH OUT FOR:

- **Arthur Lowe's slapstick performance in Ann's Pantry as Mainwaring dispenses of his glasses to impress Mrs Gray.**
- **The not-so-subtle comparisons to the 1945 film *Brief Encounter*.**
- **Jones' reaction to Mrs Fox's admission that her age is on the bottom...**

BEHIND THE SCENES:

A little more is revealed regarding the private life of George Mainwaring. In the scene where he meets Mrs Gray in the tea rooms, he takes off his glasses as she told him he looked better without them and is shown to be practically blind when without them. The tea rooms, christened Ann's Pantry, was a brand new set, which was built for the episode but was also reused many more times in the series.

David Croft revealed that the inspiration of the episode was a well-known British film, written by thespian Noel Coward.

'"Mum's Army"' was slightly based on *'Brief Encounter,'* but I didn't go as far as using the music, which was a potent factor in the movie. It was a favourite episode of mine. Arthur Lowe didn't like it to begin with. He said: "If I'd read this before we started rehearsal, I'd have had something to say." He was rather against it but within a few days was saying it was "pure genius,'8 he later recalled.

TRIVIA:

The part of Mrs Fiona Gray was played by Carmen Silvera, who would be used again by David Croft in the hit sitcom, *Allo 'Allo!* as the tone deaf wife of Rene Artois, Edith. She played the part throughout the show's run from 1982 to 1992. She was once married to John Cunliffe, who created and wrote the children's characters *'Postman Pat'* and *Rosie and Jim,* appearing as himself in the latter production.

SCORE: 10/10

EPISODE THIRTY SIX

THE TEST

RECORDED ON 20TH NOVEMBER 1970
FIRST BROADCAST ON 27TH NOVEMBER 1970
VIEWING FIGURE: 16 MILLION

PLOT:

Mainwaring is given a letter that has been written by Hodges inviting the Home Guard to a game of cricket against the ARP Wardens. When he puts the idea to the men they are enthusiastic about the prospect of a match and they accept the challenge but are dismayed when Mainwaring makes himself Captain of the team. When match day arrives, Hodges signs up a man called E C Egan who reveals himself as a professional cricket player as the ARP Wardens look to gain an unfair advantage over the platoon.

GUEST CAST:

Bill Pertwee as ARP Warden Hodges
Edward Sinclair as the Verger
Frank Williams as the Vicar
Don Estelle as Gerald
Fred Trueman as E.C. Egan

REVIEW:

The Test is the latest in a great sequence of episodes. It is a fabulous half hour, performed spectacularly by the ensemble, with the inclusion of an England cricket legend in a tight and entertaining script that is of a high standard throughout. Of course the main set piece is the cricket match itself but the buildup to the big match is flawless. The sledging, the controversy, the mistakes, the man of the match winning performances, all that you want from a cricket match! The scene in which Mainwaring attempts to teach his platoon the rules of cricket highlights his pomposity and he is well and truly embarrassed by a bowl from Pike that Fred Trueman himself would have been proud of. It is a little disappointing that we do not get a chance to see Trueman's legendary bowling skills. It is a bit of a cop out to have a man with such a big reputation in cricket make an appearance and then we don't even see him do the job that made him famous.
In conclusion, *The Test* is one that both cast and crew pass with flying colours and gives Mainwaring a one up-man ship over his close rival Hodges. How much longer can this streak of big hitters go on? Hopefully for the rest of the run!

MEMORABLE MOMENT:

The scene in which the platoon build up to the encounter with the ARP Wardens highlights Mainwaring's dominating and pompous approach, insisting on teaching his men to bat and bowl when his left hand man, Wilson, is far better equipped to handling the exercise due to his involvements in the Walmington-on-Sea cricket team. The bank manager is taught a lesson in how to deliver the perfect ball when young Pike knocks the bails off his stumps first time, making him look foolish in front of his men but it is a moment that includes a rare victory for the young Private.

LINE:

Mainwaring: That was my googly.
Verger: From where I was standing it looked like a chuck, and don't argue with the umpire or you'll be sent off.
Mainwaring: You don't send people off in cricket!
Verger: I do!
Mainwaring: I suppose I'm lucky not to be given offside!

WATCH OUT FOR:

- **Private Pike bowling Mainwaring in the practice scene in the churchyard well played sir!**
- **Corporal Jones' unorthodox style of keeping wicket for the Home Guard.**

- **The last ditch heroics of the most unlikely member of the platoon...**

BEHIND THE SCENES:

Several accidents occurred during the making of this episode, which were recorded on an 'Accident and Industrial Disease Report Form' at the BBC. According to the forms, on the 20th October 1970, both Clive Dunn and Arthur Lowe sustained injuries on location at Stanford Training Area. Dunn cut the inside of his mouth when he had to catch a ball bowled by Andy Luckhurst, which he missed and smashed into his mouth.

Lowe suffered bruising to the left side of his head as Phil Bishop, the production assistant, threw a bumper that Lowe had to duck out of but it hit him. As the report reads, 'the accident resulted from a combination of the batsmen not ducking quickly enough and the thrower throwing too low.'9

Ian Lavender was delighted at the prospect of playing cricket with his hero, Fred Trueman, but he was disappointed to have missed an opportunity with his idol. 'I was annoyed with David Croft in 'The Test' because he wouldn't let me keep wicket for Freddie Trueman, who made a special appearance in this episode. He was my boyhood hero and all I wanted to do was take a few balls from him. I pleaded with David, but to no avail. In my studio-based scene I had to bowl Arthur Lowe first ball - and I did.'10

TRIVIA:

Cricketer and guest star Fred Trueman, nicknamed 'Fiery Fred' was a famous bowler who played for Yorkshire and Derbyshire from 1949 until 1972 and also enjoyed a successful career with England and became the first bowler to take 300 wickets in Test history. His International figures stand at 307 wickets and 981 runs in 67 Test matches with a batting average of 13.81. His last appearance for his country was against New Zealand on 17th June 1965, thirteen years after his debut. He went on to build an illustrious media career before passing away on 1st July 2006, aged 75.

SCORE: 9/10

EPISODE THIRTY SEVEN

A. WILSON (MANAGER)?

RECORDED ON 27TH NOVEMBER 1970
FIRST BROADCAST ON 4TH DECEMBER 1970
VIEWING FIGURE: 15.4 MILLION

PLOT:

Wilson is fifteen minutes late for duty at the bank. Mainwaring is annoyed and answers the phone call from Head Office and he is in for a shock. He is told by Captain Pritchard that Wilson will be re-commissioned to Eastgate platoon and will act as 2nd

Lieutenant under Captain Square, which he will take up as soon as possible, leaving Mainwaring reeling. With Wilson also moving on to the Eastgate branch bank, it looks like Mainwaring is on the verge of losing his right-hand-man.

GUEST CAST:

Frank Williams as the Vicar
Edward Sinclair as the Verger
Janet Davies as Mrs. Pike
Blake Butler as Mr. West
Robert Raglan as Colonel Pritchard
Arthur Brough as Mr. Boyle
Colin Bean as Private Sponge
Hugh Hastings as Private Hastings

REVIEW:

The fledgling flies the coop. Is this the end of Sergeant Wilson's association with the Walmington-on-Sea Home Guard? In a great script from Jimmy Perry and David Croft, we bid farewell to Wilson and John Le Mesurier...for a bit. His departure to Eastgate breaks the brittle relationship between himself and Mainwaring as the difference of class, ego and ambition come to a head. It is quite clear from the outset that Mainwaring's overwhelming emotion to the news that he is losing his Sergeant is jealousy. He bubbles over with anger at having to work that much harder for his success in life and is outraged that Wilson just seems to swan along in life and reap the rewards due to his background. *A. Wilson (Manager?)* is a triumph of content and despite not being one of the funniest editions that this series has had to offer so far, it is one of the most engaging. Apart from one notable scene, there is not really a lot for the other regulars to immerse themselves in but that does not matter. This really is about Mainwaring and Wilson. The working class bank manager and the upper class gentleman. The grammar school boy and the public school graduate. You can see how sore Mainwaring is throughout the piece and he is not sorry to see Wilson go. There is a touching moment when he leaves Mainwaring's office and glances at the sign on the door. 'G. MAINWARING. MANAGER' it reads. He thinks back to the sign he owned for a short period that he found on the bomb sight. It's a moment of fantastic acting from Le Mesurier and he doesn't need to utter a single word to get across the sentiment.

MEMORABLE MOMENT:

For once my favourite moment occurs right at the very beginning of the show as Mainwaring pours out his middle-class frustrations on the upper-class, departing Wilson. After receiving the bad news regarding his Chief Clerk and Sergeant leaving for Eastgate, the bank manager boils over when Wilson arrives late and puts on his officer's hat, leaving Mainwaring to label him a 'Judas.' It is a remarkable piece of acting and I really do believe that Arthur Lowe was angry here, you watch his performance. It is hard to differentiate between his acting and his real life mood and that is the essence of a world class actor.

LINE:

The men have all mistakenly been made up to Sergeant.

Jones: Captain Mainwaring, I've fallen the Private in. What should I do with the Sergeants?

WATCH OUT FOR:

- **When Jones enquires if he can have his promotion to Sergeant in writing, Arthur Lowe's pen is not touching the paper as he writes.**
- **Janet King, the secretary to Mainwaring in the first series, is mentioned as still working in the bank but is not seen on screen.**
- **The men all turn up wearing three stripes on their arms as they have all been sent an incorrect memo that they are Sergeant, except Pike.**

BEHIND THE SCENES:

The episode was repeated on BBC1 on the 23rd November 1983 as a tribute to the late John Le Mesurier who passed away just eight days earlier. Caroline Dowdeswell, who had appeared in five episodes of the first series, believed that the air that Le Mesurier conducted himself in no one else in the cast would have got away with.

'I remember John Le Mesurier often adopted the role of Grand Seigneur. I could never find a make-up girl to powder me down as they were all fussing over John. He always seemed to have about three of them around him: one doing his hair, one giving him a manicure and another running errands or getting him a sandwich. He was always so languid and would call everyone "dear lady" in a world-wearied drawl while they fell over themselves fetching and carrying for him.

'As Arthur Lowe didn't appear to feature highly on their list of priorities, I later developed the idea that the make-up department was subconsciously reacting to the social class of the characters we played,'11 she later revealed.

TRIVIA:

In real life, John Le Mesurier had been a captain during the Second World War. After reporting for duty to the Royal Armoured Corps, in June 1941 he was commissioned to the Royal Tank Regiment and he served in the country until 1943 until he was given the rank of Captain and sent out to British India until being de-mobbed in 1946, a year after the war had ended.

SCORE: 8/10

EPISODE THIRTY EIGHT

UNINVITED GUESTS

RECORDED ON 4TH DECEMBER 1970

FIRST BROADCAST ON 11TH DECEMBER 1970
VIEWING FIGURE: 13.1 MILLION

PLOT:

During an air raid, the ARP's headquarters is levelled by the Nazis and they relocate to the Vicar's side office in the church hall. Mainwaring is irritated by his Hodge's presence at the same time as he is using the church hall, despite the Warden wanting to be fair and share the office. Mainwaring's frustrations are confounded when an air raid begins and he is forced to share the office with Hodges and his assistant. But a church fire soon forces the two enemies to cooperate.

GUEST CAST:

Bill Pertwee as ARP Warden Hodges
Frank Williams as the Vicar
Edward Sinclair as the Verger
Rose Hill as Mrs. Cole
Don Estelle as Gerald

REVIEW:

Dad's Army meets *The Odd Couple* in this strained, grating, not as funny as it should be episode. Although a damp squib in, *Uninvited Guests* is really a big opportunity for Bill Pertwee to further his mark on the programme with the wonderfully abrasive Hodges and cement his place as the main rival to Mainwaring's equilibrium. However, one performance does not make thirty minutes but luckily, the show wakes up when the chimney bursts into flames. It is a rather disappointing spectacle if I'm honest but lest we forget, this was 1970 studio-bound comedy. It does not put an end to the bickering between Mainwaring and Hodges, mind. The star of the show is definitely Pertwee, however, as he pushes Mainwaring to the limit but I also think the runner up for the week has to be John Laurie, who in one scene, upstages the pratfalls that Clive Dunn performs on top of the church roof. His monologue in the second act is brilliant and the roar it gets from the audience is enough to blow of the walls on the set. It is arguably one of the biggest laughs of the series. *Uninvited Guests* is not in the same league as the episodes of the series so far as the fourth season begins to come to a close. The inner friction with the characters ruins it though and considering that the plot revolves around this is detrimental to the overall production.

MEMORABLE MOMENT:

Frazer zones out and recalls a story about a man who had a curse put on another man that doomed him to death. With a fantastic zinger at the end (Did the Curse come true? Ay son it did, last year. He was 86!) It is a two minute long monologue from John Laurie who excels in the moment. I can imagine him doing a scary edition of *Jackanory* reading Charles Dickens' *A Christmas Carol.* The range of emotions he hits in the piece is mesmerising and easily the best moment of the episode.

LINE:

Mainwaring: (Speaking into a tin) Hello, all stations, Charlie One. Hello, all stations, Charlie One. Report my signal, all stations, Charlie One. Over. (They can't understand a word. He takes his mouth from the tin) Now, is that quite clear?
Frazer: Speaking for myself, sir. I didn't understand one single word.

WATCH OUT FOR:

- **In the scene with the men putting the tins up to their ears, Arnold Ridley delivers his line too early and is drowned out by Clive Dunn dropping his tin.**
- **The Verger cuts the men's communication wire with his garden shears.**
- **Mainwaring and Hodges behaving like children when the ARP Warden draws a chalk line through the side office to give them an equal share of the room.**

BEHIND THE SCENES:

The 1970 *Christmas with the Stars* skit that was broadcast on Christmas Day was recorded on the same day as this episode. Entitled *The Cornish Floral Dance* it involved the platoon and the ladies and the wardens of Walmington-on-Sea rehearsing a dance for a town fair. This sketch no longer exists in the BBC Archive.

Rose Hill, who played Mrs Cole during the production, later remembered how thoughtful one of her co-stars was about her moments on screen. 'Arthur Lowe was a very generous actor. I played Mrs Cole, one of the air raid wardens, in a scene in the church hall side office where the telephone kept ringing. I'd never worked with him before, and while rehearsing he must have noticed me frown or something, because he said: "Wait a minute, Rose isn't happy."

'He asked what the problem was, it was something to do with the timing of me picking up the phone, and ensured I was happy before proceeding. It was nice to see such a fine actor give me, just in a small part, such attention - I was bowled over by him.'12

TRIVIA:

Bill Pertwee was a second cousin of the actor Jon Pertwee, who among comedic roles in shows such as *The Navy Lark* is remembered for playing the third incarnation of the title character in *Doctor Who* from 1970-1974. Both appeared in the *Carry On...* franchise but in separate films as Bill performed in *Carry On Loving* in 1970 and *Carry On Girls* in 1973.

SCORE: 6/10

EPISODE THIRTY NINE

FALLEN IDOL

RECORDED ON 11TH DECEMBER 1970

FIRST BROADCAST ON 18TH DECEMBER 1970
VIEWING FIGURE: 13.1 MILLION

PLOT:

The men are sent on a weekend course at the School of Explosives. Mainwaring is quick to remind his men that the camp is a democratic one, meaning that they will sleep and eat together and there will no hierarchy, but Captain Square arrives and starts to influence Mainwaring in becoming more distant from his platoon. The men discuss Mainwaring's behaviour while he is away and when they go to sleep, they are disturbed by a drunken Mainwaring, who has taken part in drinking games with his fellow officers!

GUEST CAST:

Geoffrey Lumsden as Captain Square
Rex Garner as Captain Ashley-Jones
Michael Knowles as Captain Reed
Anthony Sagar as Sergeant Major
Tom Mennard as Mess Orderly
Robert Raglan as Captain Pritchard

REVIEW:

In Arthur Lowe, was there anybody better than him at acting like he was intoxicated? On this evidence, no. Mainwaring's further alienation from his platoon is cemented in this one despite his good will and Lowe makes the performance of the series' run. Especially when he stumbles back into the tent and his men see him completely inebriated. His comedy timing is perfect and even though his redemption is far off at this point, some of the men have already begun to doubt their Captain. The two scenes split in the middle that makes up the middle section of the episode is also well rounded and allows interaction between the men and they all have their moment of glory with a rich script. The men are having a miserable time, truly let down by the Captain's behaviour. Godfrey is right, Mainwaring has been led astray and they soon perk up but I love the contrast in both scenes occurring simultaneously. When Mainwaring returns, he is in no fit state to lead his men and wakes him up after being attacked by Jones, who believes him to be an intruder. He is truly punished the next day when his hangover is hampered by the grenade explosions. The episode feels laid back and has the air of an end of term school day about it. You have bad behaviour, a drunk and an explosion and lots of laughter at other people's expense. Sounds just like my old school, apart from the drink that is (honest...) As the final episode of series four, *Fallen Idol* is a triumph. It mixes together all that has been successful with this run. The memorable moments, the laugh a minute script, the superb acting by the regular cast and the guest stars and tighter, more character driven ideas that see us delve further into the men behind the Walmington-on-Sea Home Guard.

MEMORABLE MOMENT:

When the platoon set up camp, Private Pike seems pensive and urgent. He enquires to Sergeant Wilson whether he has seen 'Mr Snuggly.' Wilson is bemused but Pike tells him that he has slot his teddy bear and asks his 'Uncle' to help him look for it because he cannot get to sleep without it. When Wilson finds the bear rolled up in his sleeping bag, he tries to hide it but Mainwaring spots it and asks what it is. Wilson tells his superior that it is his teddy and Mainwaring rounds off the moment with a fantastic look of disapproval.

LINE:

Mainwaring: (As he enters the tent, he wobbles and grabs a tent pole to stop himself falling over) Damn revolving doors!

WATCH OUT FOR:

- **Frazer threatening to walk out on the platoon in regards to Mainwaring's behaviour.**
- **The stunt performance of the man standing in for Arthur Lowe as he cycled after Jones' dangerous van.**
- **In his drunken stupor, Mainwaring tips his drink over the head of Captain Square.**

BEHIND THE SCENES:

Exterior scenes were filmed in a genuine Grenade Training Area, once again captured at Stanford Training Area, which was owned by the Ministry of Defence. Further location filming, of Jones' van careering towards an Electric Sub Station was also captured at a real life station at Honington to Euston Road in Suffolk.

The moment when Mainwaring re-enters the tent and stumbles along in a drunken stupor was add-libbed by Arthur Lowe himself. As Don Estelle remembered, 'I remember watching *Fallen Idol* being recorded. There is a great scene where a drunken Mainwaring returns to his tent and spins round the tent pole. He didn't have any lines in the script, but during filming spun around the tent pole too much, and said: "Damn these revolving doors." The audience fell about, but the production crew nearly fell off their chairs – he'd put his own line in and it worked beautifully.'13

TRIVIA:

In 1981, David Croft received the Desmond Davis Lifetime Achievement Award and was given the award following a speech from Arthur Lowe, who the audience believed was putting on an act as he slurred his words and from what it looked like, was messing it up on purpose for comedic effect. Unfortunately, Lowe was suffering from narcolepsy and alcoholism at the time and was far from sober when he handed the award over to his former Writer, Producer and Director.

SCORE: 7/10

After yet another challenging yet enjoyable shoot, the ratings for the programme and the reviews it was obtaining continued to point towards enduring success. The average viewing figures for the series stood at 14.4 million, nearly two million up on the previous series figure. The show was also gaining more recognition from within the industry as Arthur Lowe was nominated for Best Light Entertainment Performance at the British Academy Television Awards and the show also won Best Comedy Script at the Writer's Guild of Great Britain for the second year running. As 1970 gave way to 1971, more work for the crew came, instead of in the form of a new series, a Christmas Special and a motion picture as Columbia Pictures began work on *Dad's Army: The Movie.* For a *Dad's Army* fan, it didn't get any better than this...

EPISODE FORTY

BATTLE OF THE GIANTS!

RECORDED ON 19TH SEPTEMBER 1971
FIRST BROADCAST ON 27TH DECEMBER 1971
VIEWING FIGURE: 18.7 MILLION

PLOT:

Captain Square arrives after parade to check that his memo about medals having to be worn on the parade has reached the church hall. Mainwaring inspects the men on the following parade and notices that they are all wearing their medals, except him as he has never won any. Later, Square ribs Mainwaring over his men's lack of discipline. Annoyed and insulted, Mainwaring is adamant that his men are better and fitter than Square's Eastgate platoon. In the end, the two platoons decide to go head to head in a battle of the Home Guard units...

GUEST CAST:

Bill Pertwee as ARP Warden
Frank Williams as Vicar
Edward Sinclair as Verger
Geoffrey Lumsden as Captain Square
Robert Raglan as the Colonel
Charles Hill as Sergeant Parkins
Colin Bean as Private Sponge
Rosemary Faith as Shirley, the Barmaid

REVIEW:

Battle of the Giants! is helped by its hour long duration as in some episodes in the past the final scene has seemed rushed and certain episodes have simply run out of time to round the story off. Yet here, we have a coherent pacing, a proper story with a beginning, middle and end. We have the origins of the main set piece and its resolution and the episode is all the stronger for it. It does not seem like it is carrying the weight of its run time and that is a testament to Perry and Croft's writing. When the main battle commences, the inclusion of the ARP Warden, the Vicar and the Verger is for once warranted. I moaned a couple of episodes back that there was an overcrowding of warring characters but here they are mainly kept separate from the platoon, hoping that they will fail and the Warden is the butt of the joke most of the time. Any excuse having Bill Pertwee drenched in water eh? We also see a welcome return of the shooting out of the van's portholes, a great visual joke from series three. As the pendulum swings between Eastgate and Walmington, we all know who we are backing and in the end, Walmington-on-Sea Home Guard wins fair and square...ish. In conclusion, *Battles of the Giants!* is a fantastic special. It gives Mainwaring a chance to prove himself to his men and to his rivals and allows the director to flex his muscles and bring the best out of his actors in an action packed yet funny special.

MEMORABLE MOMENT:

Mainwaring has not read out the orders for the men to wear their medals on the parade due to his lack of decoration. So when he goes to inspect the men on the next parade evening, he is shocked to find that every one of his platoon members is wearing them, even Pike who is wearing his scout badges. Mainwaring is incredibly embarrassed and confounded that Wilson has gone over his head to give the orders. But it is his true inferiority complex that shines through his anger as his lack of medals makes a mockery of his rank as Captain.

LINE:

Godfrey: Oh dear - what's wrong with Mr Jones?
Mainwaring: He's got a bout of malaria - have you got anything we can give him?
Godfrey: *(Opening his satchel)* I don't know really, sir. *(He takes out some bandages and a bottle of aspirins)* I've got some aspirins, some bicarbonate of soda and some ointment for wasp stings.
Mainwaring: Wasp stings! This is a fighting unit, not a girl guides' outing!

WATCH OUT FOR:

- **Mainwaring becoming sheepish after shouting at Pike for destroying his new hat but then being called to the phone to speak to his wife.**
- **The chair Godfrey it sitting in is lifted by members of the platoon and the lifts break, leaving him rooted as the men charge off.**

- **When the platoon has to burst the balloons, Walker puts his cigarette in his rifle to great effect.**

BEHIND THE SCENES:

As the show's first scheduled Christmas Special *Battle of the Giants!* is the first extended edition of *Dad's Army* running to sixty minutes, double the length of the standard episodes in the series. Despite the longer runtime, some scenes were still left on the cutting room floor. The explanation behind Private Walker's medal and several cutaways to the battle against Eastbourne platoon were edited back into the programme for the 2007 DVD release of the Christmas Specials release. This episode is the highest rated in the show's history, pulling in a massive 18.7 million viewers on original transmission over Christmas 1971. That accolade was never beaten with the series five episode *Brain vs Brawn* coming closest with 18.6 million viewers. Cameraman Peter Chapman described the difficulty of filming on location. 'When I filmed *Dad's Army* I used to do my own camera work and so relied on my chief electrician (aka the gaffer) to carry out my lighting plots whilst I worked out the shots and the director and the grips (the chaps responsible for tracking the camera on its dolly or crane, or for mounting it in strange places like Jones' van).

'The lighting plot must produce the correct feel for the scene whilst leaving a spot for the microphone boom to get at the actors without throwing shadows into the frame.'1

TRIVIA:

When Wilson enquires what has happened to Jones, Pike tells him that he has come down with a bout of malaria, like Leslie Banks in the film *Sanders of the River.* The film was made in 1935 and was disowned by African-American singer Paul Robeson, who accepted the role of Bosambo but when he was called in for retakes to some of his scenes, he believed that the films message had been changed in the edit to justify imperialism. He tried to buy back all the prints of the film to prevent it ever being released but he was unsuccessful.

MARK OUT OF TEN: 8/10

SERIES FIVE

MAIN CAST:

ARTHUR LOWE - CAPTAIN GEORGE MAINWARING
JOHN LE MESURIER - SERGEANT ARTHUR WILSON
CLIVE DUNN - LANCE CORPORAL JACK JONES
JOHN LAURIE - PRIVATE JAMES FRAZER
ARNOLD RIDLEY - PRIVATE CHARLES GODFREY
JAMES BECK - PRIVATE JOE WALKER
IAN LAVENDER - PRIVATE FRANK PIKE

FEATURING THE VOICE OF BUD FLANNIGAN

EPISODE FORTY ONE

ASLEEP IN THE DEEP

RECORDED ON 26TH MAY 1972
FIRST BROADCAST ON 6TH OCTOBER 1972
VIEWING FIGURE: 17 MILLION

PLOT:

The Home Guard are spending the night on duty during an air raid but their peace is disturbed by Hodges, who arrives and tells Mainwaring that two bombs have hit in the town, one in the local woods and one on the pumping station. The Captain is horrified as that is where Walker and Godfrey are on patrol. The men go with Hodges to check it out and discover that Walker is trapped behind a wall with Godfrey, who he believes is unwell as he is not able to wake him...

GUEST CAST:

Bill Pertwee as ARP Warden Hodges
Colin Bean as Private Sponge

REVIEW:

When it comes to timeless comedy, *Dad's Army* is the master of the genre and here we have a real gem. *Asleep in the Deep* is a brilliant episode, almost faultless on every level and without a shadow of a doubt my favourite of the lot. Let me tell you why. For a start, the script is among the finest Jimmy Perry and David Croft ever wrote. With 40 episodes behind them, they have got the characters and the town and the time that they lived in seamed together so well that they are so utterly memorable and the lines they have written for the cast are so funny that most of the time you forget that you are watching a programme about our nation's defence against the threat on invasion. It is a grim backdrop and premise with the prospect of comrades being killed in a bombing but this template is integral and here the episode is so funny and so engrossing you ignore the men's predicament and delight in the farcical events that lead up to the men becoming trapped. There are also a few hints at the physical inventiveness that broadened the spectrum of comedy that the programme divulged in from time to time. Seeing Hodges using his tin hat to wade across the room is simple yet effective and the inclusion of the men singing 'Underneath the Spreading Chestnut Tree' complete with actions is also memorable. The master of physical comedy, Arthur Lowe, has his stubby frame pushed up onto a foothold so that he can talk to his men through the gap in the wall and every time he falls off you can't help but let out a yelp of laughter, even if it is a recycled gag. In conclusion, is this the best *Dad's Army* episode ever? Well, of course that depends on your judgement and whilst many fans of the show choose *The Deadly Attachment* as the greatest but for my money this one is gold dust. The gags are timeless and added peril makes for a wonderful episode. *Dad's Army* doesn't get any better than this.

MEMORABLE MOMENT:

Mainwaring shows that he is a true leader of men when he displays true valour as putting himself at the front of the human chain of men who embark on removing the fallen rubble that has entombed Walker and Godfrey. He originally tells his men and Hodges to put two crosses on two pieces of paper and they will draw them from a hat and the two who get them will go at the front. Hodges draws one and Mainwaring clearly has a blank piece of paper but lies to put his life before that of the men he commands.

LINE:

(The men are stranded as the water rose higher and higher)
Godfrey: Mr Mainwaring sir, do you think I might...
Mainwaring: *(interrupting)* If you want to be excused, it's impossible!

WATCH OUT FOR:

- **When Jones closes the door in the pumping station the wall clearly bends.**
- **Another door is later replaced with a water tight one for the final act when the men are trapped.**
- **Godfrey has a vast supply of insulation stuffed down his tunic to keep the cold out.**

BEHIND THE SCENES:

The production team had to devise a way of building a set that could also act as a tank so that water could be pumped into the studio without flooding the floor and becoming a safety hazard to all. Designer Paul Joel remembered how the challenges were met.
'*Asleep in the Deep* was an interesting episode to work on because the set in which the platoon are trapped was built within a tank so we could fill it with water. It was designed so that the bottom could be taken away and the rest, with all is bunk beds, etc... could be lowered into the water. A member of the visual effects team had to don a wetsuit, get under the water and help push Hodges around in a small tank he used like a canoe.'

TRIVIA:

Pike mentions that he is reminded of the film *Each Dawn I Die.* The 1939 gangster film was based on a book written by Jerome Odlum and starred James Cagney and George Raft. The film was a box office hit for Warner Bros but it was banned in Australia until 1941 and is claimed to have been Soviet Union leader Josef Stalin's favourite American movie by Richard Schickel in his book *James Cagney: A Celebration.*

SCORE: 10/10

EPISODE FORTY TWO

KEEP YOUNG AND BEAUTIFUL

RECORDED ON 9TH JUNE 1972
FIRST BROADCAST ON 13TH OCTOBER 1972
VIEWING FIGURE: 16 MILLION

PLOT:

MP's in the Houses of Parliament have decided to shake up the Home Guard and the ARP by taking the fitter and younger men and putting them in the former and shifting the older less able bodied men into the latter. When Mainwaring hears of the proposal, he is outraged as are his men when he tells them the unfortunate news. The more senior members of the platoon contemplate on what they can do to stay in the

Home Guard and take to drastic measures to look younger...

GUEST CAST:

Bill Pertwee as ARP Warden Hodges
Derek Bond as Minister
Robert Raglan as Colonel
James Ottaway as 1st Member of Parliament
Tom Mennard as Mess Orderly
Charles Morgan as 2nd Member of Parliament

REVIEW:

After the grand *Asleep in the Deep* Jimmy Perry and David Croft are on form again as *Keep Young and Beautiful* can also stake a claim as one of the best episodes they ever wrote. The subject matter is easily plausible but of course the execution is the stand out component. It also highlights the aging process and its problems for those who do not wish to lose their hair, go grey or lose the energy and vitality they once had. But everybody ages and good on the platoon for fighting the ticking body clock all in the interest of fighting Hitler and his ever threatening Nazi army. The

episode is as close as *Dad's Army* has come to a laugh a minute script. Even the bit when Pike is trying to spot Mainwaring's hair piece under his cap still gibes viewers the giggles. Walker's sneaky revenge tactic on Hodges to make him look older and put glue in his hair so it does not wash out is also still as good after all these years. Although there is much, much better moments in the thirty minutes. It's easy to adore *Keep Young and Beautiful* with the extra verve of excellent set pieces, culminating in three members of the platoon literally aging in the rain. We have the usual pratfalls from Clive Dunn when he and James Beck and Ian Lavender fall into the river after trying to cross the banks on a pole and a lovely scene where Arthur Lowe and John Le Mesurier share a funny and quotable two hander. This is a stone cold classic from a golden era in the show's history. It has a tender narrative about the downside of growing old and shows the determination of the more senior members of the platoon to prove their worth. Plus the sight of Godfrey looking like he has had a facelift is enough to make anyone chortle like a hyena.

MEMORABLE MOMENT:

Rather tentatively, Mainwaring tip toes into the side office of the church hall and after checking to see if the coast is clear, pops an oversized, rather unconvincing toupee on his head and adjusts it to cover his bald head. He then takes his glasses off and uses a recently struck matchstick to singe his eyebrows and yelps at the heat. This is a well-crafted scene, culminating in the arrival of the corset wearing Wilson, who laughs to his heart's content when he sees the toupee. For once though, Mainwaring has the last laugh.

LINE:

(Godfrey is wearing Frazer's face paint normally reserved for the dearly departed)
Mainwaring: Get it off at once!
Godfrey: I don't think I can sir.

Mainwaring: How long does it last Frazer?
(Frazer speaks but what he says is completely illegible due to the cotton balls in his mouth)
Mainwaring: What did he say?
Jones: He says he's never dug anyone up to have a look!

WATCH OUT FOR:

- **The show's theme tune can be heard when the men are on their training exercise.**
- **When Mainwaring takes off his cap to show the men his toupee, he leaves it in the cap, leaving the platoon in fits of laughter.**
- **Hodges greyed hair is clearly a wig as his real hair pokes out from the back.**

BEHIND THE SCENES:

The location scenes of the men taking part in the exercise at the beginning of the episode and the exterior shots of the men at the very end of the piece getting caught in the rain shower parade were filmed at High Lodge in Brandon near Thetford.
Robert Raglan made another recurring appearance as the Colonel. His widow, Ms Cornewell-Walker, remembers how thrilled she was at her husband in the part and at the attention he received due to his association with the programme.
'I thought Robert was good in the series because the part of the Colonel suited him. The character was like him, a dry sense of humour and a twinkle in his eye. Robert was a very witty, amusing man, and people were always asking him about his time on '*Dad's Army*."

TRIVIA:

The episode title takes after the song *Keep Young and Beautiful,* which can also be heard in the piece. It was sung by Eddie Cantor and was written by Al Dublin and Andy Warren. The song has been covered by pop star Annie Lennox for her 1992 solo album *Diva* and was a personal favourite of Wartime Prime Minister Winston Churchill.

SCORE: 10/10

EPISODE FORTY THREE

A SOLDIER'S FAREWELL

RECORDED ON 2nd JUNE 1972
FIRST BROADCAST ON 20TH OCTOBER 1972
VIEWING FIGURE: 17.7 MILLION

PLOT:

The platoon is treated to an evening at the cinema to see a film called *Marie Walewska.* Afterwards, Mainwaring is trampled in a stampede and decides to dress the men down following the incident and to teach his men a lesson. When Mainwaring goes home after eating cheese, he sleeps in the air raid shelter in the garden with his wife and struggles to sleep as he believes that the cheese was too rich. He dreams that he is Napoleon and that he and his men are fighting at the

Battle of Trafalgar against Wilson, who is posing as the Duke of Wellington and who is assisted by Hodges and Frazer.

GUEST CAST:

Bill Pertwee as ARP Warden Hodges and British officer
Frank Williams as the Vicar
Robert Gillespie as Charles Boyer playing Napoleon
Joy Allen as Bus Conductress and Greta Garbo playing Marie Walewska
Colin Bean as Private Sponge and Marshal Ney

REVIEW:

The ball just keeps on rolling with *A Soldier's Farewell* as we are given another belter of an episode with arguably the strongest performance ever given by Arthur Lowe in an episode that evokes memories of series four's *The Two and a Half Feathers.* However, instead of a flashback we have the series' first dream sequence and it is a fantastical realisation of a period of history that plays out in Mainwaring's head with familiar faces as the key players. The dream sequence is very effective and once again it is nice to see the main cast act as different people but of course retaining certain parts of their personas. Again, the visual gags work an absolute treat. Whether it is Mainwaring getting trampled by his men three times during the episode or the lady friend of Napoleon punching a hole in his picture to confirm her similarity to the ticket inspector on the bus (ending in the classic line, 'You've punched me on the nose!') they all work brilliantly. Even the allusions to the men of Trafalgar's real identities are nice touches to the episode and an excuse to exercise some familiar catchphrases, like when Hodges shouts 'put those lights out!' and Napoleon calls Pike 'stupid drummer boy.' With regards to the increased quantity of scripts in this series - as it was for series three - nowadays, a show with over six episodes in a series would be written by a team of writers so it is a testament to Jimmy Perry and David Croft's skill in this department that the bar was still so high.

MEMORABLE MOMENT:

For my money it has to be the dream sequence involving Mainwaring placing himself in the shoes of Napoleon and the surrender of the Battle of Waterloo. The interesting part of the whole sequence is who he dreams are the aggressors against his cause. You have Hodges, his main rival, with Wilson, who in portraying the Duke of Wellington shows an indication that he is Mainwaring's biggest enemy and Frazer who from time to time doubts his Captain's capabilities and is the most likely to lead a revolution against him.

LINE:

Wilson: You know, this reminds me of the times when I was at school and we used to have midnight feasts in the dorm.

Mainwaring: Really? The school I went to, we didn't have midnight feasts. We had to manage with a few aniseed balls in the corner of the playground.

Jones: The school I went to we didn't even have a playground.

WATCH OUT FOR:

- **Mainwaring getting trampled by the men on two occasions in as rush.**
- **The record player belts out the German national anthem instead of 'God Save the Queen' in the church hall.**
- **In the dream sequence, John Le Mesurier is wearing a prosthetic nose as the Duke of Wellington.**

BEHIND THE SCENES:

Extensive location shooting was completed at the Palace Cinema in Thetford, Norfolk whilst the footage of the dream sequence was filmed at the Stanford Training Ground that the cast and crew frequented during the series run.

Joy Allen remembers her time well on the programme as it was her first appearance on the small screen and she took advice from a member of the main cast. She remembered, 'Paying the Clippie was my first TV appearance and I found Clive Dunn very helpful. I was trying to use my theatre voice to project the lines and he told me quietly to turn my voice right down. Once I did that I was OK.'3

TRIVIA:

The film that the men are watching in the cinema is the 1937 film *'Conquest'* which was Metro-Goldwyn-Mayer's biggest commercial failure of the time, as the film grossed $2,141,000 but netted a loss of $1,397,000. The film starred Gretta Garbo and Charles Boyer but since using actual footage of the picture was too much for the budget, so actors had to be drafted in to recreate the scene.

SCORE: 9/10

EPISODE FORTY FOUR

GETTING THE BIRD

RECORDED ON 19TH MAY 1972

FIRST BROADCAST ON 27TH OCTOBER 1972

VIEWING FIGURE: 17.5 MILLION

PLOT:

As Walker finds a solution to Jones' lack of meat, Mainwaring demands an explanation from a drunken Wilson for not turning up for parade. He is also distracted by the pigeons in the office, leading Mainwaring to tell Walker to put them somewhere else. Sunday arrives and the men attend a church service where Frazer spots Wilson with a young woman. During the service, Walker begins to panic. His fears are confirmed when the organ starts to play and pigeons shoot out from the pipes...

GUEST CAST:

Bill Pertwee as ARP Warden Hodges
Edward Sinclair as the Verger
Frank Williams as the Vicar
Pamela Cundell as Mrs Fox
Alvar Liddell as Newsreader
Olive Mercer as Mrs Yeatman
Seretta Wilson as the Wren

REVIEW:

Getting the Bird is an episode where the serious theme of a long lost relative of Wilson's being discovered is eclipsed by a slapstick jaunt about pigeons. That really is this episode in a nutshell, but you would have to say that it is succeeds in blending the silly with the serious and that does not make it a weak offering by any account. It is all a lot of fun and the cast appear to be enjoying themselves on the screen whilst John Le Mesurier gets his teeth stuck into a script all about him, but also one that barely features him. The inclusion of the pigeons is funny but the plot and sub-plot are the wrong way around. Wilson's predicament should be the main focus of the episode and the pigeon problems should be the light hearted relief to the more serious part of the script. John Le Mesurier is allowed much time on the screen to elaborate on his character's deep personal problems. We hear of a domestic falling out between he and the absent Mrs Pike and that he is given compassionate leave but I would have loved to have found out a little more about his enigmatic absence before the big reveal at the end just to enhance the enigma. In conclusion, *Getting the Bird* manages to balance the tender subject matter of a member of the platoon facing up to his past and the ongoing responsibilities of fatherhood and keeping a secret from his comrades. Yet it also falls into farce and brings out the best of the humour the script can offer with Walker's stolen pigeon conundrum. Frazer also gets a gold star for his keeping of Wilson's secret - showing that he is not as hard and unkind as he sometimes has been. If it were not for the pathos of the performances of Le Mesurier and Laurie at the end then the episode would just be high farce.

MEMORABLE MOMENT:

At the church service, Jones gets up to work the organ for the next hymn and Walker goes white with panic. It becomes apparent that he has hidden the pigeons in the organ pipes and as the verger starts to pump the organ, feathers begin to foam over the top of the pipes and the birds begin to fire out at the unexpected parishioners. It is a brilliant sight gag to end the episode on and after the touching and slightly sad scene where Wilson and Frazer keep the formers secret under wraps, we go from serious to silly in an instant.

LINE:

Pike: Mr Mainwaring. There's a pigeon in your pigeon hole!

WATCH OUT FOR:

- **Mrs Fox reveals that her visiting brother was one of the soldiers stranded in Dunkirk.**
- **A pigeon, obviously manned by a puppeteer, appears behind Mainwaring's desk when Wilson has a hangover and is trying to explain his absence.**
- **Jones was taught how to play the organ when he had an affair with a girl who had flat knees due to over-praying.**

BEHIND THE SCENES:

The production crew decided to ignore one of the golden rules of television by working with animals. Filming demanded live pigeons to be used in the studio and the making of glove puppets and plastic birds were made for the scene in which Wilson spots on in the pigeon hole behind Mainwaring's desk and one to balance on the top of Edward Sinclair's head.

For the final scene when Walker has hidden the feathery birds in the church organ, fake props of pigeons were thrown out from behind the organ and no animals were harmed in the making of the episode. A brand new set was built for the church, which we see for the very first time.

Mrs Fox actress Pamela Cundell is amazed to this day about the enduring success of the programme and the new generation of fans. She said, 'People still address me as Mrs Fox. When I was out shopping recently, this man stopped me and asked whether I'd meet his son, a

Dad's Army fan. This 11-year-old shook my hand and when asked why he liked the show, he said: "Because it's funny and not rude." That's what makes it so appealing, and we now have a new generation of kids who adore it.'4

TRIVIA:

We discover that Godfrey has a taste for romantic novels as he admits that he has the latest Ethel M Dell book in his library at home. Ethel M Dell was born in 1881 and wrote several romantic novels in her time and while she received praise from those who read her books, she often faced scathing reviews from critics of her work. She regarded her skills of storytelling as her biggest attribute and her best known work was called *'The Way of an Eagle.'*

SCORE: 7/10

EPISODE FORTY FIVE

THE DESPERATE DRIVE OF CORPORAL JONES

RECORDED ON 16TH JUNE 1972
FIRST BROADCAST ON 3RD NOVEMBER 1973
VIEWING FIGURE: 15.8 MILLION

PLOT:

The men are taking part in a division weekend scheme and will be using live ammunitions. Area Command call the side office and Jones goes to write down the grid reference to their hideout but his pen breaks so while he goes to get another one Godfrey picks the receiver up and writes down the numbers but in the wrong order, confusing their destination. Jones realises however, that the men are in the wrong position and that they are actually in the target area for the 25 pounders and his comrades are in danger. It's up to Jones and Godfrey to save the day...

GUEST CAST:

Bill Pertwee as ARP Warden Hodges
Frank Williams as the Vicar
Edward Sinclair as the Verger
Robert Raglan as Colonel
Larry Martyn as Signals Private
James Taylor as Artillery Officer

REVIEW:

The Desperate Drive of Corporal Jones amusing and entertaining but despite its potentially explosive plot, there are many things that contribute to its downfall - and one of them lies with the usually reliable performances from members of the cast. Arthur Lowe's performance is erratic. He seems to have a problem with his dialogue at the very beginning of the first act, his words tumble out of the sides of his mouth instead of booming towards his troops in a commanding tone. I know that unfortunately the actor suffered from narcolepsy and alcohol problems but those ailments came later, how do those two elements contribute here? He just does not look all there in the studio scenes. On location, it is another matter. He is bang on form, complete with signature double takes and perfectly timed line delivery. The platoon is given a dangerous but frankly time consuming and pointless exercise to take part in. They are only told to watch out for the enemy and are laid to waste in the script. However, Arnold Ridley and Clive Dunn are superb. Surely, the episode should have been called, *The Desperate Drive of Jones and Godfrey* because the latter plays as much of a part as the Corporal does and does not share the same billing. Poor Private Godfrey is teased for bringing a picnic hamper to provide food the men then he misunderstands the vital coordinates for the platoon and is the main *Desperate Drive* may not be as much of a big hitter as *Asleep in the Deep* or *A Soldier's Farewell* but metaphorically speaking it is rather like a middle order batsmen. In a way it is a shame that it does not quite live up to the spectacle that the title suggests but it is still a fun outing for our men from Walmington-on-Sea.

MEMORABLE MOMENT:

The men are running through the drill for the weekend's exercise and it involves Walker and Frazer shooting a door lock, Jones kinking it open, Wilson bowling a grenade into the room they are trying to capture and Pike running in to finish off any assailants who are still alive. They are unaware that Hodges is arguing with the vicar and the verger in the side room and they begin to cower in fear as the platoon shoot at them, a smoke grenade goes off near to the vicar and Pike runs in firing his rifle. After the chaos, Godfrey rushes in with bandages to tend to the shocked trio who they did not know were in there.

LINE:

Jones: You ought to get glasses, Mr Godfrey.
Godfrey: I had a pair once, you know. I didn't get on with them. They made me look rather old.

WATCH OUT FOR:

- **We discover that Private Godfrey has never been taught how to drive.**
- **Godfrey attempts to bring a wicker basket with him to the event as he believes the men will have time for a picnic.**
- **Jones steals Mainwaring's catchphrase 'you stupid boy!' before he has a chance to utter it himself.**

BEHIND THE SCENES:

For location footage, the cast and crew returned to High Lodge in Brandon, Thetford, the very same location that was used for the scene when the men's make-up begins to run off their faces at the climax of *Keep Young and Beautiful.*

Further footage was obtained from Furze Heath at Stanford Training Ground for the shots that required Jones and Godfrey to race to the rescue of the men when it is discovered that they are in the battery target. Jones is the hero of the day at the end but actor Clive Dunn was not always the number one choice to play Walmington-on-Sea's lovable old butcher:
'Someone else who read for the part was David Jason, and did it superbly. I didn't use him because I couldn't face the problem of making him look old; he was about 26 at the time, and the thought of making him up every day would have been a nuisance. So the part was eventually offered to Clive Dunn and wonderful he was, too' David Croft revealed.

TRIVIA:

The butcher's van that the platoon uses as their military vehicle is a 1935 Ford Box van. It was discovered by the BBC's assistant property master, Frank Holland, who found it in a state of disrepair in Streatham, London. The van had many modifications and repairs made to it before it debut in the series three opener *The Armoured Might of Lance Corporal Jones* and after the series finished in 1977, it stayed in a private collector's hands who lived in Finchley before being sold on again to Patrick Motor Museum in Birmingham in 1990. It was sold in auction to the Dad's Army Museum in Thetford in 2012 for £63,100.

SCORE: 5/10

EPISODE FORTY SIX

IF THE CAP FITS...

RECORDED ON 30TH JUNE 1972
FIRST BROADCAST ON 10TH NOVEMBER 1972
VIEWING FIGURE: 15.5 MILLION

PLOT:

After a lecture, Frazer barges into Mainwaring's office and lists off a number of times that he has wasted the men's time on trivial matters. The Captain is so offended by this complaint that it influences Mainwaring to offer a member of the platoon the chance to take command for a couple of days to see if they can do any better. He does not believe that anybody will take up the invite, until Frazer comes forward and demands his pips straight away...

GUEST CAST:

Bill Pertwee as ARP Warden Hodges
Robert Raglan as Colonel Pritchard
Campbell Singer as Major-General Menzies
Alex McAvoy as The Sergeant

REVIEW:

If the Cap Fits... is not one of the best editions of the series so far but is by no means a disappointment. We see the inner struggles that the platoon has developed as their time together has gone on and Frazer inadvertently gets his wish for a rank in the Home Guard, something he was not so happy about losing back in series two. But Mainwaring is the real winner in this one, despite the script being spread thin and it is only just covered by some very witty lines that delight and cover the faults well. This episode is an echo back to the lost series two episode *A Stripe for Frazer* and that should have acted as a reminder to Mainwaring that Frazer really is the worst person to lead the platoon. Mainwaring and the others really are shocked when Frazer calls his Captain's bluff and comes forward as wanting to take over for a couple of days. Jones and Godfrey are arguably Mainwaring's closest confidants and that loyalty is displayed further, especially when Jones burst into the room about to flood the floor with tears at his treatment of the craggy Scot. For all its strong points though, the main premise is sorely stretched over a thirty minute episode. There needs to be a sub-plot here to keep the ball rolling until the end. This was one of the few episodes that did not require location footage and that studio-bound atmosphere lends it a more familiar feel with the audience connection, who are clearly delighted with the entertainment in front of them. However, there is a hole in this episode that needed filling and perhaps this is a case of there being a touch of mid-series fatigue.

MEMORABLE MOMENT:

As soon as Frazer is made up to Captain he goes about making wholesale changes to the platoon as though he has been given the job on a permanent basis. Firstly, he dons an officer's hat and strips Wilson of his pips and Jones resigns before protesting with tears in his eyes to his real Captain. Their places are taken by Walker and Pike who thrive in their new roles. But really, it is Mainwaring who is getting the last laugh, especially at the expense of Wilson who is dizzied by annoyance at Frazer.

LINE:

Wilson: I cannot bear it when people are rude to me. My heart starts to pound and I just have to sit down, that's all.
Mainwaring: You don't sit down when I'm rude to you.
Wilson: I know. But, you see, I don't take any notice of you, sir.

WATCH OUT FOR:

- **During the slide show, Mainwaring alludes to people with no ear lobes being a well-known criminal trait. At once the men look at Walker.**
- **Wilson has taken to wearing a monocle as he has a weakness in his right eye.**
- **Walker's new sense of responsibility when he is made up to Sergeant.**

BEHIND THE SCENES:

Actor Evan Ross, who appeared as a member of the back row for the majority of the fifth series, recalled how John Laurie's status was looked upon by those outside of the production crew. 'Occasionally I would drive John Laurie home after rehearsals. One day we were held up at a road block when a policeman came over and started questioning where I was going. Suddenly he spotted John sat in the back, he jumped to a salute and told me to carry on – I couldn't believe it!'6
Ross was not the only member of the cast to have experienced a spot of car-related drama with Laurie as Ian Lavender, who forged a strong friendship with the elder statesman of the ensemble, recalls, 'John could be acerbic with anyone, regardless as to whether he liked you or not – but that was his style. We got on from day one, probably because I was the youngest and he was one of the oldest in the platoon.

'Often I'd drive him home. I remember driving from Brighton, where we'd been filming. As we got to the outskirts of Brighton, he asked whether I'd like him to recite something. I jumped at the offer, and from there to London he gave a splendid solo performance of *Tom O'Shanter.*'7

TRIVIA:

Haggis is a traditional Scottish savoury pudding that has been documented as far back as 1430 in the verse cook book *Liber Cure Cocorum* as 'hagese' but is famous for its inclusion in the Robert Burn's 1787 poem, *Address to a Haggis.* It is made from the heart, lungs and liver of a sheep and is minced with onion, suet, oatmeal, spices and a stock mix and is then put to simmer for three hours in an animal's stomach, or for the squeamish, a sausage casing.

SCORE: 6/10

EPISODE FORTY SEVEN

THE KING WAS IN HIS COUNTING HOUSE

RECORDED ON 23RD JUNE 1972
FIRST BROADCAST ON 17TH NOVEMBER 1972
VIEWING FIGURE: 16 MILLION

PLOT:

After a year of being in charge of the platoon, Mainwaring decides to host a party at his house and to meet the men on equal terms and out of uniform with no hierarchy attached. He lays on a spread for the troops but admits that his wife is concerned at the prospect of a rowdy bunch of men drinking and vandalising their furniture. All of a sudden, an air raid siren wails and she scarpers to the shelter. Hodges informs Mainwaring that three bombs have dropped on the town and one has hit the bank...

GUEST CAST:

Frank Williams as the Vicar
Edward Sinclair as the Verger
Bill Pertwee as ARP Warden Hodges
Wendy Richard as Shirley

REVIEW:

For a character like Mainwaring to try his best at boosting his men's morale by hosting a party, you know the war effort has taken a turn for the worse. At the same time, I feel there is a slight mid-season slump as *The King was in his Counting House* is not as good as some of its neighbours but there are the odd moments that give you the same satisfaction that you always get from a *Dad's Army* episode. The party scenario is an inspired idea, with Mainwaring desperate to be seen as one of the boys for a change. The men seem understandably pensive and on edge at the gathering, displaying just how they feel about his all of a sudden out of the ordinary sense of jovial togetherness. The sad thing about this scene is the men are so used to Mainwaring being so dominant over them that it does not feel normal to them to call him 'George' but he obviously wants them to have fun but to me it shows that they do not consider him a friend. Metaphorically speaking, it's a bit like when you are invited to the birthday party of the smelly kid in class. But there is something that occurs that happens at all house parties when Pike accidentally drains the snow and water from Mainwaring's snow globe proving that no matter how dead the party can be, something always gets broken. In conclusion, *The King was in his Counting House* is quite drab in places and in others it can keep the viewer laughing at a bad night for all involved. A star turn from Wendy Richard helps keep the humour going and her shenanigans with Walker on Mainwaring's sofa brings a brilliant look out of Arthur Lowe that could speak a thousand words of surprise and shock.

MEMORABLE MOMENT:

After interrupting Mainwaring's party by declaring that there is light showing upstairs, Hodges is present when a bombing attack commences on Walmington. He is also the first to alert Mainwaring to the damage the raid has carried out on the bank. By this point, Mainwaring's fake, jovial temperament snaps away and he marches the men down to the banks to see the damage. When Hodges refuses to leave the premises as ARP Warden he is duty bound to stay as it is an unsafe area but Mainwaring pulls a gun on him to get the brash chap out of his workplace.

LINE:

Hodges: What's going on here?
Pike: We're having a party.
Hodges: Watch the blackout. Where's Mainwaring?
Wilson: He's upstairs with his wife in the bedroom.
Hodges: Oh, it's one of those sort of parties, is it?

WATCH OUT FOR:

- **The main characters are out of uniform for the entire episode for only the second time in the series.**

- **Mainwaring reveals that his father was called Edmund who lived and worked in Eastgate. Jones tells the party that he is lying as he actually had a pokey drapers shop in a side street not a flourishing tailors business on the parade.**
- **Although Frazer is present when the men carry the wicker basket onto the cart, he disappears when they go charging after him on their bicycles.**

BEHIND THE SCENES:

Despite the majority of the episode being filmed at BBC Television Centre, the production crew ventured out to their regular haunt in Thetford to capture location filming, which was always filmed before the studio days for each series. All Saint's Church in Honington, Suffolk doubled for St Aldhelm's Church in Walmington. Further footage was captured at Frog Hill at Stanford Training Ground, whilst the Primary School in Honington acted as the hall to the church. David Croft remembered his experiences of working with Arthur Lowe. 'Arthur Lowe was a good all-round actor, very experienced, and was able to call upon all these little mannerisms. He could be obstructive and awkward but if you knew how to handle him, he was fine. The important thing was not to drive him into a corner or get fundamental opinions from him. I never asked the actors what they thought of things, it was safer that way. Arthur's character could be pedantic and like Mainwaring at times, but then all the actors were like their characters, to a point.'8

TRIVIA:

Wendy Richard, who sent on to appear in Jeremy Lloyd and David Croft's sitcom *Are You Being Served?* as Miss Brahms, makes her third appearance in the series, this time as a girl called Shirley. Richard is best remembered for her role as Pauline Fowler in the BBC soap opera '*Eastenders*' and appeared in the very first episode in 1985 and stayed in the role for twenty two years before departing in 2007. She passed away on 26th February 2009 after succumbing to breast cancer.

SCORE: 5/10

EPISODE FORTY EIGHT

ALL IS SAFELY GATHERED IN

RECORDED ON 3RD NOVEMBER 1972
FIRST BROADCAST ON 24TH NOVEMBER 1972
VIEWING FIGURE: 16.5 MILLION

PLOT:

Godfrey asks Mainwaring if he can have three days holiday from duty as a woman who he fell in love with before the Boer War. She cannot deal with the harvest alone since her husband passed away. To add to her woes, her foreman is laid up with as hernia and there are only three land girls available to work on the 100 acre of harvest. Mainwaring shows empathy towards Godfrey's story, told through Jones who is speaking up for his friend and decides that the platoon should help...

GUEST CAST:

Bill Pertwee as ARP Warden Hodges
Brenda Cowling as Mrs Prentice
Frank Williams as the Vicar
Edward Sinclair as the Verger
Colin Bean as Private Sponge
April Walker as Judy, a Land Girl
Tina Cornioli as Olive, a Land Girl

REVIEW:

Sometimes a show does not need to be loud and over the top to gain attention and stick out as perhaps the quietest, most gentle episode of *Dad's Army* ever filmed makes waves without so much as raising a voice. *All is Safely Gathered In* has a majestic, bright and fuzzy feel to it, probably helped by its authentic and well researched representation of a wartime harvest but also as it is due to the good nature of Mainwaring and the kind Private Godfrey that an elderly lady can meet the demands of the season. It is hardly surprising that Clive Dunn chews every scene he is in. He consistently mixes words up and is hilarious at doing so and this keeps him much more in the character of his age than some of his physical pratfalls that have occurred of late in the show. Yes, nowadays the sight of a man losing his trousers in a piece of farmyard machinery can seem a little old hat and insult the intelligence of the viewer but Dunn pulls it off with aplomb and even survives being chewed up by the combine harvester in the process. The harvesting scene is one that instantly pops into your head when you think of *Dad's Army* and shows off the beautiful countryside in Norfolk in all its summertime splendour. And the great thing about having a slower paced offering is that it still remains entertaining enough to not feel like a late episode of *Last of the Summer Wine.* In a way, much like the men must have felt, you welcome the temporary departure from the bombs and cramped studios. *All is Safely Gathered In* is a rather touching portrayal of how people can band together for the common good when help is needed in way many would argue a vast majority would not put themselves out today.

MEMORABLE MOMENT:

The stand out moment actually comes before the men start the harvest and they are still trying to figure out a way to make the farm machinery works. Jones steps forward to demonstrate of how the combine harvester works and hilarity ensues. It isn't so much the dialogue but the performance that Dunn brings to the camera and his add-lib murmurings and sound effects are just another showcase for a master at work.

LINE:

Jones: Mr Godfrey is a very retiring gentleman and he won't speak up for himself. So I would like to speak for him, me being privy to his intimate details, to things what he told me in his continence.

WATCH OUT FOR:

- **Pike's childlike enthusiasm to use the Tommy gun and his encyclopaedic knowledge of the fire arm.**
- **The men whistle the Laurel and Hardy theme when Hodges arrives at the barn.**
- **Walker and the land lady becoming frequently discovered in more bizarre ways on the farm.**

BEHIND THE SCENES:

Brenda Cowling's appearance as Ms Prentice was not her first experience with the show. 'I'd auditioned for Mrs Pike originally, but Janet Davies got the part; she was very good and absolutely right for the role. I was delighted to play Ms Prentice, a farmer's widow in this episode. We did the location shooting in October because it's harvest festival time. We filmed the service in a field on a chilly day, and I remember the wardrobe staff offering Arnold Ridley, John Le Mesurier and John Laurie blankets to keep them warm between scenes. John Laurie, a hardy Scot, refused adamantly and sat looking very blue!'9

The cast and crew enjoyed filming the location footage of the men working hard on the harvest and the scenes were captured in Walnut Tree Farm at Wilney Green, Fersfield in Norfolk, which doubled as Miss Prentice's farm. Extensive cine film footage of the cast working on the farm was also captured and has appeared in many documentaries regarding the series.

TRIVIA:

The scenes that show the platoon busy with the harvest is accompanied by a song called *Calling All Workers.* It was written by Viola player Eric Coates and was used as the theme tune of the BBC Radio light entertainment programme *Music While You Work,* which was broadcast twice daily from Monday to Friday from 1940 to 1969.

SCORE: 8/10

EPISODE FORTY NINE

WHEN DID YOU LAST SEE YOUR MONEY?

RECORDED ON 10TH NOVEMBER 1972
FIRST BROADCAST ON 1ST DECEMBER 1972
VIEWING FIGURE: 16 MILLION

PLOT:

Despite the bank's recent destruction at the hands of a Nazi bomb, the branch is open for business as usual but the workers are struggling with the conditions they have to put up with. Jones makes an appearance as he cashes in £500 in takings from his butcher's shop. Having wrapped it up like he would an order of sausages he realises that the payment is just that when he hands the bundle over to Pike at the kiosk. With £500 missing, Jones faints in horror!

GUEST CAST:

Bill Pertwee as ARP Warden Hodges
Edward Sinclair as the Verger
Frank Williams as the Vicar
Harold Bennett as Mr Blewitt
Tony Hughes as Mr Billings

REVIEW:

Following on from a plot device that was used a couple of show's back, Swallow's Bank is crumbling but in the grand old tradition of the British keeping calm and carrying on, that does not stop Mainwaring and his workers from their normal routine. How funny it is then that his office is a shambles, leaking water with a hole in the door to make up for the normal way of entering a room and Arthur Lowe, John Le Mesurier and Ian Lavender use the set as a playground where they pull the laughs out of the audience, who are more engrossed in the story than ever before with their spontaneous outbreaks of applause. For an edition that is mostly driven by the dialogue and integration between the main characters, there is a lot of time to explore the show's knack of physical humour. After the frolics in the first act in the bank, the platoon then mess around with a prop chicken, all in the best possible taste of course. The way the troops rally around Jones shows just how dedicated they really are to each other and how, no matter what they say on the surface, they actually care deeply for one another inside. However, here comes a grumble. The editing is rather poor in some places and a couple of scenes, especially at the start of the one with Frazer hypnotizing Jones, James Beck and John Laurie trip over each other dialogue wise and this could have been done again in a retake surely? Beck is also the subject of some quick and unnecessary cutting when the men are discussing Jones' predicament that seems a bit pointless. But really, that's the only grumble I have about this one. It's a fantastic episode, fully exploiting the acting talents of Clive Dunn, who on more than one occasion has been so good you occasionally forget that he is actually a man in his middle ages and not the old codger that Jones is.

MEMORABLE MOMENT:

The scene in which Frazer attempts to hypnotise Jones into remembering where he left the money is superb and showcases the slightly scary but always funny delivery that John Laurie could ramble out in an instant. It is an ambitious trick to use and the lighting and the mood of the scene is great and Walker's sceptical approach to the technique melts away as he realises that it is working and then as Jones retraces his footsteps, he remembers where the money is. He has stuffed the chicken he gave to Mr Blewitt with £500!

LINE:

Mainwaring: In the name of the King I demand to examine your chicken!

WATCH OUT FOR:

- **Swallows Bank is still terribly damaged by the bomb that hit it in *'The Kind was in his Counting House.'***
- **An enthusiastic audience who clap at every given opportunity - they love it!**
- **The set for Mr Blewitt's house has changed from the one the men tried to break into in the series three episode *'No Spring for Frazer.'***

BEHIND THE SCENES:

This episode was broadcast on Saturday 10th November 2012 just a few days after Clive Dunn on the 6th November had passed away aged 92. It was the latest episode to be shown in BBC Two's repeat season of the series and a picture of Dunn in character as Corporal Jones flashed up on the screen at the end in dedication to his memory.

Tony Hughes made a guest appearance and commented on his memory of the role. 'I played Mr Billings in 'When Did You Last See Your Money' and remember coming back from lunch during rehearsals to find some of the cast members asleep in their chairs. Someone turned to me and said: "My god, it's like a club for the senior citizens, they're all fast asleep!"'10

TRIVIA:

Private Pike mentions a film called *Man in the Shadows* that starred Hollywood actress Joan Blondell. She was born Rose Joan Blondell in 1906 and went on to star in over 100 film and television productions and received an Academy Award nomination Best Supporting Actress for her role as Annie Rawlins in the 1951 film *The Blue Veil.* She also made appearance in the 1978 smash hit *Grease* despite suffering from leukaemia, which eventually took her life on Christmas Day 1979.

SCORE: 9/10

EPISODE FIFTY

BRAIN VERSUS BRAWN

RECORDED ON 17TH NOVEMBER 1972
FIRST BROADCAST ON 8TH DECEMBER 1972
VIEWING FIGURE: 18.6 MILLION

PLOT:

Mainwaring attends the rotary club dinner and has asked Wilson to come along as his guest. There they meet the Colonel, who tells them about a scheme that is taking place that the Home Guard has not been invited to take part as they are seen as being over the hill. Mainwaring is annoyed by this remark and is adamant that his men are up to the task. The Colonel reluctantly invites them and they plan to show that veterans are just as capable as the youngsters...

GUEST CAST:

Bill Pertwee as ARP Warden Hodges
Robert Raglan as Colonel
Edward Sinclair as the Verger
Anthony Roye as Mr Fairbrother
Maggie Don as Waitress
Geoffrey Hughes as Bridge Corporal
David Rose as Dump Corporal

REVIEW:

*Brain versus Brawn...*or as I like to call it, *Dad's Army* does *Trumpton.* Who can watch this episode without being transported to the puppet inhabited world of Trumptonshire and hear the soft, cheerful tones of Brian Cant narrating in your head to the picture of Mainwaring et al lining up like Pugh, Pugh, Barney McGrew, Cuthbert, Dibble and Grub? I could the soft, melodic playful tune of the firemen's theme tune in my head on an old acoustic guitar as the platoon drive off to the exercise in this fun and entertaining instalment. It is ever so subtle, but the frequency of Wilson getting one over Mainwaring more often and perhaps, has started to put Mainwaring back in his place a little bit. He is invited to the rotary club dinner as Mainwaring's guest but is in fact more at home than his Captain. Indeed, there is even an old school friend there who then ignores Mainwaring as soon as he spots Wilson. Later on, it is Wilson's quick thinking that even goes on to win the exercise for the men! So in conclusion, *Brain versus Brawn* shows us the lengths the men will go to in a bid to be taken seriously but no matter how good or serious their intentions are, they always end up looking amateurish. It is nice to occasionally see how their plans sometimes work and see them victorious and the creative but slightly unbelievable ways they go about it. Although this one is not as popular as other episodes in the series, it still remains a timeless instalment and one to indulge in again and again... as long as you can get the *Trumpton* theme out of your head when you are watching it!

MEMORABLE MOMENT:

What other moment could I go for apart from the *Trumpton* homage? Okay so I know that I am banging on about it a bit but who can resist the comparison? The costumes, the fire engine, come on! It's right there on the screen. Maybe Jimmy Perry and David Croft were fans or had children who loved the show. It also highlights the ingenuity within the platoon, it is a pretty fool proof plan and allows us to have a laugh at the men's expense but in the end it is a good thing they had that fire engine when the house fire occurs!

LINE:

Walker: I wouldn't start up that engine with all those doors closed, sir.
Jones: No, sir. Because we might breathe in all the poisonous gases and we'll all get sophisticated.

WATCH OUT FOR:

- **Mainwaring announces that Wilson has been working as Chief Clerk at the bank for eight years.**
- **Private Godfrey wouldn't mind dressing up as a nun as a disguise.**
- **Mainwaring wears a silver helmet compared to his men's gold hats.**

BEHIND THE SCENES:

Jimmy Perry was thankful that he had an actor like Bill Pertwee involved in the show. 'Amongst such a bunch of tough old pros occasional friction would arise. Fortunately Bill was always able to lighten the atmosphere with a joke or impersonation. The whole cast responded to Bill in an amazing way, and I'll always be grateful top him. He was also very funny as the ARP Warden.'11
Exterior scenes involving the men in the fire engine and their journey to the exercise area were filmed at High Lodge in Brandon and Santon Downham was used near Brandon was also used as the unnamed village and

for the scene with Geoffrey Hughes on the bridge. The crew also filmed at Walnut Tree Farm for the second time in the series where they filmed the final scene when the men attempt to put a house fire out.

TRIVIA:

British actor Geoffrey Hughes makes an early career appearance as the Bridge Corporal who talks to Mainwaring as the men try to infiltrate the area in the fire engine. Hughes is perhaps best remembered for his role as bin man Eddie Yeats in the long-running soap opera *Coronation Street* from 1974 until 1983 and as Onslow in the comedy *Keeping Up Appearances* and Archie in *The Royal Family*. He also spent four years as conman Vernon Scripps in the nostalgia soap *Heartbeat*. He passed away on the 27th July 2012 after losing the fight against cancer aged 68.

SCORE: 7/10

EPISODE FIFTY ONE

A BRUSH WITH THE LAW

RECORDED ON 26TH NOVEMBER 1972
FIRST BROADCAST ON 15TH DECEMBER 1972
VIEWING FIGURE: 15.4 MILLION

PLOT:

Hodges has been frustrated for a long time over the behaviour of his rival Mainwaring but believes he has got his enemy after one of his fellow wardens, Reg, reports that he saw a light burning in the church hall side office. Hodges can barely believe his luck, this is his moment for revenge on the pompous bank manager. Meanwhile, Mainwaring and Wilson are busy inspecting the platoon's rifles. They are disturbed by Hodges, accompanied by a policeman who serves Mainwaring with a summons...

GUEST CAST:

Bill Pertwee as ARP Warden Hodges
Geoffrey Lumsden as Captain Square
Frank Williams as the Vicar
Edward Sinclair as the Verger
Stuart Sherwin as Reg Adamson (Junior Warden)
Jeffrey Gardiner as Mr Wintergreen
Marjorie Wilde as Lady Magistrate
Chris Gannon as Mr Bone, the Clerk of the Court
Toby Perkins as Usher

REVIEW:

Unfortunately, this episode is far from entertaining or amusing. But that does not mean that there are some good points about *A Brush with the Law* but you just have to delve a little deeper than usual. There are fewer laughs than previous installments and despite the heavy subject matter and the threat of Mainwaring's future with incarceration, I never felt as though Mainwaring was ever in danger of being sent down. Despite problems with the severity of the script, Arthur Lowe is outstanding and Bill Pertwee is also brilliant as Hodges, who acts like the cat who has got the cream throughout the episode. Why the Verger would be so keen to get Mainwaring off the hook if it meant that he would be in trouble instead especially when he has been belittled and mistreated at the hands of many members of the Home Guard over his time in the show? Maybe it is the divine light of the lord that gives him a guilty conscience but surely Mr Yeatman, who we know to be far from holy through small references in the series, would possibly put himself first over others like he has done in the past (stealing from the church offering plate when he takes it home to count as Jones alludes to in series three.)

The writer's decision to write Captain Square in as the magistrate is pure plot expediency and tries to squeeze a giggle or two from the viewer as Mainwaring is faced with yet another rival in his life. I'm not sure if in a real court this would be allowed to happen as surely Mainwaring would be allowed to speak against Square's appointment and declare that he would like another Judge if they have shared a tainted history, but of course, Square does not entirely play by the rules and is found out by Walker in the end to be manipulating proceedings himself. The killer one liners, brilliant set pieces and memorable moments for which this edition lacked and is one of the weakest episodes of series five.

MEMORABLE MOMENT:

The court scene is by far the biggest moment in the episode and the most memorable as Mainwaring, wearing his upper lip stiff, is pompous enough to dismiss his lawyer and defend himself. Little does he know that he will have to put up with Captain Square in the Magistrate's chair and speak over the butting in and putting down of both he and Hodges. When he calls upon his men to speak in his defence, the court session has already descended into a shambles and Walker saves the day for his Captain.

LINE:

Jones: All gentlemen are not unbiased. Lord Kitchener was a gentleman and he wasn't unbiased. Especially with the Fuzzy Wuzzies. "Shoot them," he said and you can't get more biased than that.

WATCH OUT FOR:

- **Pike reveals the secret behind his spotless rifle barrel...he uses Harpic!**
- **In the ARP Warden's HQ they discuss that night's goings on, but when they go to identify Mainwaring with haste in the church hall it is daylight outside.**
- **Frazer seems determined to send Mainwaring behind bars.**

BEHIND THE SCENES:

The Verger emerges as the culprit for all of Mainwaring's woes and David Croft fondly remembered the time he spent with actor Edward Sinclair, even if it was often a hair raising experience!

'To drive with Edward Sinclair was an experience more terrifying than Magic Mountain in Disneyland! He was always a courteous and polite person and to him, having a conversation with someone without actually looking them in the face was not to be countenanced. Having sat next to him in his car I found this habit worrying enough. Thinking to counter this idiosyncrasy by sitting behind him, imagine my horror when he continually turned round in his seat to talk to me head on. The gentle protests by Frank Williams with the words: 'Teddy, Teddy, look where you're going!' were to no avail. I never travelled with him again.'12

TRIVIA:

Mainwaring finds himself in the dock under the Emergency Powers Act (1940) which was brought onto statute law after being rushed through Parliament due to the public's demand that it was implemented. The Captain is accused of showing a light by ARP Warden Hodges and if the character had been found guilty as charged he would have been sentenced to several months in prison under the act.

SCORE: 6/10

EPISODE FIFTY TWO

ROUND AND ROUND WENT THE BIG WHEEL

RECORDED ON 1ST DECEMBER 1972
FIRST BROADCAST ON 22ND DECEMBER 1972
VIEWING FIGURE: 13.7 MILLION

PLOT:

The War Office discuss plans for a new weapon to help turn the tide in Britain's favour. It is a giant wheel that contains 2000lbs of high explosives that could knock out an enemy pillbox at a range of three miles. The device will be put to the test in Operation Catherine Wheel where it will be demonstrated near the town so the Home Guard are asked by Captain Stewart in a roundabout way to guard the area. However, thanks to Walker and Pike, it spins out of control and makes its way to Walmington-on-Sea.

GUEST CAST:

Bill Pertwee as ARP Warden Hodges
Edward Underdown as Major General Sir Charles Holland
Michael Knowles as Captain Stewart
Geoffrey Chater as Colonel Pierce
Jeffrey Segal as Minister
John Clegg as Wireless Operator

REVIEW:

Series five picks itself up again with *Round and Round went the Great Big Wheel* - a high octane thrill ride of an episode that would have given many films of the day a run for its money...if it were set in a Norfolk location in the 1940s. Here we see Mainwaring's men initially undermined by those in power but emerge triumphant saviours after a weapon exercise goes seriously wrong. The big assignment the men are send on is a massive let down to the platoon, but it is really funny to watch the men build it up as this very important and dangerous job they have been asked to do only for it to turn out to be nothing more than digging holes in the ground for latrines and peeling spuds. The smug look on Bill Pertwee's face when he realises the true job Captain Stewart eluded from telling them they were doing is priceless. Its Home Guard nil, ARP Chief Warden Hodges one. The main plot device involves a very impressive (but slow moving) Catherine Wheel chasing Jones' van off the airfield and towards Walmington-on-Sea. Of course, it is all the fault of Walker and Pike who put the lives of the men at risk and all because they wanted to tune into *High Gang*. The fools, if only they'd have waited ten years then they could catch *The Goon Show* now that's a programme still worth bunking off duty to listen to! *Round and Round went the Great Big Wheel'* is a knockabout romp, a great script from Perry and Croft that is enhanced by the stellar cast and another opportunity to get Jones' van out on location and leave the men facing mortal danger in the funniest way...if indeed that were ever possible.

MEMORABLE MOMENT:

It might be down to the fact that there is a change of scenery for the line-up sequence in this one that makes it all the more memorable but the moment Mainwaring tells his platoon about their 'secret duties' away from prying ears in the church crypt exercises the great Arthur Lowe's assets as a comedic performer. He is squished against the wall by the men and re-emerges with his glasses and hat on the wonk and then goes about unsettling his men about what they could expect, leading Frazer to slap an hysterical Jones who is then reduced to tears.

LINE:

(Mainwaring is feeling betrayed by Captain Stewart.)
Mainwaring: Oh, you'll stick up for him won't you? You both went to public school, didn't you?
Wilson: You know I can't help feeling, sir that you've got a bit of a chip on your shoulder about that.
Mainwaring: There's no chip on my shoulder, Wilson. I'll tell you what there is on my shoulder though. Three pips and don't you forget it!

WATCH OUT FOR:

- **The crypt wall wobbles as Mainwaring squeezes past his men when they are standing to attention.**
- **Private Pike's portable wireless was homemade by the teenager himself, if I were him I'd patent that, it's just the idea that might take off!**
- **There are inconsistencies with the studio and location footage as the van is chased by the wheel. On location, it is clear that the van is still**

on the airfield however when the footage cuts to the studio the CSO shows the van passing trees.

BEHIND THE SCENES:

David Croft remembered how the hardships of the location footage called for patience from the production team for the episode. 'The most difficult day's filming ever was for this episode. The plot focused on the War Office's new weapon: an explosive carrying wheel controlled by radio. Operation Catherine Wheel took place to test a new invention, with Mainwaring's men responsible for fatigues.

'We decided that the best way to get the wheel moving was to build a big hub in it and have someone inside peddling. But it didn't work because the whole mechanism collapsed. From then on we kept pushing and filming it as it gradually slowed down. We could only film about 20 feet of movement at any one time - it took ages!'13

The exterior footage with the Catherine Wheel was captured over three main areas in Thetford. Wash Lane Railway Bridge was used for the moment Jones breaks the wheel whilst Watton Airfield was used by the production team as the disused airfield where the wheel begins its journey. Both locations are at Wacton, which is owned by the Ministry of Defence.

TRIVIA:

The radio programme that Walker and Pike listen to in the episode is *Hi Gang!'*, which ran from 1940 until

1949 and was broadcast by the BBC. The programme involved a line-up that included Vic Oliver, who was Prime Minister Winston Churchill's son-in-law. Oliver's marriage into the Churchill household and was shunned by his father-in-law. He was also blacklisted on what the German army called *The Black Book* by the Nazi forces for being Jewish.

SCORE: 7/10

EPISODE FIFTY THREE

TIME ON MY HANDS

RECORDED ON 8TH DECEMBER 1972
FIRST BROADCAST ON 29TH DECEMBER 1972
VIEWING FIGURE: 16.6 MILLION

PLOT:

Before work, Mainwaring and Wilson attend the Marigold Tea Rooms and bicker over the tea and biscuits when their peace is disturbed by Pike who tells them that he has taken a call from the Police, alerting the Home Guard to a German parachutist who is dangling from the town hall clock. The trio are quickly joined by Jones, Frazer and Walker and they head off to the town hall in an attempt to capture to Nazi and also save his life!

GUEST CAST:

Bill Pertwee as ARP Warden Hodges

Frank Williams as the Vicar
Edward Sinclair as the Verger
Harold Bennett as Mr Blewitt
Colin Bean as Private Sponge
Joan Cooper as Miss Fortescue
Eric Longworth as Mr Gordon (Town Clerk)
Christopher Sandford as German Pilot

REVIEW:

With a constant stream of top notch scripts that would have made any other writers green with envy, Jimmy Perry and David Croft do it again and deliver yet another memorable, hilarious and frankly brilliant edition of the show. This is a stand out performance from Clive Dunn as he displays some fine comedic timing and one-liners. He has a glorious outing here as Corporal Jones. His retorts to the German parachutist crying for help are great and the moment he is pulled out onto the ledge by the figures and then gets the cold steel up him had me wetting myself as a child. Even the moment when he stands up to speak and launches straight into the town bell is funny. For some reason, *Dad's Army* is as its most enjoyable when the main characters are troubled by a predicament they cannot escape from or where there is high peril. Once again, when six of our favourites are stuck high up above Walmington, it gives us some lovely individual moments. Wilson irks Mainwaring yet again by retelling fairy stories, Pike gets a couple of great scenes especially the moments when he takes his comrades hats off to stop the bell chiming and breaks them against the bell.

The only one who is left out in the cold is poor old Godfrey. Oh, well, maybe next time, eh Godfrey? With a tight and resourceful script, Jimmy Perry and David Croft delivered a classic in my eyes. *Time on my Hands* hits every vein of comedy delights in an action packed thirty minutes that has me laughing over and over again.

MEMORABLE MOMENT:

After finally hauling the German inside from the clock, the attention then turns to the men's next problem, being stuck up in the tower. Mainwaring makes the mistake of asking his men for any ideas of how to get down. By the end he clearly wishes that he hadn't as he takes his glasses off and rubs his eyes wearily. The constant company of his men has not endeared them to him and he looks like he is getting fed up of them. Their suggestions are very funny but clearly mad and Frazer retells a story about how madness can set in to great effect to round off a great scene.

LINE:

German airman: Bitte, mein Herr! Oh, bitte, bitte!
Jones: It's no good trying to apologise.
German: Schnell! Schnell!
Jones: Never mind about the smell. That's got nothing to do with it.

WATCH OUT FOR:

- **Arthur Lowe's real life wife, Joan Cooper makes an appearance as a worker in Marigold Tea Rooms.**

- **Clive Dunn frequently knocks the paint off the town hall clock figures, most notably on the horse!**
- **A spot of rather unconvincing CSO is used as the men look down on the street below.**

BEHIND THE SCENES:

The exterior shots of Hodges, the vicar and the verger surrounded by towns folk as the action happens in the hall were filmed at Nether Row in Thetford, Norfolk and doubled as Percy Street, the same street that had been used several times before to represent Walmington-on-Sea. The Guildhall in the town also doubled for that of the town hall in the episode. David Croft revealed the challenges the production team were met with during the making of the episode mostly involving the figures that were to be included in the town hall clock scenes. *Time on My Hands* contains quite an elaborate clock with figures moving around every time it strikes. How to make the figures presented us with a problem. We considered plaster, cement and wood before I came up with the idea of employing some midgets. It worked well.'14

TRIVIA:

When Captain Mainwaring mentions the banks name he calls it 'Martin's Bank.' This is the first time that we hear that the bank's name has changed since the feature film a year previously. Before then the bank was known as 'Swallow Bank.' This is also only the second time in the show's history that the platoon appears out of uniform and in their everyday work uniforms.

SCORE: 9/10

As the show's fifth series concluded, there was no lingering doubt that *Dad's Army* was now truly one of the nation's favourite comedy series. It pulled in massive viewing figures for the day and by today's standards it even puts the big hitters of the 21st century to shame. Audience Ratings show that the fifth series pulled in an average of 16.3 million viewers, the highest the show had ever had. It looked as though nothing could stop Jimmy Perry and David Croft's masterpiece and the future could not have looked rosier for everybody involved. The show was riding on a crest of a wave that had gained momentum from its third series and the switch from black and white to colour. But the wave was about to crash as the death of a well-loved cast member, an integral part of the programme, was to mark the beginning of the end of the show and put its future in jeopardy...

SERIES SIX

MAIN CAST:

ARTHUR LOWE - CAPTAIN GEORGE MAINWARING
JOHN LE MESURIER - SERGEANT ARTHUR WILSON
CLIVE DUNN - LANCE CORPORAL JACK JONES
JOHN LAURIE - PRIVATE JAMES FRAZER
ARNOLD RIDLEY - PRIVATE CHARLES GODFREY
JAMES BECK - PRIVATE JOE WALKER *(UNTIL EPISODE FIFTY NINE -THINGS THAT GO BUMP IN THE NIGHT)*
IAN LAVENDER - PRIVATE FRANK PIKE

FEATURING THE VOICE OF BUD FLANNIGAN

EPISODE FIFTY FOUR

THE DEADLY ATTACHMENT

RECORDED ON 22ND JUNE 1973
FIRST BROADCAST ON 31ST OCTOBER 1973
VIEWING FIGURE: 12.9 MILLION

PLOT:

Captain Mainwaring's lecture on German parachutists is interrupted by a telephone call from GHQ. He is informed that a German U-Boat has sunk off the coast and that the Walmington-on-Sea Home Guard will hold them up in the church hall until military escort can be provided. The escort is delayed meaning that the platoon have to watch the prisoners, especially the smug U-Boat Captain, overnight. However, when Hodges is taken prisoner by the Germans, the tables turn and to make matters worse, Jones has a grenade forced down his trousers...

GUEST CAST:

Philip Madoc as U-Boat Captain
Bill Pertwee as ARP Warden Hodges
Edward Sinclair as the Verger
Robert Raglan as the Colonel
Colin Bean as Private Sponge

REVIEW:

This episode finally brings Mainwaring and his men face to face with the enemy and sets series six off like a firework. It glows with brilliance and is rightly remembered as one of the very best editions of *Dad's Army* ever produced. This is not only for one of the greatest examples of comedic writing in British television history but because everybody involved are at the peak of their powers on the show. In short, *The Deadly Attachment* is more than just a famous one-liner. Philip Madoc is by far the greatest guest star ever to appear in the programme. His delivery is malicious and sly and hits every note spot on. When the tables turn the nature of a real villain comes out but our boys come out victorious yet again in the end. The writing is superb, tighter, pitched perfectly and performed to the best of everyone's abilities. Never have Perry and Croft been so in tune with one another in a single half hour and the atmosphere switches from safe and funny to feeling quite tense when the Germans take over but we always know that the platoon will win in time. The blame can't really be laid at the feet of the men as Hodges and the Verger breaks the platoon's concentration and fall for the German U-Boat Captain's charade. Is this the best episode of *Dad's Army* of all time? Of course, *The Deadly Attachment* will forever be remembered as the one with the 'don't tell him, Pike!' line nestled in its golden lined cloud of comedy but whether it is the greatest of all time comes down to personal preference. Arguably, in the mind's eye of the viewing public, the programme would never hit the heights like it does here again.

MEMORABLE MOMENT:

Blimey, what just one? Well, since the famous exchange between Mainwaring and the German U-Boat Captain is dealt with elsewhere in this chapter (spoiler alert!) I thought I would go for the moment towards the end of the episode when the tables have turned on the men of the Home Guard and the German prisoners have gained the upper hand. Jones is chosen to have a booby trapped grenade down his trousers. Frazer comments ‘A terrible way to die’ bringing the house down once again.

LINE:

(We all know which one it is!)
U-boat Captain: I am making notes, Captain, and your name will go on the list; and when we win the war you will be brought to account.
Mainwaring: You can write what you like; you’re not going to win the war!
U-boat Captain: Oh yes we are.
Mainwaring: Oh no you're not.
U-boat Captain: Oh yes we are!
Pike: [Singing] Whistle while you work, Hitler is a twerp, he's half-barmy, so's his army, whistle while you work!
U-boat Captain: Your name will also go on the list! What is it?
Mainwaring: Don't tell him Pike!

WATCH OUT FOR:

- **Mainwaring’s stiff upper lip when the U-Boat Captain blows smoke into his face.**
- **Jones bringing the church hall roof down when he fires the Lewis gun by accident.**
- **Walker taking the Germans’ fish and chip orders.**

BEHIND THE SCENES:

The Deadly Attachment can lay claim to being the most adapted script in the history of *Dad's Army.* It was modified for the BBC Radio series and in doing so replaced Hodges for the Vicar. It was also the subject of an unsuccessful attempt to remake the series in America in 1976. As pilot for *The Rear Guard,* Jimmy Perry and David Croft kept most of the basic elements of the script but the show was not picked up...and was so bad it will not be mentioned again in this book! The episode was also chosen for the *Dad's Army Stage Show* in 2007 as the fourth in the run of recreations. Location footage was carried out at Mill Lane in Thetford, Norfolk when the men are marching down Mill Road. The plot twist consisting of the Germans taking over and putting a grenade down Jones' trousers was originally meant to be Mainwaring's trousers but as Arthur Lowe had a contract clause that stated he never wanted to remove his trousers on set, Clive Dunn came to the rescue and volunteered to take his place.

With its status as one of the most loved episodes ever, Ian Lavender also confessed his love for the show. 'I have two favourite episodes and 'The Deadly Attachment' is one. The line where Mainwaring says: 'Don't tell him, Pike!' has been a constant source of amusement. Even now, people shout it at me across the street, and I didn't even say it! Just one line in one episode and people remember it. We all loved the filming, particularly the idea of ordering fish and chips. During one scene I began to laugh; I begged David Croft to edit the bit out but he didn't.'1

TRIVIA:

The German U-Boat Captain was played by Welsh actor Philip Madoc, who in a fifty year career enjoyed a success as a small screen presence. He made several appearances as a number of villains in *Doctor Who* in the sixties and seventies and played Magua in the BBC adaptation of *The Last of the Mohicans* and DCI Noel Bain in the detective series *A Mind to Kill.* He passed away on 5th March 2012 aged 77 after a battle with cancer.

SCORE: 10/10

EPISODE FIFTY FIVE

MY BRITISH BUDDY

RECORDED ON 8TH JUNE 1973
FIRST BROADCAST ON 7TH NOVEMBER 1973
VIEWING FIGURE: 12.5 MILLION

PLOT:

The Home Guard is informed by an excited Mainwaring that the US Army have joined the war effort. They are asked to welcome a detachment of American soldiers later in the week and Jones has the idea of greeting the troops in the pub over a game of darts. To start with the two factions get on well but the platoon's girlfriends begin to flirt with the Americans much to their annoyance. It all kicks off when Hodges arrives and Mainwaring gets a black eye when he is punched by the American, Colonel Shultz...

GUEST CAST:

Bill Pertwee as ARP Warden Hodges
Alan Tilvern as Colonel Schultz
Edward Sinclair as the Verger
Frank Williams as the Vicar
Janet Davies as Mrs Pike
Wendy Richard as Shirley
Pamela Cundell as Mrs Fox
Verne Morgan as Landlord
Talfryn Thomas as Mr Cheeseman
Suzanne Kerchiss as Ivy Samways
Robert Raglan as the Colonel
Blain Fairman as US Sergeant

REVIEW:

After the brilliant *The Deadly Attachment* comes another great episode that explores the sense of empowerment being taken away from Home Guard and shows the men putting up more of a fight than ever before to stay the kings of their domain...literally. Obviously the men have mixed feelings about the Americans joining the war effort, but Mainwaring is keen on the idea of our cousins across the pond to help the British out. There is a feeling of slight discrimination against the 'yanks' especially from Walker and it mirrors perfectly what many British men felt at the time. Where else did the saying, 'oversexed, overpaid and over here!' come from but to describe the men of the UK and their feelings about the US armed forces. After all, they did bring with them all the luxuries that we had lost in the previous two and a half years like chocolate and a different sense of character to what the men in Britain displayed. This could be seen as less of a comedy and at times more of a study into the insecurities and inadequacies of men, *My British Buddy* is an entertaining effort. Mainwaring's initial branch of peace and good will is shattered by the jealousy and sense of danger that his platoon are put under from the younger better looking 'yanks.' It is still very funny in many places and the testosterone courses throughout the thirty minutes.

MEMORABLE MOMENT:

Mainwaring's hopes of a pleasant darts tournament with the Americans goes sour very quickly as they fraternize with the women of Walmington-on-Sea and pay next to no attention whatsoever to the platoon. What's more, Wilson tells Shultz that they aren't really soldiers, a remark that makes Mainwaring fume and by the time Hodges stick his awe in, the party has turned sour. As Mr Cheeseman goes to take a picture for the local paper, Shultz is so wound up he aims a punch on Hodges...but the ARP Warden ducks and he hits Mainwaring instead!

LINE:

Jones: We must take our American buddies to our bosoms and take them into our homes and fertilise with them.

WATCH OUT FOR:

- **The first appearance of Janet Davies as Mrs Pike since the series four episode *A Wilson (Manager?)***
- **The debut of Mr Cheeseman, who would go on to play a bigger part in the following run of episodes.**
- **Alan Tilvern plays the role of the American Colonel but actually made his *Dad's Army* bow in the series three episode *Battle School* as Captain Rodriguez.**

BEHIND THE SCENES:

This episode marks the very first interaction with the US army, who joined the war two and a half years after the beginning of the Second World War as Jimmy Perry and David Croft explored what effect the news would have on the Home Guard.

Talfryn Thomas makes his *Dad's Army* debut as the photographer for the town newspaper, Mr Cheeseman. His performance impressed the writers and after James Beck's death he was asked to replace the character of Walker in the line-up. This is the only time he shares the same screen time as the man he went on to replace in the Home Guard. Alan Tilvern was also recast as American Colonel Shultz after appearing in the series three episode *Battle School.*

Desmond Callum-Jones, who appeared in 63 episodes as a back row platoon member, explained that Arthur Lowe acknowledged the men at the back. 'Arthur realised very quickly that the episodes featuring the squad were most popular; he even spoke to us using our names on a couple of shows which helped to make us feel part of the family.'2

TRIVIA:

The episode is dated sometime early on in 1942 as the date the Americans joined the Second World War was on the 8th December 1941, the day after the attack on Pearl Harbour by the Japanese. Hodges also manages to offend the American Colonel that they have improved on their response time last time out as it took the USA three years to enter into the fight in the First World War when they officially allied with the United Kingdom et al in 1917.

SCORE: 9/10

EPISODE FIFTY SIX

THE ROYAL TRAIN

RECORDED ON 29TH JUNE 1973

FIRST BROADCAST ON 14TH NOVEMBER 1973

VIEWING FIGURE: 13.1 MILLION

PLOT:

Mainwaring arrives late after going to the chemist to pick up some sleeping tablets for his wife who is unable to sleep during the air raids. When he does, he informs his men that they will be greeting the King's train as it passes through the town. Unfortunately, a slow stopping train stops and the drivers get off and after having a cup of tea using the bottle of sleeping pills as sweetener by accident, it is up to the troops to move the train before the one carrying the train crashes into it!

GUEST CAST:

Bill Pertwee as ARP Warden Hodges
Edward Sinclair as the Verger
Frank Williams as the Vicar
William Moore as the Station Master
Freddie Earlle as Henry
Ronnie Brody as Bob
Fred McNaughton as the Mayor
Sue Bishop as the Ticket Collector
Bob Hornery as the City Gent

REVIEW:

The Royal Train is a delight. A memorable episode to many who saw it on its first transmission and many who have caught it in later years through repeats or videos and DVDs. One of the reasons for this is that it is highly watchable and the viewer can get lost in the excitement of the introduction of royalty like the men of Walmington-on-Sea. But as we know, nothing ever goes to plan for our protagonists. Once again it is the ineptness of the Home Guard that creates a dangerous situation as the sleeping tablets that Mainwaring has bought for his wife have fallen into the tea of the train drivers and hi farce ensues. Of course without a break wheel on the train the men decide to take charge of getting it out of the way for the King's train. The realisation that the break wheel is missing means is left in the hands of the Verger to warn Mainwaring and his men and a brilliant set-piece involving arguably one of the slowest chase sequences in TV history ensues. The speed of the chase, of course, which makes it all the more funny. Also, for once it looks as though Hodges wants to help the Home Guard, which is an odd course of action for a man who just last series wanted to send Mainwaring to prison (*A Brush With the Law*). In conclusion, the *Dad's Army* team deliver again with an episode full of action and great moments. I love how the writers actually encourage us to laugh at the characters more when they mess something up and with His Majesty the King in the area, the stakes are high yet again. Arthur Lowe is given the chance to spring into action and he and Clive Dunn are great when they are on the roof of the train.

MEMORABLE MOMENT:

With the arrival of the King's train imminent and the train drivers of the current incumbent on the platform asleep after mistakenly helping themselves to Mrs Mainwaring's sleeping pills, the Home Guard take charge of the steam engine and attempt to move it off as

Pike has previous experience. As they pull out the verger reveals that he has the worn break wheel in his mitts and Hodges panics. With the help of the vicar and the mayor, they chase after the train and enquire a handcar in a bid to save the lives of Mainwaring and his men.

LINE:

Pike: Mr Mainwaring, when you've opened your secret orders and read them, are you going to eat them?
Mainwaring: What on earth for?
Pike: So they don't fall into the hands of spies and quislings.
Jones: Sir, I'd like to volunteer to eat your secret orders, sir.

WATCH OUT FOR:

- **John Laurie is missing from the line-up when the King's train splashes past the men but he is included in the close-up.**
- **Hodges, the Mayor, the Vicar and the Verger chasing the train on a handcar but when the train goes into reverse, they are in for a shock!**
- **Pike sulking after a difference of opinions in the waiting room with Mainwaring.**

BEHIND THE SCENES:

Extensive location footage was required with the cast on the platform and involving the train. For this, the production crew decamped to Weybourne Station in Weybourne Norfolk so it could double for Walmington Station. John Laurie was absent for the majority of the location filming. To create the illusion that the train and the handcar were going faster than they were, the film editor had to speed up the footage to keep in check with the speed that the CSO display behind the cast in the studio was displaying.

There are some tail-tell signs that the scene in which the royal train comes into Walmington Station was not actually filmed as part of the location filming. The train in question features in stock footage and is a LNER Class A4 and the location of the footage is given away by the sight of Cliff Cottage on the way to Burnmouth Harbour is the background as the train was actually coming into the East Cost Mainline on the Scottish Border.

Frank Williams remembers the delights and the dangers of filming the episode. 'Filming on the railway track seemed rather hazardous. In the plot, Pikey is driving the train. But Ian, with all his talent, is not a train driver so a proper driver was out of sight and couldn't see what was happening. When the train was chasing us, Bill Pertwee said: "They can't see us and it's going to crash into us. I think we'll have to jump for it soon." I said we'd break our legs if we did, but he shouted: "Better that than have the train crash into us." It all turned out well in the end, and we were perfectly safe, but it seemed dangerous at the time.'3

TRIVIA:

The train that is used as the local train by the production crew is called Kitson 0-6-0 saddle tank "Colwyn" and it was owned by Stewarts & Lloyds of Corby at the time of recording. At the time of writing (February 2013) it is undergoing restoration by a company called T&H Engineering and is being held at Northampton and Lamport Railway Station.

SCORE: 7/10

EPISODE FIFTY SEVEN

WE KNOW OUR ONIONS

RECORDED ON 15TH JUNE 1973
FIRST BROADCAST ON 21ST NOVEMBER 1973
VIEWING FIGURE: 11.6 MILLION

PLOT:

The platoon is ready to test their new Smith gun from the back of Jones' van before they set off for a proficiency test. When they make the test site they are met by the aggressive Captain Ramsey and are given the task of obtaining twelve stars for the weekend, the maximum for a platoon. Ramsey is far from impressed by Mainwaring's charges as they fail interrogation and getting a man over an electric fence. In the final exercise they are given a chance to use their Smith gun to repel Ramsey's men...

GUEST CAST:

Bill Pertwee as ARP Warden Hodges
Edward Sinclair as the Verger
Fulton Mackay as Captain Ramsay
Alex McAvoy as the Sergeant
Pamela Manson as the NAAFI Girl
Cy Town as Mess Steward

REVIEW:

As we venture into the middle order of the sixth series, *We Know our Onions* is another piece of evidence that the writing duo of Jimmy Perry and David Croft are still at the very peak that they reached three years earlier. By introducing the Home Guard to the great outdoors, the script is strengthened by the bad luck of industrial action putting a halt to studio shooting as the show becomes more expansive and impressive in its execution. Generally speaking, its hard to see why the production team did not consign themselves to full episodes shot on film more often. The programme looks more impressive and realistic when it escapes the BBC Television Centre studios and it really does wonders for atmosphere and reality. With this being the only production in the series history that was directly affected by a strike, it is probably the best example too of a script being well adapted to the changes brought about by influences outside of the production team. The scene in which Wilson is interrogated by Ramsey in the guise as a Gestapo officer is pure comedy genius. We know by now the persona that John Le Mesurier brings to Wilson and his performance is effortless yet he gets the laughs. Fulton Mackay is doing all the work and getting wound up in the process as he fails to intimidate the Sergeant but let's be honest, it is pretty harsh that he receives no stars for the platoon here as this is the best tactic to deal with a bully. Despite not being high up in the zenith of *Dad's Army* episodes it does not its footing too badly at any stage. Yes, the joke with Jones and the electric fencing does outstay its welcome by about three minutes and the appearance of Hodges and the Verger grinds my gears this time out, it doesn't deter from a show that keeps series six ticking over nicely.

MEMORABLE MOMENT:

As the men are put through their paces Ramsey assumes the persona of a Gestapo officer. He goes about interrogating the men and after being attacked by Jones who takes his performance as genuine, he picks on Wilson. The Scout pours menace on the Sergeant and even depicts the event of matches under his fingernails burning down to his fingers but Wilson's calm, languid and composed manner infuriates Ramsey and comes across and not seeming very bothered by the pretend ordeal.

LINE:

Ramsey: What are you doing in France?
Wilson: I'm not in France.
Ramsey: Oh, yes, you are. I've captured you and now I'm interrogating you.
Wilson: Oh, I see. Well, Bonjour! What do you want to know?

WATCH OUT FOR:

- **Alex McAvoy, who plays the Sergeant, is the voice of the teacher and played the character in the flesh on rock band *Pink Floyd's The Wall'* album and film adaptation.**
- **Hodge's and the Verger's attempts to retrieve the onions from Jones' van.**
- **Wilson's reaction to the interrogation of Captain Ramsay.**

BEHIND THE SCENES:

The 1970s was a decade of strike action that disrupted many productions at the BBC and *Dad's Army* only found itself affected by industrial action once as the majority of the studio based scenes for this episode were left unfinished as the production team were unable to use BBC Television Centre at the time. Despite this set-back, the episode went ahead and was filmed largely on location at Preston Barracks in Brighton.

Further location filming was taken at Honington Primary School in Suffolk, St Aldhelm's Church doubled for All Saint's Church. An odd coincidence also occurred when the episode was repeated twenty seven years later on 20th June 2000 but a power cut occurred at Television Centre leaving only 16 minutes of *We Know Our Onions!* transmitted on BBC1 and when the channel regained its power after the failure the episode was discontinued.

TRIVIA:

Fulton Mackay makes his first appearance in *Dad's Army* as Captain Ramsey before making a return as a doctor in the series 9 episode *The Miser's Hoard.* Mackay is better known for his portrayal of prison officer Mr Mackay in the classic BBC sitcom *'Porridge'* where he was regularly thwarted by Ronnie Barker as Norman Stanley Fletcher. He also contributed plays to the BBC under the pseudonym Aeneas MacBride.

SCORE: 7/10

EPISODE FIFTY EIGHT

THE HONOURABLE MAN

RECORDED ON 8TH JULY 1973
FIRST BROADCAST ON 28TH NOVEMBER 1973
VIEWING FIGURE: 12.1 MILLION

PLOT:

At the church hall, Mainwaring chairs a meeting with members of the town about the visit of an award winning Russian worker but Hodges expresses his disgust at the bank manager chairing the committee. Later, the platoon also expresses their disgust but Mainwaring surprisingly maintains an open mind about the Russian. When he is at work the next day he is shocked to hear that Wilson has moved up a rung in the social ladder as his childless Uncle has recently passed away, making him 'The Right Honourable Arthur Wilson'....

GUEST CAST:

Bill Pertwee as ARP Warden Hodges
Edward Sinclair as the Verger
Frank Williams as the Vicar
Eric Longworth as Mr. Gordon (The Town Clerk)
Pamela Cundell as Mrs. Fox
Fred McNaughton as the Mayor
Gabor Vernon as the Russian
Hana Maria Pravda as Interpreter
Robert Raglan as Colonel Pritchard

REVIEW:

Never before has *Dad's Army* explored the class war at the heart of the series as deeply as it does here. The characters of George Mainwaring and 'The Honourable' Arthur Wilson have endured a nerve of tension between them since episode one and here I think the tension breaks like glass on a concrete floor as Mainwaring is furious and horrified at the realisation that he might not be able to keep Wilson under his thumb anymore as his status changes in the town. He seems to anger very quickly when he is told the news that Wilson's family have moved one up on the society ladder after his Uncle passes away. You can excuse his reaction as Wilson sees it does not make any difference to anything and the tipping point is the moment when

Mainwaring blows his gasket when he finds out that Wilson has been invited to join the golf club as he has spent years trying to gain a membership there. Here we have a man who swans through life and another who has to do everything the hard way. Of course, Wilson desires a quiet life and no fuss but those around him begin to change. The folk of Walmington decide they would like to honour him with the chance to present the key to the town as recognition for his status and they are overwhelmingly impressed. Jimmy Perry and David Croft have perfectly captured the way in which people in such a small community could have reacted to the news and it is very unfair in a harsh world that a man who really does not do much for the town would be selected instead of a hard worker. If Mainwaring were not so pompous he would not have such a hard time dealing with his jealousy and the reaction of the town's men. As fans, we are reassured that in the long run the relationship between Mainwaring and Wilson will remain as awkward and prickly as it has since the very first edition of the sitcom...but it is a good idea from the writers to put it to the test here.

MEMORABLE MOMENT:

Mainwaring is working another busy day at the bank Pike brings to his attention that personal post has also arrived to the bank for him but the letter is addressed to 'The Right Honourable Arthur Wilson.' Dismissing it as a practical joke, Mainwaring quizzes Wilson about the letter and despite the latter's wish for the news not to change things, it has spread all over town. He has moved up in society as his uncle had no children and has passed away. Mainwaring is furious and boils over when he discovers that Wilson has been invited to the golf club despite never playing the sport.

LINE:

Jones: Well, I look at it this way, sir. Although Sergeant Wilson has got three stripes on his honourable arm and you have got three pips on your common shoulder.

WATCH OUT FOR:

- **John Le Mesurier has a look on his face when he is being lectured by Arthur Lowe like he is trying his best not break down in laughter.**
- **Pike's reaction to the news that his Uncle Arthur is 'honourable.'**
- **Wilson nearly collides with the Vicar on his bicycle as he fails to tame the platoon's only motorbike.**

BEHIND THE SCENES:

For the scenes in which Wilson struggles to regain control of the motorcycle and ends up crashing into a trench at the side of the country lane, the location footage was captured in Sapiston in Thetford. Further location filming was made at Bardwell Green in Suffolk for the final scene and at Honington Primary School in Norfolk.

Stephen Lowe, the son of Arthur, revealed the biggest weakness of the character that his father played. 'The real chink in Mainwaring's armour is he cannot handle the fact that Wilson id a public schoolboy – it's his real hang-up. This episode makes the most of that: we really see Mainwaring the fighter, the British bulldog, because he's cut to the quick by this business of Wilson getting a title. Mainwaring goes for Wilson's jugular and this episode typifies the relationship between Mainwaring and Wilson, a major part of what *Dad's Army* is about.'4

TRIVIA:

The sub-plot mirrors the feelings many in the United Kingdom had at the time regarding the Communist Soviet Union aligning themselves with the Capitalist Great Britain. This alliance was not popular at the time and members of the Home Guard show their disgust at having to honour a 'red' and sing along to *The Red Flag* which was also used by the Labour Party until the late 1980's.

SCORE: 8/10

EPISODE FIFTY NINE

THINGS THAT GO BUMP IN THE NIGHT

RECORDED ON 15TH JULY 1973

FIRST BROADCAST ON 5TH DECEMBER 1973

VIEWING FIGURE: 12.2 MILLION

SYNOPSIS:

Following a miscalculation from Wilson, the men are lost in Jones' van as they try and make their way through a thunderstorm. With the petrol running low, the men decide to head towards a nearby manor house for shelter. There they endure an uncomfortable and frightening night, none more so than Pike, whose uniform was drenched by the rain that had collected in the tarpaulin that the men sheltered under to get to the house...

GUEST CAST:

Jonathan Cecil as Captain Cadbury
Colin Bean as Private Sponge

REVIEW:

This time *Dad's Army* has a go at trying out the spooky house motive. The scene is set for a horror ride with all the clichés in place but let's not forget this is a comedy of course and a family friendly one at that so although the first act hints at a darker, scarier edition we do in fact revert to the farcical misadventures of the Home Guard until near the very end. Speaking of which, the tone deliberately changes completely when Captain Cadbury turns up and the writers bring us back to what we are used to rather quickly. Obviously, James Beck is missing and is missed in turn. Private Joe Walker was such an important part of the *Dad's Army* puzzle, a cog in the clockwork that was key to the show's mainstream success. It was Beck's charm and ability as an actor that made the character such a fan's favourite and to be perfectly honest, his disjointed appearance here coupled with the poignant moment when Wilson writes his name on van window confirms his absence and the sense of loss at a time when Beck was already seriously ill in hospital. The scene with the dogs terrorising the platoon is *Dad's Army* doing one of the things it does best, relying on the pictures and performances to produce the laughs. The sight of grown men climbing up a tree and walking around under a shed that moves with them is great and even if the Captain Cadbury character is the sort you would find hanging out with Walter the Softy in *The Beano* comics, even his upper-class twit of a character does not cease the laughs from cascading.

MEMORABLE MOMENT:

It comes as no surprise that as soon as Captain Cadbury explains that the house is a school for dogs that the whole episode changes from a spooky feel to a more fun, entertaining one. When the dogs get out, the men are chased across a field and have to carry Godfrey on a wicker fence as they march bear foot over a small river. Mainwaring declares himself adamant that the dogs will not cross the water but they do and the men have to hide in a tree as the Captain, along with Wilson, Godfrey and Frazer are trapped in a shed and they attempt to walk off using it as protection to go and fetch help.

LINE:

Frazer: Godfrey! What do you want son?

Godfrey: I've got to go to the little boy's room. Will you come with me?

Frazer: No, nothing would induce me to budge from this room. There's too many unnatural causes.

Godfrey: It's the natural causes that worry me.

WATCH OUT FOR:

- **When in Jones' van, Mainwaring tells Wilson to take Walker's name, so he writes it onto the condensation on the window.**
- **The men attempting to escape the pack of dogs in a little shed...**
- **Even when Pike is stripped to throw the dogs off his scent, he can be seen to be wearing undergarments in the tree.**

BEHIND THE SCENES:

Production Assistant Jo Austin remembered, 'During the haunted house filming, we needed some "savage army dogs" to chase the platoon. The dogs we had, although well-trained and ferocious looking, were complete "softies" and preferred to lick everyone to death. However, in the end the handler managed to make them "smile" which passed for snarling for a brief moment. Naturally any animal filming takes time and patience, and we were some while on this sequence. None of this impressed Jimmy Beck, who was stuck up a tree for a very long time with an imminent thunderstorm getting closer. He was not too keen on dogs anyway.'5

This was the last episode to feature James Beck as he was taken ill the day before the studio scenes were due to be filmed at BBC Television Centre. His lines were distributed to Colin Bean, who had featured in nearly every episode to date as Corporal Sponge and the production team got around the absence of Beck by keeping the lighting low in the haunted house and making references to the character as being with the platoon so that when he popped up in the filmed sequences he was not completely missing from the ensemble.

The second half of the episode was completely filmed on location. Doubling for the River Crossing was The Black Bourn River in Sapiston, Suffolk with the scene with the men sheltering from the dogs captured in the neighbouring fields. The exterior of the Tracker Dog Training School was filmed at Grange Farm in the same village.

TRIVIA:

On the 14th July 1973, just one day after recording an audio play for the show with his co-stars, James Beck attended a local village fete for Guide Dogs for the Blind, when he was taken ill after complaining about a sudden pain in his stomach. Less than an hour later he was taken to the intensive care unit of Queen Mary's Hospital in Southampton and slipped into a coma. As a consequence, the actor missed the studio shoot for this episode, that were scheduled just a day later and the team were kept up to date with his condition during filming.

SCORE: 7/10

EPISODE SIXTY

THE RECRUIT

RECORDED ON 22ND JULY 1973

FIRST BROADCAST ON 12TH DECEMBER 1973

VIEWING FIGURE: 11.5 MILLION

SYNOPSIS:

Mainwaring is laid up in hospital with in growing toenails and is visited by Wilson and Jones. He is unaware that in his absence, Wilson, who is in temporary charge, had recruited both the Vicar and the Verger after the former has a moment of revelation that inspired him to join up in the fight against Hitler. When Mainwaring returns he clearly does not want the pair in his ranks and neither do many of the other platoon members and he tells them that he will not go easily on them...

GUEST CAST:

Bill Pertwee as ARP Warden Hodges
Edward Sinclair as the Verger
Frank Williams as the Vicar
Susan Majolier as Nurse
Lindsey Dunn as Hamish, the Small Boy

REVIEW:

It is a massive shame that the very last episode of such a consistent series is so baggy and weighed down by its content that it fails to round off the run with a metaphorically successful punch in the air. Then again, regarding the tragedy that was slowly occurring behind the scenes, it is no wonder that *The Recruit* rather limps to the finish line while the serious matter of James Beck's condition slowly played out its alarming and heartbreaking conclusion. Let's put ourselves in the shoes of the cast. A colleague and more importantly a friend is in a terrible state in hospital and the news is looking increasingly bleaker every day and you have to put on a brave face, march onto set and epitomize the stiff upper lip reaction we Brits have to bad news and continue as though everything is normal. But of course it was not and Mainwaring's line about having a word with Walker about his absence when he returns lingers on an eerie note. Walker was not coming back and the look on Ian Lavender and Clive Dunn's faces in the background says it all. The word grave does not cover the emotions they must have suspended in their hearts as the show went on. But it is not all doom and gloom as *The Recruit* does give us some nice extended interactions between Jones' section and gives Arnold Ridley more dialogue in a season that has seen him move more and more into the background. With regards to the uncertainty surrounding Beck, it was probably a good idea to have a shorter season and after this no future series of *Dad's Army* would be longer than six episodes long and it is a shame that the episode falls at the final hurdle but taking into account the worry the entire production must have been riddled with at the time and the re-writing that was undertaken, the lack of form can be forgiven.The series draws to a close in an uncertain fashion unfortunately as the show changes forever from here on in.

MEMORABLE MOMENT:

Mainwaring returns to parade following some time off with an in growing toenail, He hobbles along on crutches and reveals he discharged himself from hospital as they needed the beds. He makes his way along the line-up until he comes to an empty space where Walker usually stands to attention. In his place is a note. It is from the spiv, who declares that he has gone to the smoke (London) to carry out a deal. You can tell by the looks on the faces of the actors as Arthur Lowe reads the message out that shows just how worried they were for their friend.

LINE:

Vicar: Could I stand by and watch my wife being raped by a Nazi? Finally I said to myself, no I couldn't.
Mainwaring: But you're not married.
Vicar: I have a very vivid imagination.

WATCH OUT FOR:

- **The trouble maker that the vicar and the verger have problems with turns out to be ARP Warden Hodge's nephew.**

- **Jones gives Mainwaring shaved gooseberries instead of grapes, which have been scarce since the breakout of war in 1939.**
- **Ian Lavender moves Walker's note back in to position whilst in the long shot after a kerfuffle in the ranks.**

BEHIND THE SCENES:

The recording of the episode is notable for the very first time in the show's history that a main character is missing from an episode. James Beck was in intensive care as the cast recorded the episode. He had fallen ill the week before at a fete. His wife, Kay Beck remembered, 'I called the doctor and within an hour he was rushed to hospital. I wanted a specialist to see Jimmy but it seemed like none were available. Not knowing what to do, I called Arthur Lowe who was wonderful. He said: "Leave it to me." And he arranged for a specialist to see Jimmy - for that I'll always be grateful.'6

During rehearsals, an update on Beck's condition was pinned to the notice board in the room for the cast to keep an eye on his progress. Despite the episode going out nearly five months after his death, Beck still appears at the very end credits in his usual spot. It was the last time he was to be seen in the programme.

Jo Austin is one member of the production team who remembered the sadness the whole company felt during Back's final days. 'During my time on the programme Jimmy Beck died, which was totally traumatic for all of us, all the more so because this was the one unit where we got to know all the wives of the actors as most of them used to join us at weekends. We felt so much sympathy for Kay Beck. While Jimmy was still alive but on life-support machines, we had two more studio recordings and naturally the audiences wanted news. We could hardly tell them the truth that it was just a matter of time so had to keep up a facade of "slight improvements" in his condition. It was very difficult for the cast – particularly for Arthur Lowe who was very close to Jimmy.

'When it came to recording *The Recruit* David phoned me Saturday evening, the night before the recording, to say Jimmy wouldn't be able to make it. That evening him and Jimmy Perry had to rewrite the script, reallocating the lines they had written for Walker. David asked me if I could arrive at Television Centre early on the Sunday because he wanted me to retype the scripts. It was very sad.'7

TRIVIA:

When Mainwaring demands an explanation for why Pike has brought a violin case on parade, he replies that the Tommy gun is in it, just like in 'Scarface.' The 1932 gangster movie, distributed by United Artists, starred Paul Muni and George Raft and was based on the 1929 novel of the same name by author Armitage Trail. It was later used as the basis for the 1983 Al Pacino version of the film, which went on to win critical acclaim after initially finding only mixed reviews upon its original release.

SCORE: 6/10

By the time the series had finished and Christmas loomed on the horizon, 1973 had been a mixed year for *Dad's Army.* Despite boasting some of the best examples of comedy and acting that the production team had ever made the crew were rocked to the core by the death of James Beck. The actor's passing had also had a slight effect on the viewing figures as the average for season was 12.3 million, three million down on the previous run, which was also saw double the amount of episodes. The ratings were also down slightly as the show had moved to Wednesdays at 6.50pm on BBC Once, overlapping with soap opera *Crossroads.* Whilst there were question marks over the show's future, the writers had no qualms over ending and set about making changes to the line-up for the show's seventh season...

SERIES SEVEN

MAIN CAST:

ARTHUR LOWE - CAPTAIN GEORGE MAINWARING
JOHN LE MESURIER - SERGEANT ARTHUR WILSON
CLIVE DUNN - LANCE CORPORAL JACK JONES
JOHN LAURIE - PRIVATE JAMES FRAZER
ARNOLD RIDLEY - PRIVATE CHARLES GODFREY
IAN LAVENDER - PRIVATE FRANK PIKE

FEATURING THE VOICE OF BUD FLANNIGAN

EPISODE SIXTY ONE

EVERBODY'S TRUCKING

RECORDED ON 27TH OCTOBER 1974
FIRST BROADCAST ON 15TH NOVEMBER 1974
VIEWING FIGURE: 14.1 MILLION

PLOT:

Mainwaring has important news that there is going to be three battalions of troops moving into the Walmington and Eastgate areas and the men are put in charge of installing new signposts in the route to the towns. As they go about the task, they find that their route is blocked by an abandoned steam roller, with a fairground organ attached to it. Jones tries to take the van onto the grass to get past it but it gets stuck in the mud, what with all the heavy rainfall they have been having...

GUEST CAST:

Bill Pertwee as ARP Warden Hodges
Edward Sinclair as the Verger
Frank Williams as the Vicar
Pamela Cundell as Mrs Fox
Harold Bennett as Mr Blewett
Olive Mercer as Mrs Yeatman
Felix Bowness as the Driver
Colin Bean as Private Sponge

REVIEW:

After nearly four years of near comic perfection the tumultuous death of James Beck broke the team up and tested the show's resolve for the first time since its debut way back in 1968. What the programme needed after such a shock is a strong opener for the first series without the charismatic Walker and unfortunately the first episode of the show's seventh run can be summed up in just one word... its rubbish. The first problem is with the plot as Jimmy Perry and David Croft opted to play it safe and worryingly for the first script of the series, it feels tired and baggy. The premise of the platoon getting stuck in a boggy bit of mud for twenty minutes does little to enthral or entertain. Throw into the mix an appearance from Hodges that feels forced and then the entire ensemble either turning up on either a bike or a bus, who also predictably get stuck in the mud, the joke wears thinner than Bobby Charlton's barnet. Mainwaring is so unlikable and big headed and ignorant it is sad to see. It was as if the writers had taken every negative asset of his being and made a cake out of them for this episode and the key ingredient was off. I hate the way he is portrayed here and that is a bad thing because in the past it was easy to feel sympathetic towards Mainwaring. In this one, he is just a massive arse! This is an unfunny, unremarkable, instantly forgettable, over stretched, thinly written, uninspiring and generally bad opening to the seventh series which would be a solid contender for the worst episode ever if it was not for the talents of Ian Lavender who is given the chance to display a more sarcastic and strong portrayal of Pike. The premise is a simple and unimaginative one that is not good enough for a sitcom of *Dad's Army*'s calibre.

MEMORABLE MOMENT:

Well, where do I begin for an episode that is lacking in any memorable moments? Funnily enough, despite my grumblings of Mainwaring's demeanour here, the first scene is quite good, showing that the character of Pike is evolving to the point of talking back to his Captain and of course his bank manager. Ian Lavender is fabulous as the 'stupid boy' and from here on in he can be a bigger thorn in Mainwaring's side than his Uncle Arthur and arguably another rival for him to contend with. It also highlights Pike's growing nerve.

LINE:

(Mainwaring whacks Jones' van to show the signal to disembark)
Jones: Do you mind not hitting that van in the aforesaid manner, sir?
Mainwaring: Will you stop fussing, Jones? There is a war on, you know?
Jones: Yes, sir, but there's no need to spoil my van. That's up to Hitler.

WATCH OUT FOR:

- **Godfrey's homemade road sign to show the direction that Eastgate is in.**
- **The verger discovers that there is more to his wife and Mr Blewitt than meets the eye.**
- **Pike's reaction to being stuck at the rear wheel of the van as they try and get it out of the mud.**

BEHIND THE SCENES:

For a production that took place primarily in the studio frequently this episode stands out as being only the second time in the show's history that over half of the runtime was shot on location, this time quite by design as opposed to the series six episode *We Know our Onions!*, which was pushed out on location due to strike

action at the BBC at the time. The majority of the location filming took place at Stanford Training Area in Norfolk, barring the first scene that required the church yard set to be erected in Television Centre.
At the time of writing (early 2013) the fairground organ that plays the can-can was built in the 1920s by a German manufacturer called Wellerhaus and is currently held in a Thursford Collection in Norfolk.
Guest star Felix Bowness admitted that he more of an input in the episode than was originally intended and it happened quite by accident. 'The first time I was on location I laughed during the recording of a scene, but it wasn't the thing to do and it had to be shot again. I thought I'd better move away and decided to climb a nearby tree. I'm a good bird whistler so started whistling away until Bill Pertwee came over and told me to stop because it would be heard on the film. When the location shots were shown during the studio recording, you could hear a bird - that was me!'1

TRIVIA:

Felix Bowness, who plays the coach driver, went on to play a regular role as jockey Fred Quilly in the popular sitcom *Hi-de-Di!* was a frequent warm up act for *The Morecambe and Wise Show* and *The Two Ronnies* and made appearances in *The Benny Hill Show*, *Porridge* and *Sykes.* During the Second World War he played a part in the D-Day landing on Normandy but his landing craft was hit and sunk and he recovered in a French convent after the incident.

SCORE: 3/10

EPISODE SIXTY TWO

A MAN OF ACTION

RECORDED ON 7TH MAY 1974
FIRST BROADCAST ON 22ND NOVEMBER 1974
VIEWING FIGURE: 16.4 MILLION

PLOT:

Jones and Pike are taking time out towards the end of their night on patrol and the latter decides to recreate a prank he played when he was a boy by sticking his head through the park gates. Unfortunately, his head gets stuck and Mainwaring takes the platoon out during an air raid to release him. Back at the church hall, chaos ensues as the town's major services rally about an emergency that has occurred. After a heavy bombardment, the entire town is cut off and Mainwaring puts the town under martial law...

GUEST CAST:

Talfryn Thomas as Private Cheeseman
Bill Pertwee as ARP Warden Hodges
Edward Sinclair as the Verger
Frank Williams as the Vicar

REVIEW:

No sooner has the programme served up a clunker that they soon rectify a poor script with one that brings the show back to basics. *A Man of Action* is multi-layered delight and a surprisingly good episode after the last one. It brings the heroic and duty bound nature inside Mainwaring to the fore and despite becoming Napoleonic in his conviction towards the end, his character is much more likable than last time out and he boldly stands forward when an emergency situation arises in the town and no one else can stand up to take charge. *A Man of Action* also makes the bold move of replacing James Beck as Talfryn Thomas returns after his small role as Eastgate Gazette reporter Mr Cheeseman (in series six episode *My British Buddy*) to make up the seventh member of the main cast. From the outset, Thomas is just fine as the reporter and brings a new dimension to the dynamic. He is subtly funny, with his native Welsh tongue bamboozling Mainwaring and sometimes the viewers. Wilson and Frazer clearly have reservations about his inclusion as his background as a journalist leaves them to debate he would report on the follies of the men and scrutinize the mistakes Mainwaring makes. Of course, they are going on previous experience here but it shows just how untrustworthy the profession of journalism was even then. Still, the new recruit is just a small sub-plot in an otherwise busy episode. When the town is completely cut off by an air raid, Mainwaring takes the situation into his own hands - and for once Wilson is quite behind him. He can hardly believe his ears, and neither can we. Even if it is not within his authority, it is obvious that he is the only cool head in the position to form some sort of action. Arthur Lowe's stand-off with the policeman is great and shows just how confident he is in his own abilities - even if Mainwaring is quite heavy handed in his threats during the emergency.

MEMORABLE MOMENT:

With the railway badly damaged, phone lines down and a devastating air raid leaving the town in crisis, Mainwaring is greeted by Hodges, the vicar and the verger and policeman forming an emergency committee but getting nowhere in conversation. Mainwaring decides to put the town under martial law and proceeds to tell the panic-stricken committee after grabbing their attention with the help of his men. The Policeman stands up to the Captain at the insistence of Hodges and ponders on what authority Mainwaring has to do such a thing. He quietly puts his gun on the table and shows his intent.

LINE:

Mainwaring: No liquor is to be taken without my permission.
Frazer: Hold on! That is undemocratic!
Mainwaring: You, Frazer, will be in charge of all liquor permits.
Frazer: I'm right behind you, Cap'n!

WATCH OUT FOR:

- **Wilson and Frazer's reaction to the news that a reporter will join the platoon temporarily to report on the Home Guard's adventures.**
- **Mr. Blewitt obtaining a bath permit from Corporal Jones...and then handing it back to the**

butcher who is in temporary charge of bath time.

- **The frequent observation that Pike is under some form of punishment after getting his head stuck in between iron bars.**

BEHIND THE SCENES:

Robert Mill remembered that he was impressed with the way the show was brought to the screen and the team behind the programme. 'The production was well organised. All the characters were beautifully related to each other and the merest look or word would be a cue for a laugh. But I remember David Croft was anxious that scenes which wouldn't create a laugh, namely me marching or whatever, should be done as expeditiously as possible so it wouldn't encroach on the laughter time!2

The episode was the first script to go into production for the series and was recorded five months before the rest of the series, making it the first episode to be recorded since James Beck's death on 6th August the previous year.

TRIVIA:

In the very first scene, Pike comments on Jones eating a pear and questions if the British will ever be treated to a banana again. The British Government banned the selling of the fruit to the country through the Ministry of Food in November 1940. The reason for this was that the food had to be imported from around the globe and it was not lifted until September 1945, mere months after the war ended and this was only a partial lift on the ban. When British citizens were treated to the fruit once more, some children had to be shown how to eat it as they had not prior experience of eating a banana.

SCORE: 7/10

EPISODE SIXTY THREE

GORILLA WARFARE

RECORDED ON 27TH OCTOBER 1974
FIRST BROADCAST ON 29TH NOVEMBER 1974
VIEWING FIGURE: 14.4 MILLION

PLOT:

The platoon pack up Jones' van as they prepare for a weekend exercise that will see them take part in Guerrilla Warfare and transport a highly important agent - that Mainwaring decides will be him – to a secret destination while avoiding the enemies efforts to capture him.. On the exercise they are met by obstacles designed to lure them to defeat. They also dismiss a message from a soldier telling them that a gorilla has escaped...

GUEST CAST:

Talfryn Thomas as Private Cheeseman

Bill Pertwee as ARP Warden Hodges
Edward Sinclair as the Verger
Robert Raglan as the Colonel
Robin Parkinson as Lieutenant Wood
Erik Chitty as Mr. Clerk
Rachel Thomas as the Mother Superior
Michael Sharvell-Martin as the Lieutenant
Verne Morgan as the Farmer
Joy Allen as The Lady with the pram

REVIEW:

There seems to be a trend in the pitch of the episodes so far this series which suggests that the *Dad's Army* peak may well be over by the time it comes to *Gorilla Warfare*. Not only is this a hard one to sell to even the most fanatical of fans with a highly unrealistic ape on screen but it also divides those who have seen it. Does the unconvincing costume ruin the fun and act as a distraction that takes the viewer out of the story. The writer's confidence in Mr Cheeseman appears to be on the wane already. Apart from the fiasco with the initials on his armband and wanting to bring his camera on the exercise he is given very little to do. It appears to me that he is just here to make the numbers up this time out but more screen time rightly goes to Ian Lavender and the supporting characters that have already established themselves as mainstays in the programme. It is they who eat up the minutes at the expense of the relative newcomer. Was this a purposeful tactic from Perry and Croft? If so, why go out if the way to employ a new actor in a regular spot if all they were going to do was effectively make Cheeseman a less important character than the likes of ARP Chief Hodges? There are some good points to be said about the episode. Perry and Croft seem to be firmly back in the groove when it comes to the moulding of their scripts. Firstly, the sight gags are very good. The distrust of Mainwaring towards anybody dressed as a woman, especially nuns, can seem a little sexist but he and his men have been conditioned to ignore those who dress as nuns as this was something the British forces thought Hitler's charges might disguise themselves as if they invaded. Even when they are clearly women, the men leave the stranded ladies behind. It seems harsh on them and yes actually attacking a lady pushing a baby in a pram is taking it to extremes and kind of ruins the first use of misinterpretation but oh well, let's hope the nun's have got their Hayes book on hand for their broken car!

MEMORABLE MOMENT:

This episode seems to make up for the lack of memorable moments so far this series by putting several in the same script. Not only do we have the scene in which the men suspect the two nuns as being Nazis in disguise but we also have Private Frazer story about the Auld Empty Barn. As he pulls Mainwaring in with his suspenseful build up and the rest of the men huddle closer to hear the tale, he declares there was nothing in it. Cue howls of laughter from the audience and a great punch line from Arthur Lowe that adds to the gag beautifully.

LINE:

Frazer: Captain Mainwaring. Did I ever tell you the story about the old, empty barn?
Mainwaring: Um. No.
Frazer: Would you like to hear the story about the old, empty barn?
Mainwaring: Um. Yes. Listen everybody. Frazer's going to tell us the story about the old empty barn.
Frazer: Right. The story of the old empty barn. Well. There was nothing in it.

WATCH OUT FOR:

- **The edge of the back drop can be seen as Pike enters shot in the opening scene.**
- **Cheeseman wears an armband reading W.C, standing for War Correspondent, of course.**
- **Hodges and the verger's plan to sabotage the platoon's effort but see their plan backfire spectacularly in a messy way.**

BEHIND THE SCENES:

Although mainly a studio-bound production, the production team had embarked on All Saint's Church in Honington, Suffolk for location filming where the church doubled for Walmington's own St Aldhelm's House. Croxton Heath at Stanford Training Ground was also used as the Pinner Fields.

Ian Lavender commented that although James Beck was gone, he was always greatly missed by the cast and crew. 'All kinds of silly things used to set us off. There was the a cappella singing, for example. We had this habit, on location, of sitting around in the fields, while we were waiting to film something, and singing. It was never planned, it always just happened: someone would start singing - 'You'll never know how much I love you' - and then someone else would join in ' You'll never know just how much I care' - and it would just grow and grow, until all of us were together, singing, with Arthur, of course, conducting.
Well the first time we went filming after Jimmy died, we were sitting around the van, waiting to begin filming, and somebody started it - 'You'll never know...' - and nobody took it up. We never did it again after Jimmy died. And that was how it was. Something had gone. No matter how good the things were that we went on to do without Jimmy, something was missing.'3

TRIVIA:

Hodges does his best to get the escaped monkey off his back by ringing the Royal Society for the Prevention of Cruelty to Animals (RSPCA.) The RSPCA was formed in 1824 by 22 reformers led by Members of Parliament Richard Martin and William Wilberforce with Reverend Arthur Broome. It was the first animal welfare charity to be formed in the world and is still going strong to this day with four animal hospitals in Putney in South London, Birmingham, Greater Manchester and Holloway in North London and clinics across the United Kingdom. Their mission status is to by all lawful means prevent cruelty, promote kindness to and alleviate suffering of animals.

SCORE: 6/10

EPISODE SIXTY FOUR

THE GODIVA AFFAIR

RECORDED ON 3RD NOVEMBER 1974
FIRST BROADCAST ON 6TH DECEMBER 1974
VIEWING FIGURE: 13.8 MILLION

PLOT:

The platoon spent their parade night practising a Morris dance they will take part in for the Spitfire fundraiser at the weekend. All is not well with Jones, however, and he has a quiet chat with Mainwaring in which he admits that he has feelings for Mrs Fox and she has become involved with the town clerk. He begs Mainwaring to talk to her and he agrees to meet with the widow at Marigold's Tea Rooms the next day, setting tongues wagging about his relationship with the woman who shall portray Lady Godiva at the fundraiser...

GUEST CAST:

Bill Pertwee as ARP Warden Hodges
Frank Williams as the Vicar
Edward Sinclair as the Verger

Janet Davies as Mrs Pike
Pamela Cundell as Mrs Fox
Talfryn Thomas as Private Cheeseman
Colin Bean as Private Sponge
George Hancock as Private Hancock
Peter Honri as Private Day
Eric Longworth as Town Clerk
Rosemary Faith as Waitress

REVIEW:

The Godiva Affair is frequently hilarious and entertaining from the word go. It has a couple of iffy moments, but on the whole it has character and depth and at the centre of it Arthur Lowe is also back to his best.

But despite this set piece, the spitfire fund is more of a back story as we are given a more character driven plot and an in depth at the relationship between Corporal Jones and Mrs Fox. We are seeing the foundations of their romance that developed all the way to the finale of the programme and although we have seen them smooching together in the cinema in *The Big Parade* here Jones expresses his deeper emotions and gets Mainwaring into all kinds of trouble in the process. The tearoom's scene is great and Arthur Lowe illuminates the screen, trying his best to talk about a delicate matter as the Home Guard members tongue's wag all around him. The moment Pike arrives to tell him he has told Mrs Mainwaring that he is busy having tea with another woman, we get the ever trusty catchphrase and even Pike himself realises what a stupid boy he has been.

The script is multi layered and very funny, highlighting the strengths in the writing of Jimmy Perry and David Croft and bringing the best out of the performers. It is as good as the series got so far in this run. However, it is apparent that the character of Mr Cheeseman as a replacement for Private Walker is not working out as he is given nowhere near the same exposure as the departed spiv.

MEMORABLE MOMENT:

At his Corporal's insistence, Mainwaring goes to meet Mrs Fox to discuss the feelings both Jones has for her and also the town clerk, who has designs on her himself. As the meeting takes place in Marigold Tearooms, Mainwaring realises that some of the members of his platoon are also present, including Jones in a thin disguise. He risks becoming the talk of the town and is frequently interrupted by Pike who tells him that his wife is on the phone. He is also startled by Mrs Fox making clear that she believes that he is a handsome man and can offer her much.

LINE:

(Captain Mainwaring collapses after seeing his wife as Lady Godiva.)
Jones: Speak to me sir, speak to me. Poor Mr Mainwaring, he'll never get over the shock.
Frazer: Aye, and neither will the horse.

WATCH OUT FOR:

- **Jones and Frazer's rivalry during the Morris dancing scene.**
- **The platoon's reaction to Mainwaring and Mrs Fox meeting over Jones and the spying that ensues.**
- **Private Pike imitating the town clerk's pronunciation of 'fleshings.'**

BEHIND THE SCENES:

Eric Longworth remarked that he thoroughly enjoyed making this episode. 'The town clerk was a rather pompous, northerner, but he was wonderful to play. The Godiva Affair is my favourite episode. Mrs Fox is auditioning for the part of Lady Godiva. I claim she'll be perfectly respectable covered from top to toe in fleshings and wearing a wig of long golden tresses. I mouthed every syllable of it while drooling over the thought of Mrs Fox with her ample figure wearing fleshings.'4

The idea to have the platoon morris dance to raise money for a spitfire fund was inspired by similar fundraisers that occurred during the Second World War as people rallied around to help in any way they could to help in the war effort. From the cash that was raised a Spitfire would then be constructed.

TRIVIA:

The episode makes many references to the legend of Lady Godiva. Godiva was an 11th century noblewoman, who as the story goes, once rode on a horseback naked through the streets of Medieval Coventry. She did so after her husband imposed taxation on his tenants and to gain remission. A statue of Lady Godiva was erected in the city on 22nd August 1949 and was made by Sir William Reid Dick.

SCORE: 7/10

EPISODE SIXTY FIVE

THE CAPTAIN'S CAR

RECORDED ON 17TH NOVEMBER 1974
FIRST BROADCAST ON 13TH DECEMBER 1974
VIEWING FIGURE: 14.4 MILLION

PLOT:

Lady Matlby graces Mainwaring and Wilson with her presence and donates her Rolls-Royce to the Home Guard as she would like to see it used in the war effort and does not want to give it to Hodges who she believes is common. The town is also getting ready for the arrival of a French General, leaving Hodges to argue with Mainwaring over who gets to lead the Guard of Honour...

GUEST CAST:

Bill Pertwee as ARP Warden Hodges
Talfryn Thomas as Private Cheeseman
Frank Williams as the Vicar
Edward Sinclair as the Verger

Colin Bean as Private Sponge
John Hart Dyke as the French General
Eric Longworth as Town Clerk
Fred McNaughton as the Mayor
Mavis Pugh as Lady Maltby
Robert Raglan as Colonel
Donald Morley as Glossip

REVIEW:

The Captain's Car is without doubt the best episode in this series. It sees Jimmy Perry and David Croft on fine form and back to the zenith of their writing abilities in a way in which makes me forgive them for the mess that was *Everybody's Trucking'*. This is the funniest thirty minutes *Dad's Army* had to offer since *The Deadly Attachment.* The opening few minutes sees Mainwaring at arguably his most pompous. He berates Wilson for sitting in his chair but as always, the Sergeant gets the last laugh as the chair Mainwaring sits in is broken and Mainwaring slips backwards as Arthur Lowe displays his fantastic physical ability to bring the laughs in early and his snobbery is also flying high when the lady of the manor is introduced.

Luckily the behaviour of his men around him, when Lady Maltby is in the side office, means that they bring him crashing back down to earth by repeatedly showing him up. First of all, Frazer yells at him for being late and then the icing on the cake is supplied by Pike, who dumps a bucket full of manure on his desk and guarantees the lady of the manor gets an unexpected waft of it. The farcical twist is amusing and results in the platoon camouflaging two Rolls-Royce cars inadvertently. The final scene when the French General is unveiled is almost a laugh a second. First you have the Verger clipping the horn player, followed by the choir led by the vicar only having time to learn a little bit of *La Marseillaise* and Frazer admitting that his paint work has not dried yet on the Mayor's Rolls-Royce. Then Mainwaring's reaction to Wilson's statement spoken in French is also funny and then the French General gets intimate with the stiff upper lip of the British way (kind of) to add to the hilarity. Then of course, the pay off comes with a simple touch of paint on Bill Pertwee's chops that brings the house down as the 'You Have Been Watching' card comes up at the bottom of the screen. A perfect way to round off the episode.

MEMORABLE MOMENT:

Hodges is upset that he has been left out of the affectionate greetings given from the French General and after Cheeseman's flash bulb on his camera startles the dignitary into falling back onto the Rolls-Royce, covering his palms with the black paint the Frazer has just put to disguise the camouflaged coat it mistakenly got earlier on, he finally gets a kiss from the French General. To Mainwaring's amusement, the Chief Warden stands grinning with black car paint on his face. It is a fantastic and a great way to round of a great episode.

LINE:

Lady Maltby: That Mr Hodges is most awfully common. And, of course, I know Mr Jones and Arthur is such a darling. (To Mainwaring) Well, I'm sure you are very nice to, when one gets to know you.
Mainwaring: Yes. Well, I can assure you we'd look after it most carefully, Lady Maltby. My men are very reliable. Very particular about who I have in my platoon. They're all handpicked.
(Knock on the side office door and Frazer enters)
Frazer: Hey! We're all lined up out here waiting, waiting and if you don't come soon, we're all off home! I thought you'd just like to know.

WATCH OUT FOR:

- **Mainwaring has a very low opinion of the French army and is made uncomfortable by their affectionate kissing.**
- **Jones has been supplying Lady Maltby with meat since 1933, when her late husband fell out with the JR Sainsbury.**
- **When Mainwaring is introduced to his new staff car, he pats it despite the fresh paintwork having just been completed and not getting any paint on his hands.**

BEHIND THE SCENES:

Mavis Pugh was grateful to the writers and for her links to Jimmy Perry as she made her television debut. 'Jimmy Perry and David Croft were very loyal to the people who had worked for them. The part of Lady

Maltby, which was actually my first TV role, was designed by Jimmy with me in mind. I'd worked with him at Watford Rep. It was a lovely part.'5
All Saint's Church in Honington was used once again to double for St Aldhelm's Church in the programme and further location filming was completed at the Honington Primary School and the Guildhall in Thetford acted as the Town Hall in Walmington.

TRIVIA:

Jones recounts his take on the inspiration behind Lord Kitchener's iconic recruitment poster with the slogan 'Your country needs you!' The real story behind the poster can be traced back to the very beginning of the First World War when the British Prime Minister Herbert Asquith appointed Kitchener as the Secretary of State for War, the first man ever recruited to the newly created post. His main job was to recruit an army of volunteers in the country to fight the German forces. The poster was designed by Alfred Leete and it made its debut on the cover on London Opinion, one of the most popular and influential magazines in the world at the time on 5th September 1914.

SCORE: 9/10

EPISODE SIXTY SIX

TURKEY DINNER

RECORDED ON 10TH NOVEMBER 1974

FIRST BROADCAST ON 23RD DECEMBER 1974
VIEWING FIGURE: 15.8 MILLION

PLOT:

Mainwaring has noticed that the platoon have been rather quiet of late. Jones' section admit they have been feeling guilty lately after an unexpected drunken night led to the him shooting a turkey he found as he mistook it for a Nazi. Mainwaring is shocked by his men's admission and insists that they pay the farmer for the turkey but they discover that it did not come from his farm. Instead, Jones' section believes they should hold a turkey dinner for the pensioners of the town...

GUEST CAST:

Bill Pertwee as ARP Warden Hodges
Talfryn Thomas as Private Cheeseman
Edward Sinclair as the Verger
Frank Williams as the Vicar
Harold Bennett as Mr Blewett
Pamela Cundell as Mrs Fox
Janet Davies as Mrs Pike
Olive Mercer as Mrs Yeatman
Dave Butler as Farmhand

REVIEW:

We round off the seventh series with a turkey, with a little stuffing. Let that not be a criticism on the turkey part but the latter of the statement is suitable for such an aptly named episode. It makes for a nice jaunt for the last of the series and an exploration into the behaviour of its central character and the karma that comes around to bite him on the bum by the end. Mainwaring is at his most pompous again and he is frequently looking for one up over Wilson. His joke that he tells the men to boost morale does little to bring a cascade of laughter but Wilson gets one for his anecdote, once again underlining Mainwaring and fuelling his jealousy. Unfortunately, the episode does suffer from a slow start that is only really kept awake by the story Jones recounts about the eventful night for his section on patrol. It is here that the we really get going and there a couple of details in Clive Dunn's speech, including the one about Godfrey becoming drunk and the shooting of a rogue turkey, that are very funny. Mainwaring is not best pleased by the tale and expects the men to make up for the shooting and he is confounded by the men's pub crawl on patrol. That piece of exposition in ways of a flashback would have been fun or maybe it could have replaced the whole line-up sequence completely. As the unofficial Christmas Special, it this the most festive treat ever given to the series. Once again Captain Mainwaring is the main butt of the joke and his descent into gravy stained farce at the end of the episode is very funny. Private Cheeseman once again falls into the background as the chance to develop the character bypasses as he makes his final bow.

MEMORABLE MOMENT:

On the day of the Rotary Club dinner that Mainwaring is giving a speech at, the men are busy organising the turkey dinner for the elderly of Walmington-on-Sea. Instead of doing the sensible thing and letting somebody else cut the turkey up, Mainwaring does his best to cover his dinner attire as he is leaving as soon as the last person has their meal. As he reveals his smart clothes, Pike walks into him with a plate covered in gravy that spoils his shirt. In the side office, the men try to get the gravy out and Jones paints over the stain with white paint, only to leave the paint tin resting on his Captain's jacket and ruining that too!

LINE:

Mainwaring: Where is Mr Boggis?
Worker: It's Wednesday!
Mainwaring (slowly): Where is your master?
Worker: It's Wednesday!
Mainwaring (to Wilson): The man's an idiot, Wilson.

WATCH OUT FOR:

- **Mainwaring's joke about the Englishman, Scotsman and Welshman gets a rather tepid response from the men.**
- **Jones' account of his patrol's unexpected pub crawl and an even more unexpected turn out from a less than sober Godfrey.**
- **The studio audience give the cast a big cheer at the end credits and an even bigger cheer for Ian Lavender.**

BEHIND THE SCENES:

Caston Hall in Attleborough, Norfolk was used as North Berrington Farm for location scenes and filmed earlier on in the year with the bulk of location filming. The episode was meant to go out on the 6th December but was pushed back to the final episode of the series and its original broadcast on the 23rd December makes it an unofficial Christmas Special, despite being written with that as the intention.

Hugh Cecil, who appeared in 50 episodes as a back row platoon member of the Home Guard, remarked on his time on the programme. 'Appearing in *Dad's Army* was a good job insofar as we were booked for two days a week for six or seven weeks. In addition there were periods of four days upwards when we were on location in Thetford where we would do all the pre-filming for the coming six or seven episodes. Several of us knew each other from previous TV shows, and we were all experienced professionals from one branch or another of show business. This meant, of course, that there was always plenty to talk about - the usual thing when a bunch of pros get together!'6

TRIVIA:

Turkey Dinner marks the final appearance of Talfryn Thomas as Eastgate Platoon journalist Private Cheeseman. Although the actor had impressed both Jimmy Perry and David Croft with his performances, the character had only been brought into the series on a temporary basis to see if the character could eventually replace Private Walker. Thomas, who had also made appearances in *Doctor Who, The Saint* and *The Avengers* died on 4th November 1982 from a heart attack, just four days before his 60th birthday.

SCORE: 7/10

After the disappointing audience figures that greeted the sixth series a year earlier, *Dad's Army* found itself in another new slot on Sunday evenings where the schedule was less competitive than it had been before. This saw an increase in the ratings for the series as the run averaged 14.8 million viewers. For the first time since 1969, the programme only produced six episodes, an episode count that had doubled in the early 1970s. It did not include many episodes that hold up to previous classics, but *The Godiva Affair* and *The Captain's Car* are personal highlights. So, the show had improved in this respect, but some of the show's fans had not taken to the character of Mr Cheeseman and Jimmy Perry and David Croft decided not to include the journalist in the next series, although as they pondered whether to end the series soon, the pair spent the early months of 1975 wondering whether there would even be another run...

SERIES EIGHT

MAIN CAST:

ARTHUR LOWE - CAPTAIN GEORGE MAINWARING
JOHN LE MESURIER - SERGEANT ARTHUR WILSON
CLIVE DUNN - LANCE CORPORAL JACK JONES
JOHN LAURIE - PRIVATE JAMES FRAZER
ARNOLD RIDLEY - PRIVATE CHARLES GODFREY
IAN LAVENDER - PRIVATE FRANK PIKE

FEATURING THE VOICE OF BUD FLANNIGAN

EPISODE SIXTY SEVEN

RING DEM BELLS

RECORDED ON 3RD JULY 1975
FIRST BROADCAST ON 5TH SEPTEMBER 1975
VIEWING FIGURE: 11.3 MILLION

PLOT:

The platoon is on parade, with Pike in an excited mood. The men are to feature in a film that is being made to help the war effort. However, it becomes apparent that the men will be playing the roles of Nazi soldiers, much to their horror. After a less than inconspicuous visit to the local pub, Hodges, the Vicar and the Verger see the backs of the platoon and sound the alarm of invasion by ringing the church bells...

GUEST CAST:

Bill Pertwee as ARP Warden Hodges
Frank Williams as the Vicar
Edward Sinclair as the Verger
Jack Haig as Mr Palethorpe, the Landlord
Robert Raglan as the Colonel
Felix Bowness as Special Constable
John Bardon as Harold Forster
Hilda Fenemore as Queenie Beal
Janet Mahoney as Doris, the Barmaid
Adele Strong as Lady with the Umbrella
Colin Bean as Private Sponge

REVIEW:

We are out of the blocks in quick fashion this time out as *Ring Dem Bells* is one of the best episodes of *Dad's Army* made post-Walker and rightly deserves a place in my any fans' top ten-list. The writing is so inventive but simple and the acting is superb, notably from Mr Ian Lavender but we will get onto him soon enough. Firstly, the premise regarding the men taking part in a film and brings out the naive and excitable side of Pike and the pragmatic, seen-it-all-before, non-impressed mood in Frazer to counterpoint this the young man's youthful enthusiasm. An early exchange between youth and experience leads to an excellent opening exchange of dialogue and a funny moment in which Jones makes the men about turn on more than one occasion to highlight the men's 'all-round qualities.' It is a silly visual gag but one that works. The pace of the episode is well judged and as soon as the main plot starts up, the rest of the episode really does just write itself. Of course, the episode peaks with the men's appearance at the Six Bells Pub in full Nazi uniform in aN hilarious encounter with a startled landlord. The cast show no signs of slowing down despite this being the eighth year of the series and the writing duo seem to have tailored the script to the ensemble's strengths, allowing for high farce and more laughs than were available at any point during the almost unfocused and unconfident seventh series. Ian Lavender is at the centre of attention and at the front of most of what makes this episode so good. His performance is spell binding, making it easy to forget the gap in his biological age and the age of his character has stretched and grown as time has moved on and he had lent a more assured and trusted performance as a consequence.

MEMORABLE MOMENT:

Hodges, the Vicar and Mr Yeatman witness Captain Mainwaring giving a lecture to a platoon of Nazi storm troopers, much to their horror. They decide to ring the church bells to sound the invasion alarm. Hearing this, Mainwaring and Wilson act quickly to try to put the townsfolk at ease and Pike goes to ring GHQ to tell them of the false alarm but the church bells continue ringing and the men are unable to get into the bell tower to stop them as they have locked themselves in. Mainwaring decides to shoot the lock, making the bell ringers jump, leaving them dangling off the bells high up in the tower.

LINE:

(The platoon has gone into a pub dressed as Nazis, without Mainwaring's permission)
Jones: We shouldn't do this, Sergeant Wilson.
Wilson: Well, what are you going to have?
Jones: A pint.
(Later in the scene...)
Landlord: Good morning, Gentlemen. What can I get...? *(Turns and sees the platoon dressed as Nazis)*
Pike: *(in a German accent)* Gut afternoon, mein host. 16 shandies mit the ginger beer.
Landlord: *(stammering)* Pints or 'alves?
Pike: Pints!

WATCH OUT FOR:

- **The safety harness that are holding up Bill Pertwee, Frank Williams and Edward Sinclair as they dangles from the church bells.**
- **Jack Haig, who was considered for the part of Corporal Jones and went on to star in 'Allo! Allo!' guest stars as the Pub Landlord.**
- **John Bardon, who went on to find fame as the lovable Jim Branning in *Eastenders* makes an**

appearance. He also played Walker in the *Dad's Army* stage show.

BEHIND THE SCENES:

Despite being enlisted as a replacement for the Private Walker character, Mr Cheeseman was not written into the eighth series cast list on purpose by Jimmy Perry and David Croft, but the pair's decision was not a personal one towards Welsh actor Talfryn Thomas. David Croft reflected, 'It had been our mistake. It wasn't Talfryn's fault - he was a good actor - but it had just been wrong to try to bring such a strong character into such a well-established show.'1

The news went down well with one prominent member of the ensemble who had been irked by the actor's intention to steal the same scene he had picked out - and the man was John Laurie. 'John had come up me to complain. He said: "James, can I have a word please? Is yon Welsh fellow going to be in the new series next year?" I said: "I don't know, John." So he said: "Well, make sure he isn't - he's getting far too many laughs!" Totally ruthless pro! But that didn't influence our decision; we just came to the conclusion that the character wasn't quite right.'2

The location filming was completed at All Saint's Church, Honington Suffolk and the Primary School in the same village whilst The Six Bells Public House in Bardwell, Thetford, a frequent stomping ground for the cast and crew when filming the show was added to the programme and even given the honour of keeping its real name in the episode. Ian Lavender also holds the episode in high regard. '*Ring Dem Bells* is my other favourite episode, purely for practical reasons. Wilson and Pike were chosen to play German officers in a training film because the uniforms fitted. So, for five days filming in Norfolk and throughout the studio work, we had comfortable costumes to wear. It was a fun episode.'3

TRIVIA:

The title is taken from a 1930 song by Duke Ellington of the same name. It reached number 17b in the charts in the United States charts, referred to nowadays as the Billboard Hot 100. Ellington was an American composer, big-band leader and pianist, born on 29th April 1899. His orchestrations trended many music genres including classical, gospel, and blues and even scored a number of films. He called his brand of music 'American Music.' He remained a big-band leader until his death in 1974.

SCORE: 9/10

EPISODE SIXTY EIGHT

WHEN YOU'VE GOT TO GO

RECORDED ON 6TH JUNE 1975

FIRST BROADCAST ON 12TH SEPTEMBER 1975

VIEWING FIGURE: 12.6 MILLION

PLOT:

Wilson is having evening tea with Mavis at the Pike residence, waiting for Frank to return with the results of his medical. When he gets home, he announces that he has been passed A1 and has requested to join the RAF, much to his Mother's horror who believes she should have gone along with him as he has what she refers to as 'a chest.' Later, Mainwaring breaks the news to the platoon of Pike's call-up and that he will be leaving in a few weeks...

GUEST CAST:

Janet Davies as Mrs Pike
Bill Pertwee as ARP Warden Hodges
Frank Williams as the Vicar
Edward Sinclair as the Verger
Eric Longworth as Town Clerk
Freddie Earlle as Italian Sergeant
Tim Barrett as Doctor
Colin Bean as Private Sponge
Frankie Holmes as Fishfryer

REVIEW:

There are many great things to say about the episode. First of all, we see a rarc sight in *Dad's Army* - a domestic dinner scene. It's taken nearly 60 episodes since the last one in series two's *Sgt. Wilson's Little Secret* and it's a wonder that we have not seen more into the life of Wilson and Mavis away from the main ensemble because the relationship is such an intriguing one and the chemistry between John Le Mesurier and Janet Davies is great. I think the character of Mrs Pike has improved immensely over the years and here she is still rather overbearing towards her son and understandably so when she hears his news. She is horrified when she hears he has been passed fit for call-up, something so many Mother's with children in the armed forces must feel when they are called into active service. This is also another very good episode for Private Pike, who finds himself at the heart of the narrative. The character of Pike was one of the characters who benefited from the absence of both Walker and Cheeseman and Ian Lavender is in fine form once again, even eclipsing the more seasoned actors with his performance. The facial expression he pulls to display his nervous twitch is very funny and it is made even funnier when Arthur Lowe witnesses him make the face for the very first time. There is a sub-plot involving a chance to test the limits of the rivalry between Mainwaring and Hodges when they decide to wager on how many people they can recruit to give blood. It does not detract from the main narrative but adds to it nicely and allows the viewer to boo and hiss at Bill Pertwee's pantomime villain on a couple of occasions. In conclusion, the series was still kicking bottom and the whole team were still on great form and a real star had emerged in the form of Lavender who once again showed how well he can hold his own. The pay-off at the end does not feel cheap or pinned on and also assures us that, like the men of the Home Guard, Pike will be around for a little while yet.

MEMORABLE MOMENT:

To celebrate the departure of Private Pike, who is off on his way to the RAF, Mainwaring decides to ask Pike to leave the church hall and go into the side office whilst the men discuss what they should do to mark the occasion. Wilson, who knows the boy better than anybody in the room, believes that he would love a Fish and Chip supper. Mainwaring agrees that this would be a good idea and the men decide to keep this a surprise. When Pike is called in he is told that something has been organised but the boy has obviously overheard the conversation and says he loves Fish and Chips!

LINE:

Pike: I got a letter to say I wasn't fit enough to join the army.
Mainwaring: When did you hear this?
Pike: About three days ago.
Mainwaring: Well, why didn't you say anything?
Pike: No one's ever done a meal in my honour before and I didn't want to miss my Fish and Chips, I like Fish and Chips.
Mainwaring: You stupid boy.

WATCH OUT FOR:

- **The facial expression that has become a habit for Pike and Mainwaring's imitation of it.**
- **Mrs Pike method of curing Pike's sinus problems involved him sleeping with a hot water bottle on his face.**

- **Pike decides to help out Mainwaring with the salt shaker but forgets to screw the top on the dispenser and spoils his Captain's tea.**

BEHIND THE SCENES:

Freddie Earlle, who portrayed the Italian Sergeant, reminisced on his performance in the programme.

'Playing Italians is one of my specialities so I enjoyed this one. But I have vivid memories of the first episode I worked on. I turned up for rehearsals and sat down. When John Laurie arrived I said: "Morning, Mr Laurie." He walked past mumbling. Next morning, the same thing.

'So I asked Clive Dunn, an old friend, what was wrong. Clive said: "The problem is you're sitting in his chair, he likes sitting there in the corner doing the crossword." I went up to John and apologised. He turned to me and asked where I was from. After replying "Glasgow", he said: "Oh, a fellow Scotsman, you can sit there if you want."'4

TRIVIA:

Tim Barrett makes a guest appearance as the Doctor but will be more recognisable for his regular appearances in the popular BBC sitcom *Terry and June* where he played the role of Terry Scott's Manager, Malcolm Harris from 1980 to 1983. Barrett was born on 31st May 1929 and made a number of television appearances during his long career. His role as Sir Trafford Leigh-Mallory in the 1989 short series *War and Remembrance* was his last before his death in 1990.

SCORE: 8/10

EPISODE SIXTY NINE

IS THERE STILL HONEY FOR TEA?

RECORDED ON 26TH JUNE 1975
FIRST BROADCAST ON 19TH SEPTEMBER 1975
VIEWING FIGURE: 12.8 MILLION

PLOT:

Mainwaring is informed by the Colonel that Godfrey's cottage is due for demolition as it is in the way of a proposed aerodrome. Mainwaring calls over Jones and Frazer and asks them to break the news to the platoon's most elderly member. They all try and fail in their own unique way, apart from Frazer and when Jones eventually manages to tell Godfrey the news, the pensioner's reaction is far from predictable...

GUEST CAST:

Bill Pertwee as ARP Warden Hodges
Gordon Peters as the man with the door
Robert Raglan as the Colonel
Campbell Singer as Sir Charles McAllister
Joan Cooper as Dolly
Kathleen Saintsbury as Cissy

REVIEW:

With the main cast of characters reduced to just six for the very first time in the shows history this series, in theory there should be more for the actors playing their parts to do. However, perhaps the oldest member had been given less and less to do as time wore on and it meant that poor old Arnold Ridley had slipped further and further into the background – especially since the emergence of Ian Lavender's Private Pike. But in this one, we get more Godfrey than we have had in a while in a pleasant sequel to *The Battle of Godfrey's Cottage.* In fact, that would have been a more apt title here than with the episode it occupies in series two. The episode is an excuse to play physical pranks on the main characters and I for one am a sucker for physical jokes. The great gag regarding Mainwaring and his paper office door is actually a little tedious until Jones completely destroys it by running through it, by which time you are laughing, not at Clive Dunn, but the reaction from Arthur Lowe, whose face is nearly as red as the fake hair dye he has on his back and sides. The other main visual joke occurs right at the very end and is brilliantly funny mainly for the reason that people who normally try to hold themselves in high regard in a dignified situation are blown about severe downwind from an aeroplane. If only for a fake toupee flying off somebody's head then that really would have put the icing on the cake. But for all this tomfoolery one of the more subtle moments of the episode is between Jones and Godfrey. The characters have bickered the whole way through the episode about who should break the and news to the gentle old man and Mainwaring has failed in his task miserably so it is down to the old butcher to try his hand at the difficult subject. As we expect, he makes a royal hash at it and Godfrey inadvertently reveals that he already knows the fate of his quaint home - but now believes Jones will lose his too. It is a fun two-hander between Dunn and Ridley and allows for more Godfrey screen time which is scarce but always welcome. So with normality restored and a highly surprising gag at the very end that quite literally blows the characters away Godfrey's cottage lives to see another bright, sunny wartime day. The show was still pulling the laughs out of the bag this late in the run and it boded well for the final half of the series.

MEMORABLE MOMENT:

The bank is still suffering from the bomb damage it suffered the night of Mainwaring's party (series five's *When Did You Last See Your Money)* but Mainwaring is delighted when his door replacement arrives. He is dismayed, however, to find that the door is nothing but paper. He demands something less flimsy but is refused due to cut backs affected by the war. That morning, the Colonel sets fire to it, Pike gets it wet and when the door will refuse to budge Jones decides to give it the old heave-ho resulting in its total destruction, much to Mainwaring's frustration.

LINE:

Sir Charles: What the hell do you think you're doing ringing me up in the middle of the night?
Frazer: Ah! It's quiet and peaceful... and it's cheaper!

WATCH OUT FOR:

- **When the Colonel sets fire to Mainwaring's paper door Pike puts water in his mouth and spits it on the hole that it's left, hitting his manager on the other side.**
- **Jones' tactile effort in breaking the news to Godfrey that his house is soon to be demolished.**
- **The noisy, windy disruption to the tea party at the end.**

BEHIND THE SCENES:

Doubling for Godfrey's cottage that he shares with his sisters was tough but the production crew eventually found a 500-year-old cottage in East Wretham, Thetford. Jo Austin remembered, 'Finding a suitable property to act as Godfrey's cottage in *Is There Still Honey for Tea?* was an absolute nightmare. The original brief: thatch roof, pink wash walls, quiet lance, beautiful garden, easy to reach of our base, seemed a doddle in Norfolk. Not so.

'After several fruitless searches I was told about the place we eventually used. When I went to check it out I took the designer, Bob Perk, with me as we were getting very close to filming dates. Although the situation was perfect, from the front the place was useless; we trailed round to the back which had a lovely big garden and was more promising. Bob reckoned that with a lot of dressing to cut off the front shape of the house we could do it.

'Later I took David (Croft) to see it - his face when he saw the frontage was a picture of horror - but we hurried him round the back which he passed as OK.'5

TRIVIA:

Pike shares his movie knowledge by referring to the British made 1941 film *Dangerous Moonlight,* starring Anton Walbrook and distributed by RKO Radio British Productions. It was renamed when it was released in the United States as *Suicide Squadron.* The film was a box office hit in the United Kingdom and the song *Warsaw Concerto* which was orchestrated by Roy Douglas. Its mention in the episode was intended as an in-joke from the writers as John Laurie played the British Commander in the film.

SCORE: 7/10

EPISODE SEVENTY

COME IN, YOUR TIME IS UP

RECORDED ON 10TH JULY 1975

FIRST BROADCAST ON 26TH SEPTEMBER 1975

VIEWING FIGURE: 14.6 MILLION

PLOT:

The men set off to camp to test out their new tents but are annoyed when Hodges arrives with the Sea Scouts for the very same reason. Mainwaring believes that the Chief Warden is trying to sabotage their weekend but when he runs out of petrol, he is forced to stay on and camp. Their night under the stars is interrupted by an enemy plane and in the morning the platoon finds three Nazi soldiers in a rubber dingy stranded in the middle of the lake...

GUEST CAST:

Janet Davies as Mrs Pike
Bill Pertwee as ARP Warden Hodges
Frank Williams as the Vicar
Edward Sinclair as the Verger
Harold Bennett as Mr Blewitt
Colin Bean as Private Sponge

REVIEW:

The high standards of series eight slip here as *Come In, Your Time is Up* does little to enthral and seems much more strained and forced than the three previous instalments. But how is this, I hear you say? What could be better than a camping trip for the men and a plot involving three Nazi's stuck in a rubber boat? Well, for a start the Germans that are caught are little more than background characters, extras to the show, who contribute very little to proceedings. What a shame as we have seen how strong performances from actors playing Nazis, standing eye-to-eye against Mainwaring can be (Philip Madoc's turn as the U-Boat Captain in *The Deadly Attachment* instantly springs to mind). But here, they might as well be shop mannequins dressed up in costume floating on a dingy for all the material and involvement they are given. When the action moves to the camp site, we get to see the men going through exercises, a less than flattering position for many of them and Clive Dunn's Jones steals the whole routine. But the introduction of Hodges, the Vicar, the Verger and the sea scouts actually spoils it for me despite the feeling that the writers were trying to add more opportunity for comedy. This must have been filmed on one of the hottest days of the year as the location footage looks beautiful and desirable. It is sad to say that this looks like the moment that Jimmy Perry and David Croft were beginning to wind down with their ideas for *Dad's Army*. The episode feels like it could have done with an additional re-write before going before the camera to make it tighter and less over drawn. Of course this could just be blip on the otherwise high standards we are used to with *Dad's Army* but nonetheless it is far from a shining moment in the show's canon. There are redeeming moments, such as the opening scene in the vicar's garden, but even this feels too long. Bill Pertwee's common 'falling in the water' act does little to raise more than a smirk and there are less laughs on offer than in recent efforts. *Come In, Your Time is Up is* not at all enthralling and gets forgotten among better episodes in the series.

MEMORABLE MOMENT:

Mainwaring is given a rude awakening by the bugle playing sea scout, but when he fully stirs he spots three German soldiers floating in a rubber dingy in the nearby lake. He commandeers the pirate ship that the scouts have brought with them and along with Wilson, Jones, Pike and Hodges who can speak German they set out to bring them in to dry land. They attempt to tie a rope to the dingy but Hodges fall in and they realise that the ship is sinking, much to the delight of the laughing Germans.

LINE:

Jones: See, I put the gas mask on Sir and then I attach this pipe to a little raft that's camouflaged. Then I'd be able to swim under water and breathe through the pipe. When I get near to that German 'dingy' I'll dive underneath it and pierce it with my bayonet Sir and it'll sink!

Mainwaring: What do you think Wilson?

Wilson: I think he'll drown.

WATCH OUT FOR:

- **Wilson's auction-like style of showcasing the new bivouac tents.**
- **The vicar's funny camping attire when he Hodges and the verger bring the seas scouts to the Home Guard's camp site.**
- **Jones' attempt to sink the dingy ends in a rather wet plunge for Hodges.**

BEHIND THE SCENES:

On the day of location filming involving the platoon improving on their fitness at the campsite, Clive Dunn received news that he had been made an OBE by Her Majesty the Queen. It was well known at the time that The Royal Family were fans of the show, with the Queen Mother herself admitting that her favourite episode was the series six instalment *The Royal Train.* The news came as a shock to Dunn and as an annoyance to Arthur Lowe.

Production Assistant Jo Austin remembered, 'Any mishaps during filming had to be reported on a form. We were at Stanford Training Area by the river for *Come In, Your Time is Up,* the episode where the German aircrew were on a lake; the weather was absolutely roasting and we had a troop of sea scouts with Teddy Sinclair as their senior.

'He, of course, had to wear the uniform of shorts and his knees (and those of several of the children) got quite scorched. So I had to continually coat his knees with sun cream - which led to a lot of merriment to all and a very strange report form. In fact the recipient of the form actually asked me if it was a wind-up!6

Visual Effects man Peter Day revealed how the sinking of the German dingy was achieved. 'For the scene in where the Germans are stuck in the middle of a lake in an inflatable raft, we cut a section from the bottom and replaced it with a piece of ply that was well and truly greased. When we wanted it to sink, the wood was pulled out and rushed in at quite a rate.'7

TRIVIA:

Frank Williams, who by this point was well established within the series as the Reverend Timothy Farthing, had previous experience of starring in a sitcom concerning the British Forces as he starred in the ITV comedy series *The Army Game* as Captain T R Pocket from 1958 to 1961. The series, which was based on the National Service Conscription that was compulsory for young, fit men in the United Kingdom in the 1950s and early 1960s, was a forerunner to the very first *Carry On...* film, 1958's *Carry on Sergeant* which shared William Hartnell and Charles Hawtrey in both productions.

SCORE: 4/10

EPISODE SEVENTY ONE

HIGH FINANCE

RECORDED ON 30TH MAY 1975
FIRST BROADCAST ON 3RD OCTOBER 1975
VIEWING FIGURE: 14.3 MILLION

PLOT:

Mainwaring come to the conclusion that Jones is £50 short on the business side of things and Jones tells him that a £50 bill for the orphanage has disappeared from his pocket. Mainwaring decides to track down the missing £50 and puts together a meeting where he discovers that Mrs Pike used the money to pay her rent off to Hodges, who is her landlord...

GUEST CAST:

Bill Pertwee as ARP Warden Hodges
Edward Sinclair as the Verger
Frank Williams as the Vicar
Harold Bennett as Mr Blewitt
Colin Bean as Private Sponge
Natalie Kent as Miss Twelvetrees

REVIEW:

High Finance sees Mainwaring put on his detective hat and investigate the case of Jones' missing £50. This episode sees the members of the Home Guard band together in the name of Corporal Jones and discover a disturbing underbelly of loans and blackmail. That could be the synopsis for a dark prime-time drama so it is weird to see it used in a usually fun and hilarious situation comedy, although we do still have time for those serious moments too in the script. Wilson then goes on to make a lovely, patriotic and sentimental speech regarding Jones' predicament and he admits just how much he loves walking past thc butcher's shop on his daily walk to work. It is this that changes Mainwaring's mind and reminds him that they need to help their friend and comrade out. I reckon that this is the longest speech John Le Mesurier ever had to give in *Dad's Army* and he sells it so well, painting an idealistic painting in our head of the simple joys of everyday life and the familiarities that keep us going.

When the action moves to Jones' shop the laughs become more frequent and this is the best part of the whole episode for me. When the fly paper gets stuck to Mainwaring's bowler hat, Pike cuts it off and leaves Mainwaring with less of a hat than he had walked into the shop with. It is the reaction of Clive Dunn and Arthur Lowe that sells the gag and it is another great visual gag in a surprisingly creative episode. As Mainwaring conducts his investigation, it actually all gets a little bit boring but my interest really perks up when he calls a meeting and we witness ARP Chief Warden Hodges at his most repugnant. During proceedings, we discover that the main culprit is Mrs Pike, who is being bullied by Hodges, her landlord. I love Wilson's reaction to the fact that the horrible greengrocer will only lower the rent if she gives him sexual favours. It is actually a little unnerving and you do feel sorry for Mrs Pike and instantly hate Hodges that little bit more. So by the end of the episode, the gags do tend to dry up as they are sacrificed to round the show off on a slightly underwhelming yet serious feel.

MEMORABLE MOMENT:

Determined to get to the bottom of the mystery that has caused Corporal Jones to go overdrawn, Mainwaring, Wilson and Pike embark on the old man's butcher's shop to check over his account. As they go over the books, Mainwaring somehow manages to get fly paper attached to his hat and it refuses to come off. Pike offers to wet it but Mainwaring is adamant for his hat not to be ruined. All out of other ideas, Pike decides to cut it off and he takes the meat cleaver to it. On quick chop later, he returns the hat to Mainwaring, who when putting on his head, realises that he has machete the peak off.

LINE:

Hodges: *(about lowering Mrs. Pike's rent)* I'll do nothing of the sort. It's my property, and I'll charge what I want for it.
Jones: Oh, no you won't. I shall report you to the Chamber of Commerce, and they'll throw you out on your ear.
Frazer: And, as a member of the chamber of commerce (taps the table), I second that.
Godfrey: And I third it.
Frazer: *(Amid much noise)* You're not a shopkeeper, so shut up.

WATCH OUT FOR:

- **The look on Frazer's face when Miss Twelvetrees calls him a 'kind and religious man.'**
- **The aforementioned Twelvetrees shares the same name as the footman in Perry and Croft's series *You Rang M'Lord?***
- **The reaction from Wilson when Mrs Pike reveals Hodges suggestion in exchange for lowering the housekeeping fees.**

BEHIND THE SCENES:

The scene in which Frazer comments on Jones becoming doomed when Mainwaring announces that he will study the butcher's finances was cut prior to transmission. A much longer scene would have seen further dialogue between Frazer, Godfrey and Jones and later on in the piece another scene was cut down to make the show thirty minutes long when Mainwaring is reviewing the possessions that Jones could sell to recoup the money he has lost.

Hilda Fenemore guest starred during the eighth series run and revealed that she had met the show's main man before she was due to film on the series. 'Just before filming I was at Pinewood doing a film and shared a dinner with Arthur Lowe. I was being made up to play a filthy old landlady, but as lunchtime was approaching the make-up assistant decided just to put the artificial warts on.

'He filled my face with very realistic warts but I forgot they were there when I went to the restaurant. I ended up sitting next to Arthur and when Terry Thomas, who I knew, came over and stared at my face, I remembered I was smothered in warts. Next day on the *Dad's Army* set, Arthur said: "Oh, you're the one with my warts!"'8

TRIVIA:

Pike makes references to the fictional crime character Charlie Chan, a character created by novelist Earl Der Biggers and star of a series of films made throughout the 1930s to the 1950s starring Warner Oland. The film he refers to is *Charlie Chan in London,* which was released in 1934 by 20th Century Fox. Pike believes that Mainwaring's claim to meet the villain to reveal his identity mirrors a piece of the plot in the film. The film itself is only the second earliest film that has not been lost in the American film archives to star Oland as the title character.

SCORE: 7/10

EPISODE SEVENTY TWO

THE FACE ON THE POSTER

RECORDED ON 17TH JULY 1975
FIRST BROADCAST ON 10TH OCTOBER 1975
VIEWING FIGURE: 15.5 MILLION

PLOT:

Wilson is surprised to walk in on Mainwaring writing a confidential report about him. He scoffs at the report but Mainwaring reveals that it could lead to him being made up to Major and the platoon size tripling as soon as he starts a recruitment campaign. When he tells the platoon of his plan, a ballot is drawn up to see who will be chosen to be the face of the poster and Jones wins by a large majority. However, the men find out that there has been a mix-up at the printers and Jones has appeared on a poster labelling him as a wanted man...

GUEST CAST:

Bill Pertwee as ARP Warden Hodges
Edward Sinclair as the Verger
Frank Williams as the Vicar
Harold Bennett as Mr Blewitt
Colin Bean as Private Sponge
Peter Butterworth as Mr Bugden, the Printer
Bill Tasker as Fred
Michael Bevis as Police Sergeant
Gabor Vernon as Polish Army Major

REVIEW:

The Face on the Poster is not a big fanfare moment for *Dad's Army* nor is it a tour de force of laughter and although it succeeds at the beginning in being entertaining and witty it spends too much time padding itself up in the middle and then rushes to the finish line when those final ten minutes should be building to the biggest laughs in the episode. In fact, the joke of Jones being captured and held as a prisoner of war actually ends up being rather sad in my eyes but let's look at what the episode has going for it first. When Jones is chosen to become the face on the recruitment poster, it leads to an enjoyable skit with Mr Blewitt but all the repeated failings in taking the picture does get boring and repetitive after a couple of minutes. It feels as though the scene has been stretched to pad the episode out and it really isn't that funny, apart from the moment when it looks like Pike has misread Mainwaring's wishes for only Jones' head to be used in the picture and it looks like he is taking the butcher off to have his head cut off. It does seem odd to see Peter Butterworth in a *Dad's Army* episode as he is more associated with his memorable appearances in the *Carry On...* films. But his cameo here is still great and although it may not be as funny as it could have been, it is great to see an icon of British comedy turn up in one of the greatest sitcoms ever. If only his appearance was not so fleeting... *The Face on the Poster* is not as funny as the earlier helpings in the eighth series and wastes the comedy talents of one of its guest stars, which is a big shame. By this point, the series is no longer meeting the high standard it once obtained and the final half of this series is certainly not up to scratch with the first three episodes.

MEMORABLE MOMENT:

Unaware that there has been a mix-up at the printers and that his face is now plastered all over the town on a 'Wanted! Prisoner of War' poster, Jones waits outside the Free Polish Club to hand over some eggs to one of the old ladies that he looks after. He spots the poster and recognises his likeness. A Polish Officer comes out of the club and also sees the poster and the man standing next to it. Jones tries to walk away incognito but is stalked by the officer and eventually captured.

LINE:

Frazer: Can ye use a flash?
Mr. Blewitt: I can't get any bulbs.
Frazer: What about flash powder?

Mr. Blewitt: Ah yes, now I tried that once at a wedding and I must say the picture had a lovely quality... but the hall burned down.

WATCH OUT FOR:

- **Mainwaring going through the confidential report with Wilson and labelling him 'almost a friend.'**
- **Jones experiences problems holding still for the six seconds it takes for his image to be captured on camera.**
- **Outside the Free Polish club, Pike misinterprets the sign and thinks that they are giving away free polish.**

BEHIND THE SCENES:

The episode's extensive location footage took the production team to Gorse Industrial Estate in Barnham, Thetford that doubled for the POW camp. Old Bury Road was also used as the Free Polish Club. After transmission selected viewers were selected by the BBC to take part in an Audience Report and here is an extract from official documentation and I believe it makes for interesting viewing for the profile of the programme in 1975...

'In the main, reporting viewers continued to enjoy the hilarious comedy...finding the "crazy" theme of this edition most amusing. A few said they felt they had been "seen it all before", or that they regretted seeing little of Ian Lavender this week.

'The response to the series as a whole was mainly most favourable; several reporting viewers remarking on how it seemed to have retained its original freshness, with perhaps a tendency in this series to focus rather more on individual characters. Though a small group said it had deteriorated somewhat nowadays or appeared to have run out of ideas ("could do with a rest"), the vast majority evidently agreed that it was "first class fun and well acted". In fact, for a sizeable number of fans it seems that "anything these lads do appeals"; always buck me up"; "something I try and stay in for".'9

TRIVIA:

Peter Butterworth, who is remembered as a regular cast member of the *Carry On...* film series, plays Mr Bugden, the printer. During the Second World War he had served as a Lieutenant Commander in the Royal Navy. He spent some of the war as a prisoner after being captured in Holland in 1940 and escaping through a tunnel from Dulag Luft near Frankfurt a year later. After covering 27 miles in three days he was captured again, this time by a member of the Hitler Youth.

SCORE: 6/10

By the end of 1975, Jimmy Perry and David Croft were beginning to think that *Dad's Army* should probably end. They had believed that the show had run its course. The ratings for the series had proved that the viewing public still had an appetite for the programme as the eighth run averaged 13.5 million, although this was slightly down on the previous year's total. It was clear that some of the focus and enthusiasm in the scripts were a little tired by the end of production but the then Controller of BBC1, David Attenborough managed to convince the pair to continue and they set about writing that year's Christmas episode, *My Brother and I.* However, after production on that episode finished, the team took a break and there would be no series the following year...

THE 1975 AND 1976 CHRISTMAS SPECIALS

MAIN CAST:

ARTHUR LOWE - CAPTAIN GEORGE MAINWARING
JOHN LE MESURIER - SERGEANT ARTHUR WILSON
CLIVE DUNN - LANCE CORPORAL JACK JONES
JOHN LAURIE - PRIVATE JAMES FRAZER
ARNOLD RIDLEY - PRIVATE CHARLES GODFREY
IAN LAVENDER - PRIVATE FRANK PIKE

FEATURING THE VOICE OF BUD FLANNIGAN

EPISODE SEVENTY THREE

MY BROTHER AND I

RECORDED ON 23RD AND 24TH MAY 1975
FIRST BROADCAST ON 26TH DECEMBER 1975
VIEWING FIGURE: 13.6 MILLION

PLOT:

Pike has written to Hotspur Magazine retailing a story involving visits to pubs while on patrol. Mainwaring is disgusted and tells his men he does not want to hear anymore about his men drinking. He then declares that he will be hosting a sherry party for local dignitaries and officers. Meanwhile, Frazer is returning to the town by train and meets Barry Mainwaring, his Captain's drunken brother, who turns out to be the black sheep of the family and who is on his way to visit his brother...

GUEST CAST:

Bill Pertwee as ARP Warden Hodges
Edward Sinclair as the Verger
Frank Williams as the Vicar
Arthur Lowe as Barry Mainwaring
Penny Irving as Chambermaid
Arnold Diamond as Major-General Anstruther-Stevens
Colin Bean as Private Sponge

REVIEW:

Despite seeming like a rather odd concept for a Christmas Special, *My Brother and I* is a good opportunity to showcase the acting talents of the programme's main man and for the team to explore a little more than just comedy. Here we see the strained relations of two very different people personified by the same man and as Frazer would say, a chance to 'expose' Captain Mainwaring as somebody other than the man he has shown himself to be in the little town of Walmington-on-Sea. Arthur Lowe's characterization of Barry Mainwaring is like watching a completely different actor at work. His poise, his speech, his whole body shape is totally different to that we have come to know and love. This is his finest hour within the programme make no mistake. His ability to play two polar opposites so convincingly and match them with the right balance of funny lines, touching moments and all -round bravado and make them believable is breathtaking. Just watch the scene when the two brothers are left alone together in the pub room. However, some of the jokes suffer from the same ailment as the latter half of the previous season. They do seem tired. That is only to be expected when it was filmed within the same production block but still, there are moments to savour but not all of them funny. Maybe that is just a testament to Jimmy Perry and David Croft's writing talents and just how well they know their characters and the actors who play them. Lowe's performance as the drunken Barry is the complete opposite of the tee-total and pompous Captain we all know and love and this makes for a fantastic scene when they meet. Overall it is a fun portrait of what made Lowe such a well-loved actor.

MEMORABLE MOMENT:

Just over half way through the episode, we get the scene we have been waiting for. The meeting of the Mainwaring brothers in Barry's room. It soon becomes clear that these are two very different people and their conversation is prickly and cautious - well from Captain Mainwaring anyway. Barry on the other hand is crass, rude and after the watch that rightfully belongs to him. It is obvious that this is the man that George could have been if his life had taken a different turn and the effects are brilliant for the time.

LINE:

Barry: Do you want a drink?
George: No, thank you.
Barry: Please yourself.
George: I should have thought 5.30 in the afternoon was a bit early even for you.
Barry: Po-face! Look at you: rolled umbrella, striped trousers, pot hat! 'Course, you've 'got on', haven't you?
George: I'm the Branch Manager.
Barry: Nice for you. Put your hand in the till when you get a bit short, do you?
George: Don't be ridiculous!

WATCH OUT FOR:

- **Mainwaring by now has become accustomed to Jones' lack of timing when standing to attention.**
- **Sergeant Wilson has a talent for playing the piano and is recruited by the men to play it at the sherry party.**
- **The look on Godfrey's face as Hodges, the vicar and the verger scoffs down the batch of his sister's cucumber sandwiches.**

BEHIND THE SCENES:

For the very first time in the series history, the studio recording day was stretched over two sessions sue to the complex nature of the scene involving Arthur Lowe portraying both George and Barry Mainwaring at the Red Lion hotel. Lowe did his lines as one character and then went off to the dressing room to have his make-up and costume changed in time to play the other to create the illusion that he both characters were in the room together. This was further enhanced by a filming technique called Colour Separation Overlay (CSO) which the production team had used before if the cast were filming an interior shot with moving scenery behind them.

Ian Lavender recalls the making of the episode- and a revelation he had at the time. 'That episode was a real eye-opener for me, because it was just about the conflict between these two characters, Mainwaring and his awful brother, and the setting for it could have been just about anything. I thought: "Ah! Jimmy and David obviously feel, now, that they can write about things that have no reference at all to either the Home Guard or the war." That's when I realised; "Oh, I see - we've really made it. It's made it. This is something rather special."'1

TRIVIA:

The Hotspur was a British magazine for boys that was first published by D.C Thomson & Co, the same company who produce The Beano, on 2nd September 1933. It was instantly popular, selling 350,000 copies of its first issue and ending the year with as one of the company's biggest hitters in the market. At the breakout of war, the magazine's output was rationed to a fortnightly print instead of a weekly edition and by the 1950s it had been re-launched as a comic book. After 1,197 issues and several mergers throughout the 1970s, the magazine's publication ended on 24th January 1981.

SCORE: 6/10

EPISODE SEVENTY FOUR

THE LOVE OF THREE ORANGES

RECORDED ON 10TH DECEMBER 1976

FIRST BROADCAST ON 26TH DECEMBER 1976

VIEWING FIGURE: 13.7 MILLION

PLOT:

At the church hall, the men are trying out the snow camouflage that they have all made of found at home in the event of a snow based invasion. The parade is interrupted by the Vicar and the Verger who inform Mainwaring that there will be as church bazaar for Comforts of the Church Fund. Amongst the ideas that many of the attendees come up with, Hodges reveals that he could auction off three oranges that he has in his possession...

GUEST CAST:

Bill Pertwee as ARP Warden Hodges
Edward Sinclair as the Verger
Frank Williams as the Vicar
Pamela Cundell as Mrs Fox
Janet Davies as Mrs Pike
Olive Mercer as Mrs Yeatman
Joan Cooper as Dolly

Eric Longworth as Claude Gordon, the Town Clerk
Colin Bean as Private Sponge

REVIEW:

The plodding nature of the episode is really rather boring. It also seems as though the character of Pike has regressed somewhat as his maturing personality in the preceding series is now reduced to the 'stupid boy' motive, especially when he insults an overacting Mrs Fox at the benefit meeting. Also, the nature of the plot leads to more time spent in the company of the show's secondary characters, who tend to be hit and miss. Hodges and the Vicar are on fine form here, frustrating Mainwaring but Mr Yeatman is so fusty he comes across as annoying and Edward Sinclair appears to struggle with what little material he is given.
The highlight of the episode is definitely the first scene when the men test their winter camouflage - with hilarious results. Not only do they look ridiculous but when John Laurie hones into view, dressed in an old wedding dress, it is perhaps the only laugh out loud moment of the whole episode. He managed to upstage everybody else in the scene and the image lingers like a bad nightmare for a few minutes after it has passed.
We are given a bit of character development in the progression of Jones and Mrs Fox's relationship, which seems to be at its most stable and stronger than it has ever been on screen. But Jones still faces a little competition for the widow's heart. It is a great moment

when Frazer finds out that he can spend five minutes with her and you can tell what devilish thought are racing through his mind just by looking at his eyes. All in all, this is a rather low-key, un-significant special after a year off and lacks the punch of the shows past glories. The cast are beginning to look their age even more and are doing their best with the material but it is clear that Perry and Croft have their mind on other things by this point. *The Love of the Oranges* is by far the less successful of the two Christmas Specials and really does not justify its extended run time. The premise is not strong enough for a festive edition of the programme and the main scene involving the characters in the church hall drags on far too long and does not have enough in it to keep the viewer interested or laughing.

MEMORABLE MOMENT:

The benefit in the church hall is about to commence and the members of the committee ready themselves for the afternoon. Jones brings out his monster brawn, which Pike slaps to watch it wobble and Godfrey reveals that he and his sister Dolly have come up with a unique idea to allow people to taste the wine before they purchase it (it will never catch on.) Wilson is up first and approaches the sample with all the grace and expertise of a wine connoisseur, much to the frustration and bemusement of Mainwaring.

LINE:

Mainwaring: As chairman, uh, may I just bring the meeting to order and welcome all...

Hodges: Oi! Hold on a minute, hold on...why is it that whenever we have a meeting about anything, you're always the chairman? Who elected you, that's what I want to know?
Mainwaring: It was perfectly above board and legal. I was elected by the steering committee.
Hodges: And who elected the steering committee?
Mainwaring: I did!

WATCH OUT FOR:

- **The men have a varied, imaginative and downright surprising selection of snow camouflage.**
- **Wilson reveals that Pike has sensitive skin, a condition that runs in the family, leading to a quizzical look from Mainwaring.**
- **The state of Jones' brawn when the bike runs through it.**

BEHIND THE SCENES:

This was the first and only episode of *Dad's Army* that was both broadcast and made in 1976 but it was still a very busy year of the cast and crew. Both Jimmy Perry and David Croft had taken a conscience decision to give the how a rest as they concentrated on other projects as another series the pair wrote *It Ain't Half Hot Mum* and the Croft/Jeremy Lloyd series *Are You Being Served* had both entered production on their fourth series while the writers attempts to launch the show in America failed with just one pilot, mostly based on the series six classic *The Deadly Attachment* being made by ABC under the show title of *The Rear Guard.* Despite this commercial failure, the BBC had also agreed that it would be a good thing for the programme if it were to take a rest as both members of the cast and the writers especially, had grown weary of its demands. 'Success...demands a self-discipline by television companies. Somebody coined the phrase...that one was obliged to exert 'management of creativity.' The temptations of a hit show are to flog it into the ground... [but the BBC's] policy is to try to sustain the series. This entails a form of rationing so that the standards of production can be maintained over as long a period as possible. Showbusiness *is* a business. There is no reason why a series should not last as long as 10 years if its exposure is handled in the right way.'2 Explained the BBC producer and executive and current Head of Light Entertainment, Bill Cotton.

The cast had also been busy during the hiatus. To add to their separate projects, the team also went on a tour of the English theatres from 4th September 1975 to the same day a year later, taking in such venues as The Shaftesbury Theatre, the Birmingham Hippodrome and the Theatre Royal in Bath along the way. It was while on this tour that Private Godfrey actor celebrated his 80th birthday.

TRIVIA:

There seems to be some confusion over the dating of the episode when Mainwaring mentions 'our Finnish allies.' Despite being set in 1942, the year the Home Guard disbanded, Mainwaring mentions that Great Britain is still allying itself with Finland when in fact the Finns effectively ended the alliance on 25th June 1941 when the country invaded the USSR and aligned itself with the German forces that the Brits were fighting.

SCORE: 5/10

With just two shows in the space of a year, the viewing figures held strong at 13.6 and 13.7 million respectively, suggesting that although the programme had been a mainstay on British television screens for eight years, there was still life in the show yet. However, the clock was ticking for some of the members of the cast who were beginning to feel their age. It was clear that mother time was catching up on the team and both Jimmy Perry and David Croft decided that the next series, that was to commence filming a few months into 1977, was to be *Dad's Army's* last. Much to the shock of the cast and crew, a vital member of the team was to be stuck down with illness before filming, threatening a repeat of James Beck's death a few year earlier. For a while, it was unclear whether *Dad's Army,* despite going into its last year, would survive another tragedy before the end...

SERIES NINE

MAIN CAST:

ARTHUR LOWE - CAPTAIN GEORGE MAINWARING
JOHN LE MESURIER - SERGEANT ARTHUR WILSON
CLIVE DUNN - LANCE CORPORAL JACK JONES
JOHN LAURIE - PRIVATE JAMES FRAZER
ARNOLD RIDLEY - PRIVATE CHARLES GODFREY
IAN LAVENDER - PRIVATE FRANK PIKE

FEATURING THE VOICE OF BUD FLANNIGAN

EPISODE SEVENTY FIVE

WAKE-UP WALMINGTON

RECORDED ON 8TH JULY 1977
FIRST BROADCAST ON 2ND OCTOBER 1977
VIEWING FIGURE: 10.2 MILLION

PLOT:

The men are practising on a firing range at the town's manor house when His Lordship's butler Perkins inadvertently makes Captain Mainwaring lose a shooting bet by demanding that they stop their target practice while his master is asleep. Captain Mainwaring is annoyed and later agrees with Hodges that there is lack of respect to their war effort in the town. To improve the situation, Mainwaring agrees to simulate a fifth column attack. The Colonel hears of the plans and somewhat reluctantly allows "Operation Wake-Up" to go ahead...

GUEST CAST:

Bill Pertwee as ARP Warden Hodges
Frank Williams as the Vicar
Edward Sinclair as the Verger
Geoffrey Lumsden as Captain Square
Sam Kydd as the Yokel
Harold Bennett as Mr. Blewitt
Robert Raglan as the Colonel
Charles Hill as the Butler
Jeffrey Holland as the Soldier
Barry Linehan as the Van Driver
Colin Bean as Private Sponge
Alister Williamson as Bert
Michael Stainton as Frenchy

REVIEW:

Wake-Up Walmington does little to stir the belly laughs in this, a disappointing loose sequel to the much better series opener from the series 8, *Ring Dem Bells.* All of the key components to what make a successful, long lasting *Dad's Army* episode funny, its dialogue, the cast's sense of timing and a stand-out performance to take the production up a notch is sadly missing here, and it does not help that Sergeant Wilson looks so gaunt. It is almost uncomfortable to watch John Le Mesurier here as he looks so ill. You can really tell in the studio that the actor was not at his best and it almost feels cruel to watch him. I'm surprised that the series was not suspended until he was better. Sure studio days must have already been booked and of course then you have other people's commitments could have potentially conflicted.

The Mainwaring/Hodges truce is a good plot device if not a weird one. Why would Mainwaring put his bitter differences aside for once to let rotten Hodges in on his gang on this occasion? If you had somebody who was THAT reviled within your group, would you let them spend time with you and take part in a plan just because he breaks into tears after an old man did a silly impression of him? So in conclusion, *Wake-Up Walmington* is far from spectacular and is let down by the condition of its main actors, which is sad as if this had been made in the programme's hay-day it would have been tighter and funnier.

MEMORABLE MOMENT:

The platoon - plus there temporary recruit Hodges, are walking through the country roads to Walmington to commence 'Operation Wake-Up' dressed as desperados and cut throats. They come across men who are dressed identically to Mainwaring and Hodge's costumes, leading to a confrontation between the two factions and an argument over who should present their papers to prove the credibility of the platoon and the three hard men.

LINE:

Mainwaring; When he *[Godfrey]* comes back, give him this message. 'Operation, wake-up, roger' and tell him to ring Walmington 633 at once, it's very urgent.
Verger: Yes, I got it, 633.
(The Verger hangs up and Godfrey enters the room)
Verger: Captain Mainwaring's just been on the phone for you, he left a message. Someone named Roger, he's just gonna have an operation, you got to ring that number at once! It must be the hospital! Could be appendicitis, it comes on very quick you know!
(Godfrey telephones 633, Mainwaring answers)
Godfrey: Is that the hospital?
Mainwaring: What? Is that you Godfrey?
Godfrey: How's Roger, is he going to be all right?
Mainwaring: What are you babbling about?
Godfrey: I just had a message that Roger had been taken ill with appendicitis and had to have an operation.

WATCH OUT FOR:

- **Geoffrey Lumsden's final appearance as Captain Square in the series.**
- **The location of Walmington-on-Sea is situated twenty miles away from Dover.**
- **The cast regulars dressed as gangsters and nuns for 'Operation Wake-up.'**

BEHIND THE SCENES:

Location footage was captured at Blackrabbit Warren at Stanford Training Area with the cast on the firing range while further shoots were also carried out Ixworth House, Ixworth in Suffolk, which doubled for the flour mill and the Six Bells pub was also used for the second series in a row whilst Lynford Hall near Mundford in Thetford was also used for the big hall.

The last series was almost marred by the risk of losing yet another member of the cast as in early 1977 John Le Mesurier had been taken seriously ill in Australia whilst rehearsing for a play. His wife, Joan, recalls meeting him at Heathrow Airport and she was shocked by his appearance. 'He was in a wheelchair looking desperately ill. He seemed to have aged ten years in the few weeks he had been away and I was hard pressed to hold back the tears. He was out of danger, but so weak he could hardly walk unaided. He was as thin as a stick, and his eyes were great sunken hollows in his craggy face. People who came to visit were shocked at his appearance.'1

Le Mesurier was taken to a hospital near his home in Ramsgate and diagnosed with cirrhosis of the liver. He was put on a strict diet on raw vegetables and fruit and his condition began to improve, but when the team got back together to commence location filming in June of that year, David Croft could not believe how ill his friend and colleague still looked.

'He was pathetic, he looked so ill. I remember one day in particular, when the weather had turned rather cold, being so concerned about him that I ordered all the lights to be arranged around him in a sort of six-foot square area and then turning them all on to warm him up a bit. He was in such a bad way. It was very hard, very sad. And when we went on to do the last episode in the studio and I remember thinking, "Well, that's the last we shall see of John Le Mesurier."'2

TRIVIA:

Despite appearing in every series since the first in 1968, Geoffrey Lumsden only appeared in eight episodes of *Dad's Army.* Although his performance in *Wake-Up Walmington* would be his last, he went on to appear in the 1978 TV mini-series *Edward and Mrs Simpson* as Sir Lewis Gurney and also made an appearance in a 1981 episode of the drama *Bergerac.* He continued to make further television and theatre appearances up to his death on 4TH March 1984 aged 69.

SCORE: 4/10

EPISODE SEVENTY SIX

THE MAKING OF PRIVATE PIKE

RECORDED ON 1ST JULY 1977
FIRST BROADCAST ON 9TH OCTOBER 1977
VIEWING FIGURE: 10.3 MILLION

PLOT:

Captain Mainwaring accepts an invitation to act as an umpire for manoeuvre exercises when he discovers quickly that a perk of the job comes in the form of a non-assigned staff car. The car spells trouble for Pike, who after expressing his enthusiasm to be allowed in it as runner, is convinced by Hodges's flirtatious niece Sylvia to take her in the car to the pictures leaving him in a difficult situation with the platoon...

GUEST CAST:

Bill Pertwee as ARP Warden Hodges
Frank Williams as the Vicar
Edward Sinclair as the Verger
Jean Gilpin as Sylvia
Anthony Sharp as the Colonel
Jeffrey Segal as the Brigadier
Pamela Cundell as Mrs Fox
Janet Davies as Mrs Pike
Melita Manger as Nora

REVIEW:

It took far too long for Ian Lavender to have the chance to really cement his place in the Dad's Army line-up and with the show in its final series, he delivers a superior and ultimately impressive performance to take *The Making of Private Pike* better than it probably should be. The plot is a good one from Perry and Croft and delivers more laughs than their previous attempt but the studio-bound segments and the moments away from Pike and Sylvia tend to drag their heels. Lavender is the star performer and as Pike, he continues to get his own back on the many times his Captain has called him a 'stupid boy' by repeatedly pulling him out of the car like a portly rag doll and then slams the car door on his elbow. I like that by this time, Pike has become a more significant person in the Walmington-on-Sea Home Guard and how strong and integral his character now is to the whole programme. Arguably, he is now the best and most interesting character in the show by this point. *The Making of Private Pike* does not such 'maketh the man' but cement the innocence and naivety of the youngest member of the platoon. It is hardly surprising that as Ian Lavender matured and grew in confidence as an actor that he became more central to the script. I bemoaned the fact that he was not given his moment back in the black and white days of the first two series but he really bloomed among the great pillars of talent in the cast alongside Arthur Lowe, John Le Mesurier, and John Laurie et al. It is his performance that makes this episode interesting, that's for sure and in the hands of another actor, Frank Pike would never have been so brilliantly realised and likeable. Viva le Stupid Boy!

MEMORABLE MOMENT:

The best and funniest moment of the whole episode is the touching final scene when Wilson and Pike have an almost father to son conversation in the car about his behaviour with Sylvia. Wilson is honest and upfront with Pike, who is exasperated at how nobody will buy his pleas of innocent behaviour but Wilson is apologetic for not being the father figure he should be and tells the boy that both he and Sylvia should not be ashamed of what they did when the car broke down.

Pike retorts 'I was pushing, she was steering!' It's a lovely moment, made all the better by John Le Mesurier's gentle delivery and Ian Lavender's strong performance.

LINE:

Pike: Did you have staff cars in the Sudan, Mr Jones?
Jones: No, nothing like that in those days. We had a staff camel once. It was very good in the desert, but it didn't have a horn and windscreen wipers, or anything like that.

WATCH OUT FOR:

- **When introduced to Sylvia, Jones gets confused and tells Wilson he is delighted to meet him!**
- **Godfrey wears slippers instead of marching boots when on parade.**
- **Pike's over enthusiasm with his role as runner in the car leads to embarrassment and pain for Mainwaring.**

BEHIND THE SCENES:

Actress Jean Gilpin recalled her memories on working on the programme. 'At the time I was cast as Sylvia I couldn't drive, and of course, the episode involves the character driving Pikey to the pictures at Eastgate. At the end of my interview with David Croft, he said: "You're too intelligent for this role and you don't drive, but if I don't find anybody more suitable I'll cast you." I went away thinking that was the end of that, but then I got a call from my agent saying I'd better learn how to drive quickly because he was offering me the role.

'I immediately took some lessons but didn't have time to take my test before we went off to film some of my scenes on location; private land was used for the driving scenes, which meant it didn't matter that I hadn't passed my test. Ian Lavender was extremely apprehensive about being driven by me and I was equally nervous about driving!

'It was a wonderful experience doing *Dad's Army* because it was not the kind of role that I tended to get at that point in my career. I was usually offered more offbeat characters, so I was grateful to David for his willingness to take a chance and offer me something different. It was enormous fun working with those lovely men, and was the first time I'd gone to the BBC to rehearse and no one wore jeans.

'It was one of my more memorable jobs because of the wonderful characters I worked with. They were mostly experiences, distinguished character actors, and it was a rare opportunity to work with such people at the end of a special and successful series.'3

TRIVIA:

1977 was a busy year in television for Jean Gilpin who also appeared in other distinguished programmes within the BBC such as *Z-Cars* and *Survivors.* The following year she also took the role of Debra in the ITV hit series *The Professionals.* In recent years she has become a voice actor, appearing in such animated productions as *Max Steel* and has also lent her tones to Hollywood in films such as *Garfield 2* and the Twentieth Century Fox production *Rio* in 2011.

SCORE: 6/10

EPISODE SEVENTY SEVEN

KNIGHTS OF MADNESS

RECORDED ON 22ND JULY 1977
FIRST BROADCAST ON 16TH OCTOBER 1977
VIEWING FIGURE: 10 MILLION

PLOT:

The council are organising events for St Georges Day and both the Home Guard and the ARP will both be involved but neither Mainwaring nor Hodges want to reveal their roles in the proceedings. Mainwaring later reveals that the platoon will mirror the country's fight against Hitler by taking on a dragon, with the Captain as St George. However, when the men rehearse the battle, Mainwaring experiences problems...

GUEST CAST:

Bill Pertwee as ARP Warden Hodges
Frank Williams as the Vicar
Edward Sinclair as the Verger
Colin Bean as Private Sponge
Janet Davies as Mrs Pike

Olive Mercer as Mrs. Yeatman
Eric Longworth as the Town Clerk
Fred McNaughton as the Mayor

REVIEW:

One of the main comparisons with *Dad's Army* and real life is that sometimes adults behave like little children. They can bicker, argue, talk back, put down, ridicule and more often than not, compete with each other for supremacy. These are the main ingredients that go into the relationship between up-tight and pompous Captain Mainwaring and the rude and abrupt ARP Warden Hodges. Both characters had never been displayed as raw and childlike anything like what the way they are written in *Knights of Madness.* In the middle of a tepid and less than funny committee scene, which looks as though it has replaced the familiar line-up scene, Mainwaring is knocked off his perch by not being granted the chance to chair the committee like he had done so many times before. To regain his pride, he declines to reveal the involvement that the Home Guard will play in the proceedings just so he can prevent Hodges from finding out and sabotaging it. The majority of the cast are well beyond their peak here and it shows in come laboured, tired performances. There's much in this script, like a few episodes previously, that would have been more invigorated if it had been written a few years before, when the series was extended to a 14-episode run and when the cast were younger and fitter and the brilliant James Beck was still around. But alas, all these things have gone and the cast struggle on. *Knights of Madness* could be so much more. It has the potential to be one of the funniest and memorable editions of *Dad's Army* but it is let down in its overall presentation and pacing of the scenes. The team really do look tired and if it was not for the sight of Ian Lavender's legs and the clash between Mainwaring and Hodges in the end, the laughs would also be largely inconsequential. The dragon prop is fun and Arthur Lowe manages to squeeze the amusement out of the script. But it is clear that the potential of the script is not fully realised and at the halfway point of the last series, *Dad's Army* was running out of steam.

MEMORABLE MOMENT:

After resigning to the fact that the heavy armour will not work for him, and a couple of high falls from horses and ropes confirm this, Mainwaring decides to wear a knitted set of armour courtesy of Private Godfrey's sister. But since he decided to withhold the Home Guard's presentation at the event has meant that Hodges has had exactly the same idea as his bitter rival. This leads to a stand-off between Captain and Chief ARP Warden. The two factions of men acting as the dragon end up battering each other and the two figure heads take each other on in a sword fight!

LINE:

Mainwaring: A man in my position can't be seen fighting a dragon in cardboard armour!

WATCH OUT FOR:

- **Olive Mercer is wearing an eye patch over her left eye as the actress' health had deteriorated by this point.**
- **Pike trying to guess what Mainwaring is trying to build as he overhears his manager's telephone call requesting for a 12 foot tail and 22 legs!**
- **The dragon costume has Nazi swastikas drawn all over it to represent the fight against Hitler.**

BEHIND THE SCENES:

The location footage was completed during the cast and crew's annual stay in and around Thetford and Suffolk in June 1977 at Sapiston Church in Suffolk for the scenes outside Walmington Church and the green in which the battle for the St George parade takes place. Bill Pertwee recalled how much he enjoyed filming in Thetford and the legacy of *Dad's Army*. 'I'll always remember the early morning coach trip from the hotel to where we filmed the battle scenes. It was only three or four miles and the countryside was beautiful. The weather was always good. We had nothing but sunshine for our filming; in all the years we went there, we only had three days of rain and one day of snow.

It's extraordinary, I've been to places all over the British Isles and people will come up and talk to me about *Dad's Army*. I was in a small Scottish village once and I visited the only shop to buy a postcard. As I went out, this lady followed me. She said: "Oh, I've got to talk to you. You're from *Dad's Army*, I can't believe it - what are you doing here?" By the time I'd finished speaking to her a crowd of villagers had gathered round.'4

TRIVIA:

Olive Mercer graduated from RADA but in 1931 left acting to devote herself to family life. She eventually returned to acting during the 1950s and was a member of the Watford rep that included series creator and writer Jimmy Perry. She made various appearances as Mrs Yeatman throughout the series and appeared in an additional three roles in the programme during series three. She also made appearances in such ground-breaking programmes as *Monty Python's Flying Circus, The Forsyte Saga* and *Emergency Ward 10.* When she was 70 she contacted shingles and her health continued to decline until her death in 1983.

SCORE: 5/10

EPISODE SEVENTY EIGHT

THE MISER'S HOARD

RECORDED ON 24TH JUNE 1977

FIRST BROADCAST ON 23RD OCTOBER 1977

VIEWING FIGURE: 11.1 MILLION

PLOT:

Mainwaring is informed by Doctor McCeavedy - who signs off the deaths for Frazer at the undertakers - that he has accidentally discovered his life savings in the form of hundreds of gold sovereigns and implores Mainwaring to persuade the Scot to put the fortune in a savings account. Soon, a rumour spreads regarding Frazer's wealth and it inspires many of the townsfolk to appeal to Frazer in vain for generosity financially but unfortunately he does not relent...

GUEST CAST:

Bill Pertwee as ARP Warden Hodges
Frank Williams as the Vicar
Edward Sinclair as the Verger
Colin Bean as Private Sponge
Fulton Mackay as Doctor McCeavedy

REVIEW:

The Miser's Hoard is a definite improvement on the quality of the series thus far but it still fails to hit the same high notes of earlier episodes. That does not mean, however that it is not a highly entertaining episode and it allows Jimmy Perry and David Croft the last chance for an episode to focus on one of the best characters in the series and the final opportunity for John Laurie to snatch the limelight and act the rest of his peers off the screen and back into acting school. John Laurie was arguably the greatest actor to have never played Ebenezer Scrooge on screen. This is the closest he ever got to that role. Just look at the scene when he is standing in the dark, cold and unwelcoming undertaker's parlour, working by candlelight like a man of the Victorian era. So, *The Miser's Hoard* might not be a spectacular episode in any way but there are delightful moments that remind you just how funny this show was. The scene in which Jones attempts to give a lecture on how to apply respirators is brilliant as is the moment that Wilson staggers in from his impromptu pub crawl well and truly incapacitated - allowing his true personality to come out and make a mockery of Mainwaring's command - leading to an expression from Arthur Lowe that is funnier and more sincere than any line of dialogue ever could be. However, the series was looking more and more fatigued as the finish line drew closer. While the acting side of things are quite natural by this stage which explains away the odd slip up from time to time as these characters were getting older too and they were still unmistakably the characters we all know and love. But the writing is, in my humble opinion, the flawed piece in this worn-out jigsaw. It still has not picked up from the slump that began halfway through the eighth series.

MEMORABLE MOMENT:

When Frazer does not show up for parade, Mainwaring is worried as this is not something he has ever done before so he sends his men out to go look for him, After failing to obtain him on the telephone at his house, Wilson and Pike stumble into the side office. They have been searching the pubs of the town and it is obvious that Wilson has had more than his fair share of drinks. Pike goes on to lecture him on what his Mother would say and remarks that they even went to the cafe where they had a black coffee - not that it helped sober his Uncle up!

LINE:

(Frazer reads out loud a letter he's written to one of his funeral customers).

Frazer: Dear Mrs. Pickering. I hope you found the funeral arrangements for your late husband entirely satisfactory. May I say how sorry I was that the hearse ran out of petrol just outside the cemetery. I'm sure your dearly departed husband would have been proud of the way you helped to push him to his final resting place and what a fine strong women your mother is. I hope you managed to get the mud off her skirt.

WATCH OUT FOR:

- **Fulton Mackay makes his second appearance in the series, this time as Dr McCeavedy.**
- **Godfrey corrects Jones on not using the correct term for the gas masks...I mean, err...respirators. It is a remark that was also made in the first series by Mainwaring.**
- **When Frazer goes missing, Wilson and Pike report back to Mainwaring, with the former a little worse for wear after visiting several pubs...**

BEHIND THE SCENES:

Colin Bean, who had played back-row regular Private Sponge in more episodes than any other extra, was rewarded with a more prominent position in the platoon towards the end of the series. 'By the time of *The Miser's Hoard* I'd ended up on the front row of the platoon, it was a lovely feeling. Instead of peering and smirking over Jones' shoulder, I was on the front line. It was very satisfying.'5

TRIVIA:

The film that Pike mentions *Miser's Gold* when he explains his idea that Frazer might have buried his loot, was made circa 1911 and was directed by David Alyott. Not a lot of information is known about this film as it is no longer in existence but according to the *British Film Institute's (BFI)* website it was made by the production company Pathe Frères and it was a French silent production. The film is so obscure that not even a cast roll call exists and it remains elusive to this day.

SCORE: 4/10

EPISODE SEVENTY NINE

NUMBER ENGAGED

RECORDED ON 15TH JULY 1977

FIRST BROADCAST ON 6TH NOVEMBER 1977

VIEWING FIGURE: 9.6 MILLION

PLOT:

Mainwaring reveals to his men on parade that they have been placed in charge of guarding a one-mile stretch of telephone wires that hold a great deal of importance in the war effort. When they head to the site, they camp over night during an air raid and Pike overcooks the volume of porridge for the men. Later in the morning, the Vicar holds a communion service for the men and they realise that an unexploded bomb had got caught in the telephone wires...

GUEST CAST:

Bill Pertwee as ARP Warden Hodges
Frank Williams as the Vicar
Edward Sinclair as the Verger
Colin Bean as Private Sponge
Ronnie Brody as the GPO Man
Robert Mill as the Army Captain
Kenneth MacDonald as the Army Sergeant
Felix Bowness as the Van Driver
Stuart McGugan as the Scottish Sergeant
Bernice Adams as the ATS Girl

REVIEW:

Number Engaged is a slight improvement on its predecessors, but not by much. However, that is not to say that it is without its moments of greatness. It's the simple things that win me over in this one, like Pike messing up the water to oats ratio of the porridge the men eat on camp and inadvertently saving the day as a consequence and his two-handed scene with Corporal Jones and they discuss the (not so subtle) rumours behind General Kitchener's sexuality. Arthur Lowe is also still on hand to supply some slapstick moments and John Le Mesurier's clever wit and dry retorts to his overbearing Captain are still in place. With this being the penultimate *Dad's Army* episode, you would expect some build up towards the grand finale in today's world of television. But back then, TV shows were plotted in a completely different way and sadly, this is all rather irrelevant and would have given nothing away to the viewer back in 1977 about what to expect the following week. Still, this does at least allow the cast and crew to have a lot of fun for the very last time as things get a bit sad after this one. While *Number Engaged* is not quite a romp, it does display the trademark slapstick moments of a *Dad's Army* episode. Mainwaring emerging from a platoon scrum with his hat and glasses on the wonk does have an alluring charm to it but it's the reliability on tried and tested jokes. It is without doubt that John Le Mesurier's illness had a detrimental influence on the making of the series as a whole but there is also a simple case of momentum and personal distraction from the men behind the screen that adds to that dip in quality that had been prevalent throughout the ninth series. At least in the last episode, viewers would see *Dad's Army* make a final, glorious return to form...

MEMORABLE MOMENT:

When Hodges, the Vicar and the Verger arrive at the camp site, they proceed to give a service for the Home Guard. As the Vicar urges the men to look up to the skies in prayer, the platoon can't believe their eyes. There is bomb lodged in the all-important telephone wires that the men are supposed to be protecting. Panic ensues and Mainwaring enlists himself as the man to shimmy up the pole to get the bomb down. However, when he puts on the safety harness, he somehow manages to tear his trouser leg, much to the fury of the ARP Warden.

LINE:

Vicar: Let us give thought to those things above that control our destiny. Let us raise our faces to heaven and give thanks.
Mainwaring: *(Looking up)* Good Lord!
Vicar: He is indeed, Captain Mainwaring.
Verger: *(Looking up)* Heaven's above!
Vicar: I'll do the praying, Mr Yeatman.
Jones: There's a bomb in the wire, don't panic, there's a bomb in the wire!

WATCH OUT FOR:

- **Kenneth MacDonald, who also starred as a regular in *Only Fools and Horses* and *It Ain't Half Hot Mum!* appears as an Army Sergeant.**
- **Captain Mainwaring reveals that he does not like corned beef.**
- **Mainwaring's top bunk has a hole in it and he begins to sink in his sleep!**

BEHIND THE SCENES:

Ian Lavender remembered that everything went to plan on location for the episode. 'A stunt went wrong during

Number Engaged. A small bomb had got lodged in the telephone wires, so the platoon commandeered a furniture van and built a tower with all the furniture. A rigid structure, it was built to fall back onto the hay and manure strategically positioned.

'Although I pleaded with David Croft to let me do the stunt, he refused. Just as well because it was filmed with a stuntman, the tower collapsed and he ended up in hospital. David turned to me afterwards with this lovely wide smile, and said: "Fancy doing it now?"'6

For the scene in question, the team filmed at Blackrabbit Warren at the frequent destination for the *Dad's Army* team, Stanford Training Ground. Some of the sequences of Jones trying to dislodge the bomb were acted out by Clive Dunn, himself.

TRIVIA:

Actor Ronald Brody makes an appearance as the GPO man but he also appeared in many other films and TV programmes besides his three episode stint in *Dad's Army.* He also appeared frequently with Eric Sykes and John Le Mesurier's former wife Hattie Jacques in the sitcom *Sykes* and also enjoyed an appearance in the 1983 superhero movie, *Superman III.* In his later years he continued to make appearances in sketch shows such as *The Lenny Henry Show* before he passed away in 1991, aged 72.

SCORE: 4/10

EPISODE EIGHTY
NEVER TOO OLD
RECORDED ON 29TH JULY 1977
FIRST BROADCAST ON 13TH NOVEMBER 1977
VIEWING FIGURE: 12.5 MILLION

PLOT:

Godfrey awaits the men to arrive back from a march and he is met by Mrs Fox, who tells him that she wants to put Jones 'out of his misery.' When they get back, Jones reveals that he has proposed to her as he declares his undying love for the widow. After a few nail biting moments she rings the hall to tell him that her answer is 'yes.' The preparations for the wedding go ahead and the newlyweds enjoy a delightful wedding but the reception is cut short as Walmington-on-Sea is put on invasion alert...

GUEST CAST:

Bill Pertwee as ARP Warden Hodges
Frank Williams as the Vicar
Edward Sinclair as the Verger
Colin Bean as Private Sponge
Pamela Cundell as Mrs Fox
Janet Davies as Mrs Pike
Joan Cooper as Dolly
Robert Raglan as the Colonel

REVIEW:

We'll meet again. Don't know where, don't know when. After forty-eight hours and ten minutes of television, *Dad's Army* hung up its tin hat and called it a day. The legs had been getting ropey and the wheels have tried to keep rolling in the face of adversity surrounding production but father time had called last orders on one of the greatest comedy series the BBC ever produced. Under the studio lights of Television Centre, we said farewell to Mainwaring, Wilson, Jones, Frazer, Godfrey, Pike and all the rest of the cast. Like the old soldiers that they were, the team had managed to nurse themselves through one final run and come out smiling at the end. Arnold Ridley, now into his eighties, had suffered with mobility problems as Arthur Lowe's narcolepsy had worsened and John Le Mesurier, although he had begun to look slowly better as each episode went along, was still suffering with cirrhosis. Even John Laurie had been hampered with emphysema in recent times and although he does not show it on screen was also suffering as much as his colleagues. So although they might not be as quick and sharp as they had been, they all click back together here and pull the whole script by the scruff of its neck and collectively say 'We'll make sure we go out with a bang!' And they do, because *Never Too Old* is arguably the best post-Walker episode of them all. It carries an awful lot of melancholy and inevitability with it and you do get the sense that even if the cast could and would have liked to have carried on, this was the appropriate stopping point for the series. Of course, its main plot consists of the union between Jones and Mrs Fox and as soon as they are given a guard of honour in the church hall, the dynamic of the gang is changed forever and we realise that we are losing not just one friend but a whole host of them. But despite its poignancy, there are many great moments of comedy still to remember. Overall, this is a fitting end to the series which ties up all the loose ends and marries off Jones in a convincing and touching way with his relationship with the flirtatious Mrs Fox. The cast really pull it out of the bag one last time and the script services them well as it looks like Jimmy Perry and David Croft had been saving the best of this series to the very last. It is sad not to see James Beck involved in some way as his absence is felt, what better excuse to get the whole gang together for their grand finale. A fitting end to a brilliant programme.

MEMORABLE MOMENT:

With Walmington-on-Sea on invasion alert, Jones has to make do with a very different wedding night to the one he expected. As he and Mrs Fox, now Jones, spend some time together, Mainwaring, Wilson, Frazer and Godfrey join Pike on the pier. Hodges also arrives and berates the old guard and ridicules their chances against Hitler's charges. Jones joins them and they all dismiss Hodge's jibes and declare that they are ready for whatever the Nazis can throw at them. Wilson proposes a toast to those in a similar situation as them and the platoon raise their mess tins in a salute to 'Britain's Home Guard.'

LINE:

Pike: Warden wasn't right was he, when he said the Nazi's would walk straight through us?
Mainwaring: Of course he wasn't right!
Jones: I know one thing; they're not walking straight through me!
Frazer: Nor me. I'll be beside you Jonesey.
Mainwaring: We'll all be beside you Jonesey. We'll stick together, you can rely on that. If anybody tries to take our homes and freedom away from us, they'll find out what we can do. We'll fight. And we're not alone; there are thousands of us all over England.
Frazer: And Scotland!
Mainwaring: And Scotland. All over Great Britain in fact. Men who'll stand together when their country needs them.
Wilson: 'scuse me sir, don't think it'd be a nice idea if we were to pay our tribute to them.
Mainwaring: For once, Wilson, I agree with you. (Raises cup) to Britain's Home Guard!
Jones, Mainwaring, Pike, Wilson, Godfrey and Frazer: (raising cups and looking towards the camera) To Britain's Home Guard!

WATCH OUT FOR:

- **Mainwaring's awkwardness and subsequent embarrassment as he waits in Mrs Fox's house while she gets changed, and stuffs her stray bra in his hat to erase suspicion!**
- **Corporal Jones and Mrs Fox's wedding cake being less spectacular than originally expected!**

- **ARP Chief Warden Hodges and the verger's impromptu confetti fight at the wedding reception.**

BEHIND THE SCENES:

One of the funniest visual gags of the episode happened quite by accident as Pamela Cundell remembers. 'There's a scene where Mainwaring, who gives Mrs Fox away, gets stuck between the wall and a pillar when he walks through with Mrs Fox. Well, that wasn't planned. It was during rehearsals that this happened; Arthur thought it very funny and suggested not saying anything to anybody and doing it for the recording. The scene worked well.'7

Susie Belbin joined the team for the final seven episodes of the series and remembered how difficult it was to get through the final studio day. 'Working on the final episode, *Never Too Old,* was extremely emotional, and on the actual recording day, it suddenly dawned on me that this really was the last one. David (Croft) played it for everything it had, and it was so moving. I found myself sobbing at the side of the set, and thought: "This is ridiculous, I'll have to leave the studio otherwise I'm going to interfere with the recording, blubbing away in the corner." So I went and watched the very last scene from the make-up room. 'There's a huge elation when you've recorded a programme that has gone well, but with *Dad's Army* a lot of people were sub-dued or over happy, covering up the sadness. It was a very touching time.'8

The episode intentionally went out on Remembrance Sunday on its original transmission and the scene in which Mainwaring and his men toast the real heroes of Britain's Home Guard was written as a conscious decision to commemorate those who had battled and fought for their country during the Second World War.

TRIVIA:

Although the show ended its original run with *Never Too Old* this did not end the association of the series with the members of the cast. In 1981, BBC Radio 4 commissioned a pilot spin-off episode called *It Sticks Out Half a Mile* which starred Arthur Lowe and John Le Mesurier, in which Mainwaring moves to a seaside town in 1948 and goes to the local bank to take out a loan and is shocked to discover that the manager of the branch is Wilson. However, as Lowe was ill during the recording and died soon after, the pilot was not broadcast until December 2004. The pilot was reworked and a full series was commissioned and broadcast in 1983 and featured some of Le Mesurier's last work before his death.

SCORE: 8/10

And that was it. After nine series, 80 episodes, one feature-length film, four shorts, a radio series and a stage show, *Dad's Army* was no more. But it went out with a bang and although the series had only managed to pull in an average of 10.5 million viewers, it was clear that the series had left an impression on its doting audience. As the BBC's Audience Report confirms at the time...
'The majority of reporting viewers greeted this; the last ever episode of *Dad's Army,* warmly. It was generally felt to have been a very enjoyable story which provided an excellent, if somewhat final ending to the series. It was also widely agreed that the programme had been one of the most consistently amusing on television and that this episode had been no exception. There were a few who thought the story too contrived or who felt it had been rather melancholy and sentimental but, despite this, the overwhelming majority found it a pleasant and appropriate finish to what many regarded as a very good series.

It continues...

'The acting and production were almost universally commended, as it was felt that both had been of a consistently high standard ("acting very good and production always very smooth"). It was felt that all the characters had been beautifully portrayed ("a superb performance from all") and special mention was made of Arthur Lowe as Captain Mainwaring and Ian

Lavender as Private Pike. The production, too, was highly praised for bringing out a convincing sense of period and for paying great attention to detail. Altogether, it was generally agreed that the programme had always been magnificent, that the cast could not have been better chosen and that it was sad to see the series come to an end.'9

I couldn't put it better myself. Although the cast and crew's recollections of when the news broke to them that the series was not coming back (Clive Dunn recalled that he had been told as early as 1975 and Ian Lavender remembers that he had not been told that the ninth series was the last) there could be no doubt when on 29th August, a month to the day since the final studio day on the series, Edward Sinclair suffered a heart attack and died aged just 63. The news came as a big shock to the cast and crew, as it had done with James Beck's death in 1973. The cast were thrown a special party in their honour by the British Tabloid newspaper, the *Daily Mirror* at London's Cafe Royal. The actors were also presented medals, each inscribed with the words, 'FOR SERVICES TO TELEVISION ENTERTAINMENT.' Although the party was an opportunity to show up the BBC for not doing something similar, the sentiment was there. *Dad's Army* was, and always will be, a national institution.

DAD'S ARMY: THE MOVIE

RECORDED ON LOCATION AND AT SHEPPERTON STUDIOS, ENGLAND FROM 10TH AUGUST UNTIL 25TH SEPTEMBER 1970
RELEASED IN THE UNITED KINGDOM 12th MARCH 1971

PLOT:

On the 14th May 1940, Anthony Eden announces over the wireless that a home defence shall be formed in the guise of the Local Defence Volunteers and a bank manager called George Mainwaring, sees this as his chance to take command of his own fighting unit in the town of Walmington-on-Sea. When three desperate Nazi soldiers take the local church by force the bumbling members of the Home Guard turn out to be unlikely heroes and save the day.

CAST:

Arthur Lowe as Captain Mainwaring
John Le Mesurier as Sergeant Wilson
Clive Dunn as Lance Corporal Jones
John Laurie as Private Frazer
James Beck as Private Walker
Arnold Ridley as Private Godfrey
Ian Lavender as Private Pike

Liz Fraser as Mrs. Pike
Bernard Archard as Major General Fullard
Derek Newark as R.S.M.
Bill Pertwee as Hodges
Frank Williams as Vicar
Edward Sinclair as Verger Henry Yeatman
Anthony Sagar as Police Sergeant
Pat Coombs as Mrs. Hall
Roger Maxwell as Peppery Old Gent
Paul Dawkins as Nazi General
Sam Kydd as Nazi Orderly
Michael Knowles as Staff Captain
Fred Griffiths as Bert King
John Baskcomb as Mayor
George Roubicek as German Radio Operator
Scott Frederick as Nazi Photographer
Ingo Mogendorf as Nazi Pilot
Franz Van Norde as Nazi Co-Pilot
John Henderson as Radio Shop Assistant
Harriet Rhys as Janet King
Dervis Ward as A.A. Man
Robert Raglan as Inspector Hardcastle
John D. Collins as Naval Officer
Alan Haines as Marine Officer
Desmond Cullum-Jones as Platoon (as Desmond Cullen-Jones)
Colin Bean as Private Sponge
Frank Godfrey as Platoon
Freddie Wiles as Platoon
Freddie White as Platoon
Leslie Noyes as Platoon
David Fennell as Platoon

Hugh Hastings as Private Hastings
George Hancock as Platoon
Bernard Severn as Platoon
Alvar Liddell as Newsreader (voice) (as Alvar Lidell)
Anthony Eden as Himself (archive sound) (uncredited)

TECHNICAL CAST:

Screenplay by Jimmy Perry and David Croft
Based on an idea by Jimmy Perry
Produced by John R. Sloan
Original Music by Wilfred Burns
Cinematography by Terry Maher (director of photography)
Film Editing by Willy Kemplen
Art Direction by Terry Knight
Jimmy Evans - Makeup Artist (as Jim Evans)
Merwyn Medalie - Hairdressing (as Mervyn Medalie)
L.C. Rudkin - Production Manager (as Leonard C. Rudkin)
Douglas Hermes - Assistant Director
Dimity Collins - Set Dresser
Dino Di Campo – Sound Editor
Bob Jones – Sound Recorder
Ken Ritchie – Sound Recorder
Gerry Anstiss - Camera Operator
Harvey Woods - Casting
Bridget Sellers - Wardrobe Supervisor
Wilfred Burns - Conductor and Composer
'Who Do You Think You Are Kidding, Mr Hitler?'
Sung by Bud Flanagan
Music by Jimmy Perry and Derek Taverner
Words by Jimmy Perry

Zelda Barron - Continuity
Robert Simmonds - Location Manager (as Bob Simmonds)

REVIEW:

Back in the early seventies, it was common place for a popular sitcom to make the switch to the movie screens at some point and *Dad's Army: the Movie* somehow manages to succeed and fail at exactly the same time. It has an awful lot going for it. The team seem to be at the peak of their powers as it was made during the break in between the filming of the fourth and fifth series – the most consistent run in the series' history - and it is obvious that the confidence is high here.

It is not surprising that the movie picks the best from the first three series if it's counterpart programme but in a way this is just a safe house for the grounding of the project. This is nothing new for the fans and although it is brilliant to see this nostalgic world in a more expansive and realistic setting than one that was realised inside one of the studios in Television Centre, I think that one of the film's stumbling blocks is that we have seen this story told before. How the platoon assembles and the struggle to be taken seriously and the early days of limited ammunition and resources is a story we have seen before.

So what we get is a rather stifled finished article and it comes as no surprise that the best parts of the movie are those that have been written FOR the movie and not plucked like a pick 'n' mix assortment from bits that worked in the series. The moment when the Major

General and his horse drift down the river on a piece of the sabotaged bridge is instantly synonymous with the movie and one of the first scenes that pops into your head when you watch it on a repeated viewing. Then of course there is the hostage situation at the very end which is where the film stops being funny and actually turns very tense and gripping. Also, the Home Guard's journey to the exercise is a fun piece and also lays the seeds of doubt over Mainwaring's leadership on a weekend that the men would do well to forget.

There is an argument that in order to make the film accessible for a wider audience, that the writers plumped for a more saucy, tongue in cheek approach to the dialogue. For example, here we get more of an idea of the real reason why Wilson stays over at the Pike's house while all we had in the series up until this point was nothing more than little hints. There is also the line when Mainwaring insists that Hodges takes his hands off his privates...yep, that really is the level of humour we are at during certain stages of the picture. This does tend to look a little out of place with the sharp dialogue we have expected from the townsfolk of Walmington but at least it is not too bawdy. I can also see David Croft's argument that he thought the film was edited badly. We do not see any of the reaction shots we have come to sometimes rely on for the laughs in the series. The star of the film is without a doubt Arthur Lowe, who seems to revel in the script and snatch the limelight for all its worth. *Dad's Army: the Movie* is actually Mainwaring's story about how he goes from being a fusty, pompous bank manager to being the man who leads a small troop of elderly men to thwart Nazi parachutists and thus win the respect and gratitude of the people of the town and prove himself as a born leader.

Furthermore, why on earth did they replace Janet Davies for Liz Fraser? Considering she is the only semi-regular not to appear in the film I am not surprised that Davies was upset by her exclusion. Fraser brings more of a flirtatious and sexy look and feel to the role but all she is doing is stepping on the toes of the woman who the audience knew as Mrs Pike. It was a bizarre decision and it might not be a coincidence that after this, Davies did not appear in the next series that was made a famous face and that Mrs Pike's role was rather diminished for the rest of the series after the release of the film.

What works in the movie's favour is its comforting familiarity with the feel of the series. It feels like a hot water bottle - warm and cosy. It might not be the best adaptation of a sitcom on the big-screen. But it is not the worst, either, not by a long chalk. So while the main gags and laughs are more visual than dialogue-led, I still think that although it is a wasted opportunity to further explore the essence of the show and those who bring so much to it, there is a charm to the production and one that draws it above the other catastrophic attempts to transfer a winning sitcom to the big screen, like *Are You Being Served?*

The direction makes full use of the absence of the crammed studio sets and both the location and filmic finish makes for a more believable world.

In the end, *Dad's Army: the Movie* may have it's problems but that does not stop it from being an essential Bank Holiday favourite in the UK.

MEMORABLE MOMENT:

While on their exercise, Jones and his section discover that the bridge linking the banks together has been sabotaged and the ropes have been cut. As they try their best to pull the floating section back and keep it steady, Major General Fullard comes along on his horse and orders Jones to salute him as he is an NCO. This results in Jones letting go of the rope and Fullard is trapped on his horse as the loose section of the bridge floats away. Despite the men's best efforts, they lose Jones on the piece of debris when they rescue the disgruntled Major.

LINE:

Mainwaring: We have an invaluable weapon in our army, ingenuity and improvisation.
Frazer: That's two.

WATCH OUT FOR:

- **A clue is given to the true whereabouts of Walmington-on-Sea when the volunteers leave the police station. It says on the notice board in clear white letters 'Kent Constabulary.'**
- **In the series, the men wear armbands labelled 'CP' which stands for 'Croft/Perry' after the show's creators. However, in the film, the letters**

have been replaced with the words 'Home Guard.'

- **In the scene in which Mainwaring and Jones accidentally steamroller over the camp, the footage is not-so-subtly sped up.**

BEHIND THE SCENES:

The idea to bring the concept of *Dad's Army* to the big screen came from Jimmy Perry and David Croft themselves and with the help of Norman Cohen, who would go on to direct the film, they sent the idea around a number of the big-hitters in the industry to try and get their plans off the ground. Sadly, their desire hit several brick walls and the idea was not picked up until Columbia Pictures snapped up the project and the plans on paper were soon put into practise.

Compared to the budget that the comedy series was getting at the BBC, Columbia had been generous to Perry and Croft and they set about expanding the world of Walmington-on-Sea in the dark days of 1940. The money in the budget was spent on populating the town as this had been restricted in the sitcom version. Also, the film would be made entirely on location and for the interior scenes, Shepperton Studios was used for inside the church hall and the German's Operation Room as well as the interiors of the shops that some of the platoon members worked in.

The shooting schedule was issued to the cast and crew on 5th August 1970 and just five days later filming commenced at Chobham Common for the scene involving the platoon and Jones' van. Other locations were used included Chalfont St Giles in Buckinghamshire which doubled impressively for the town and gave it an authentic wartime feel. The scenes when the platoon is on the exercise were recorded on the lot at the back of Shepperton Studios. The schedule continued for another six weeks and concluded on Friday 25th September when the entire squad was required for pick-up shots.

One decision that had been taken out of Perry and Croft's hands was the recasting of Mrs Pike. Janet Davies, who had appeared in many episodes up to this point, was replaced by well-known actress and *Carry-On* regular Liz Fraser. The decision did not sit well with either the cast or crew. 'I don't think the recasting worked in the audience's eyes. It was a mistake, in my view, not to cast Janet in the role because the viewing public had come to recognise her as Mrs Pike. But that was a decision taken by Columbia.'1 David Croft remembered.

Andrew Gardiner, Janet's son, recalled how his Mother was affected by the news. 'I think the production company wanted a bigger name as far as the film was concerned, but being dropped from the movie hit my mother hard because she'd done so many TV episodes.'2

When the film was released the following March, it was met by mixed reviews from the British press, although the views of the fans and the watching audience was more positive and it is still a staple of Bank Holiday Weekends on British Television 40 years later. Some of the reviews even noted on how there were too many

similarities between some episodes of the TV series, most notably *The Man and the Hour* and *The Armoured Might of Lance Corporal Jones.*
At the time, the *Daily Express,* dated 15th March 1971 wrote: 'The familiar characters of the successful TV series march over well-trodden ground and never plant a boot in new territory. The main incident with the chaps capturing German airmen in the local church is not at all entertaining.'3 Alexander Walker of the *Evening Standard* wrote two days later: 'It seems a bit slow and stiff in the limbs; it's probably hard to galvanise the senior citizens whose own bumbling pace sets the scene for easy and affectionate laughter.'4
The response from Perry and Croft was also less than enthusiastic as the pair thought that the film lacked reaction shots and the feel of the series. However, this did not stop them from planning a sequel entitled *Dad's Army and the Secret U-Boat Base.* In its planning stages, it attracted the attention of perhaps the biggest star of stage and screen of all time. 'Laurence Olivier loved the show so much, he had indicated he was interested in playing the lead, which was the part of the villain. The story was that British ships were being sunk in the Irish Sea, and in North Wales there was an inlet where a German U-Boat used to go under the rocks and into a base that was sited there, manned by Germans. There was a country house above and all the sailors masqueraded as the staff, with the Nazi leader acting as the lord of the manor.
'We never finished the plot and would have probably completed several treatments, but it didn't go any

further because David and I were very busy; we also didn't think the first film had succeeded, so we dropped the whole idea.'5

TRIVIA:

Arthur Lowe had an unexpected and slight odd clause written into his contract that stated that he would not appear on screen without his trousers on. Ironically, in the film there is such a scene when the men are out marching and they are wearing white long johns and Mainwaring is not present. In Lowe's absence, John Le Mesurier led the platoon on screen and the actor's uncomfortable view on the matter meant a re-write was required in the series six episode *The Deadly Attachment* so that Jones took a grenade down his trousers and not Mainwaring.

SCORE: 7/10

APPENDIX I - THE RADIO SERIES

All episodes were adapted for radio by Harold Snoad and Michael Knowles and based on the original scripts by Jimmy Perry and David Croft. The pair made a conscious decision to adapt scripts that were less action-orientated and more dialogue driven first and some episodes, such as 'The Day the Balloon Went Up' had wholesale changes to the script so that the action could be described in the absence of the visual element. Snoad later acknowledged this challenge. 'Some scenes were just too visual so we had no alternative but to go back to the drawing board and write a completely different scene. But Jimmy Perry and David Croft always saw the scripts before they were transmitted.'1 On some occasions the schedule for both the TV series and the radio series clashed, leading to the cast recording two episodes each day for a period of two weeks. The cast were also given a day off rehearsals for the latest TV edition of the programme and with such a tiring schedule, Ian Lavender remembered the difficulty in making both incarnations of '*Dad's Army*.' 'We all felt brain dead by the time we'd finished. But they were great fun and worked well, even though, at times, they felt like a chore.'2

STARRING:

ARTHUR LOWE AS CAPTAIN MAINWARING, JOHN LE MESURIER AS SERGEANT WILSON AND CLIVE DUNN AS LANCE CORPORAL JONES.

PRODUCTION CREDITS:

Producer: John Dyas

Every episode was introduced by BBC Announcer John Snagge and recorded at The Playhouse Theatre, Northumberland Avenue and the Paris Studios, Lower Regent Street, London.

NOTE: All episodes are adaptations of the same scripts recorded for the TV Series with the exception of *'Gorilla Warfare'* (Series 7), *'Ring Dem Bells', 'When You've Got To Go', 'Come In, Your Time is Up', 'The Face of the Poster'* (Series 8), *'Wake-Up Walmington', 'The Making of Private Pike', 'Knights of Madness', 'The Miser's Hoard', 'Number Engaged'* and *'Never Too Old'* (Series 9). The short *'Christmas Night With the Stars'* sketch *'Broadcast to the Empire'* kept its original script and was the only one used with no changes or used at all.

SERIES ONE:

TITLE:	DATE RECORDED	DATE FIRST BROADCAST:	AUDIENCE:	ADDITIONAL CAST:
THE MAN AND THE HOUR	3/6/73	28/1/74	0.9 MILLION	ARNOLD RIDLEY, JAMES BECK, IANLAVENDER, JOHN LAURIE, TIMOTHY BATESON (ELLIOTT/GENERA

				L WILKINSON, GHQ DRIVER)
MUSEUM PIECE	7/6/73	4/2/74	0.9 MILLION	JAMES BECK, JOHN LAURIE, IAN LAVENDER, ERIC WOODBURN (GEORGE JONES)
COMMAND DECISION	21/6/73	11/2/74	0.6 MILLION	JOHN LAURIE, JAMES BECK, GEOFFREY LUMSDEN (COLONEL SQUARE), DAVID SINCLAIR (GHQ DRIVER)
THE ENEMY WITHIN THE GATES	21/6/73	18/2/74	1 MILLION	JAMES BECK, ARNOLD RIDLEY, IAN LAVENDER, CARL JAFFE (CAPTAIN WINOGRODSKI), DAVID SINCLAIR (GERMAN AIRMAN)
THE BATTLE OF GODFREY'S COTTAGE	6/7/73	25/2/74	1.1 MILLION	JOHN LAURIE, ARNOLD RIDLEY, IAN LAVENDER, BILL PERTWEE (ARP WARDEN), NANA BRAUNTON (CISSY GODFREY), PERCY EDWARDS (PERCY THE PARROT)
THE ARMOURED MIGHT OF LANCE CORPORAL JONES	6/7/73	4/3/74	0.9 MILLION	JOHN LAURIE, JAMES BECK, BILL PERTWEE, PEARL HACKNEY (MRS PIKE), RICHARD DAVIES (THE VOLUNTEER), ELIZABETH MORGAN (MRS LEONARD), DIANA BISHOP (MISS MEADOWS)
SGT. WILSON'S LITTLE SECRET	13/7/73	11/3/74	1.3 MILLION	JAMES BECK, ARNOLD RIDLEY, IAN LAVENDER, BILL PERTWEE,

				PEARL HACKNEY
A STRIPE FOR FRAZER	13/7/73	18/3/74	1 MILLION	JOHN LAURIE, JAMES BECK (FINAL APPERANCE AS WALKER. CHARACTER CONTINUED AFTER EPISODE WITH GRAHAM STARK AND LARRY MARTYN IN THE ROLE) GEOFFREY LUMSDEN, MICHAEL KNOWLES (CAPTAIN BAILEY)
OPERATION KILT	23/7/73	25/3/74	1.3 MILLION	JOHN LAURIE, IAN LAVENDER, ARNOLD RIDLEY, PEARL HACKNEY, JACK WATSON (CAPTAIN OGILVY)
BATTLE SCHOOL	28/6/73	1/4/74	1 MILLION	JOHN LAURIE, ARNOLD RIDLEY, IAN LAVENDER, JACK WATSON (MAJOR SMITH) ALAN TILVERN (CAPTAIN RODRIGUES)
UNDER FIRE	27/7/73	8/4/74	0.8 MILLION	JOHN LAURIE, ARNOLD RIDLEY, PEARL HACKNEY, GEOFFREY LUMSDEN, AVRIL ANGERS (MRS KEANE), DAVID GOODERSON (MR MURPHY)
SOMETHING NASTY IN THE VAULT	23/7/73	15/4/74	0.7 MILLION	JOHN LAURIE, IAN LAVENDER, BILL PERTWEE, JOHN BARRON (MR WEST) FRANK THORNTON (CAPTAIN ROGERS) ELIZABETH MORGAN (JANET

				KING)
THE SHOWING UP OF CORPORAL JONES	20/7/73	22/4/74	0.7 MILLION	JOHN LAURIE, ARNOLD RIDLEY, GRAHAM STARK, JACK WATSON (MAJOR REGAN)
THE LONELINESS OF THE LONG DISTANCE WALKER	20/7/73	29/4/74	0.9 MILLION	JOHN LAURIE, ARNOLD RIDLEY, GRAHAM STARK, JACK WATSON, JUDITH FURSE (CHAIRWOMAN), MICHAEL KNOWLES (THE CAPTAIN/MR REES)
SORRY, WRONG NUMBER (RADIO EQUIVALENT OF 'THE LION HAS PHONES'	27/7/73	6/5/74	1 MILLION	JOHN LAURIE, IAN LAVENDER, GRAHAM STARK, BILL PERTWEE, PEARL HACKNEY, AVRIL ANGERS (TELEPHONE OPERATOR) JOHN FOREST (LIEUTENANT HOPE-BRUCE)
THE BULLET IS NOT FOR FIRING	26/7/73	13/5/74	0.9 MILLION	ARNOLD RIDLEY, GRAHAM STARK, FRANK WILLIAMS (THE VICAR), MICHAEL KNOWLES (CAPTAIN PRINGLE), TIMOTHY BATESON (CAPTAIN MARSH), JOHN WHITEHALL (MEMBERS OF THE CHOIR)
ROOM AT THE BOTTOM	23/7/73	20/5/74	0.7 MILLION	JOHN LAURIE, ARNOLD RIDLEY, JOHN RINGHAM (CAPTAIN TURNER), JACK WATSON (SERGEANT GREGORY)
MENACE	24/7/73	27/5/74	0.6	JOHN LAURIE, IAN

FROM THE DEEP			MILLION	LAVENDER, BILL PERTWEE, DAVID SINCLAIR (2ND ARP WARDEN)
NO SPRING FOR FRAZER	26/7/73	3/6/74	1 MILLION	JOHN LAURIE, ARNOLD RIDLEY, EDWARD SINCLAIR (THE VERGER), JOAN COOPER (MISS BAKER), TIMOTHY BATESON (MR BLEWITT/ CAPTAIN TURNER)
SONS OF THE SEA	25/7/73	10/6/74	0.9 MILLION	IAN LAVENDER, JOHN LAURIE, ARNOLD RIDLEY, TIMOTHY BATESON (MR MAXWELL AND ALL OTHRER CHARACTERS)
CHRISTMAS SPECIAL - PRESENT ARMS (TV EQUIVALEN T OF 'BATTLE OF THE GIANTS' AND 'SHOOTING PAINS'	18/7/74	25/12/74	0.7 MILLION	JOHN LAURIE, IAN LAVENDER, ARNOLD RIDLEY, LARRY MARTYN, BILL PERTWEE, PEARL HACKNEY,GEOFFR EY LUMSDEN, JACK WATSON (THE BRIGADIER/ CHARLIE CHEESEMAN), NORMAN BIRD (BERT POSTLEWAITE)

SERIES TWO:

TITLE:	DATE RECORDED:	DATE FIRST BROADCAST:	AUDIENCE:	ADDITIONAL CAST:
DON'T FORGET THE	16/7/74	11/2/75	0.6 MILLION	JOHN LAURIE, IAN LAVENDER, ARNOLD

DIVER				RIDLEY, BILL PERTWEE, FRANK WILLIAMS, EDWARD SINCLAIR, GEOFFREY LUMSDEN, NORMAN ETTLINGER (THE SERGEANT)
IF THE CAP FITS...	17/4/74	18/2/75	1 MILLION	JOHN LAURIE, IAN LAVENDER, ARNOLD RIDLEY, EDWARD SINCLAIR, FRASER KERR (MAJOR GENERAL MENZIES/SERGEANT MACKENZIE)
PUT THAT LIGHT OUT!	30/4//74	25/2/75	0.9 MILLION	JOHN LAURIE, IAN LAVENDER, ARNOLD RIDLEY, BILL PERTWEE, AVRIL ANGERS (TELEPHONE OPERATOR), STUART SHERWIN (LIGHTHOUSE KEEPER)
BOOTS, BOOTS, BOOTS	16/4/74	4/3/75	1.1 MILLION	JOHN LAURIE, IAN LAVENDER, ARNOLD RIDLEY, ERIK CHITTY (MR SEDGEWICK)
SGT - SAVE MY BOY!	16/4/74	11/3/75	0.9 MILLION	JOHN LAURIE, IAN LAVENDER, ARNOLD RIDLEY, PEARL HACKNEY
BRANDED	17/7/74	18/3/75	0.7 MILLION	JOHN LAURIE, IAN LAVENDER,

				ARNOLD RIDLEY, BILL PERTWEE, NANA BRAUNTON, MICHAEL SEGAL (2ND WARDEN), NORMAN ETTLINGER (THE DOCTOR)
UNINVITED GUESTS	18/4/74	25/3/75	0.9 MILLION	JOHN LAURIE, IAN LAVENDER, ARNOLD RIDLEY, BILL PERTWEE, FRANK WILLIAMS, EDWARD SINCLAIR
A BRUSH WITH THE LAW	17/7/74	1/4/75	1 MILLION	JOHN LAURIE, IAN LAVENDER, ARNOLD RIDLEY, LARRY MARTYN, BILL PERTWEE, GEOFFREY LUMSDEN, EDWARD SINCLAIR, MICHAEL SEGAL (2ND WARDEN), MICHAEL KNOWLES (MR WINTERGREEN), NORMAN ETTLINGER (CLERK OF THE COURT)
A SOLDIER'S FAREWELL	15/5/74	8/4/75	1.4 MILLION	JOHN LAURIE, IAN LAVENDER, ARNOLD RIDLEY, LARRY MARTYN, BILL PERTWEE, PAT COOMBS (THE CLIPPIE/MARIE)
BRAIN VERSUS BRAWN	30/4/74	22/4/75	0.8 MILLION	JOHN LAURIE, IAN LAVENDER, ARNOLD

				RIDLEY, LARRY MARTYN, AVRIL ANGERS (THE WAITRESS/THE POLICEWOMAN), ROBERT RAGLAN (COLONEL PRITCHARD), STUART SHERWIN (THE CORPORAL)
WAR DANCE	12/5/74	22/4/75	1.2 MILLION	JOHN LAURIE, IAN LAVENDER, ARNOLD RIDLEY, LARRY MARTYN, PEARL HACKNEY, WENDY RICHARD (VIOLET GIBBONS)
MUM'S ARMY	12/5/74	29/4/75	0.7 MILLION	JOHN LAURIE, IAN LAVENDER, ARNOLD RIDLEY, LARRY MARTYN, CARMEN SILVERA (MRS GRAY), MOLLIE SUGDEN (MRS FOX/THE WAITRESS), WENDY RICHARD (EDITH PARISH)
GETTING THE BIRD	15/7/74	6/5/75	0.9 MILLION	JOHN LAURIE, IAN LAVENDER, ARNOLD RIDLEY, LARRY MARTYN, FRANK WILLIAMS, DIANA BISHOP (SERGEANT WILSON'S DAUGHTER)
DON'T FENCE ME IN	16/5/74	13/5/75	0.9 MILLION	JOHN LAURIE, IAN LAVENDER, ARNOLD

				RIDLEY, LARRY MARTYN, CYRIL SHAPS (GENERAL MONTEVERDI), JOHN RINGHAM, SION PROBERT (THE POW, THE SENTRY)
THE KING WAS IN HIS COUNTING HOUSE	15/5/74	20/5/75	1.2 MILLION	JOHN LAURIE, IAN LAVENDER, ARNOLD RIDLEY, LARRY MARTYN, BILL PERTWEE, WENDY RICHARD (SHIRLEY)
WHEN DID YOU LAST SEE YOUR MONEY	15/5/74	27/5/75	0.7 MILLION	JOHN LAURIE, ARNOLD RIDLEY, TIMOTHY BATESON (MR BLEWITT/MR BILLINGS)
FALLEN IDOL	16/7/74	3/6/75	0.9 MILLION	JOHN LAURIE, IAN LAVENDER, ARNOLD RIDLEY, GEOFFREY LUMSDEN, JACK WATSON (CAPTAIN REED), MICHAEL BRENNAN (THE SERGEANT-MAJOR), NORMAN ETTLINGER (PRITCHARD)
A WILSON (MANAGER?)	17/4/74	10/6/75	0.9 MILLION	JOHN LAURIE, IAN LAVENDER, ARNOLD RIDLEY, EDWARD SINCLAIR, MICHAEL KNOWLES, FRASER KERR

				(MR WEST)
ALL IS SAFELY GATHERED IN	15/7/74	17/6/75	0.8 MILLION	JOHN LAURIE, IAN LAVENDER, ARNOLD RIDLEY, BILL PERTWEE, FRANK WILLIAMS, NANA KENWAY (MRS PRENTICE)
THE DAY THE BALLOON WENT UP	18/4/75	24/6/75	0.9 MILLION	JOHN LAURIE, IAN LAVENDER, ARNOLD RIDLEY, BILL PERTWEE, FRANK WILLIAMS, EDWARD SINCLAIR, MICHAEL KNOWLES (SQUADRON LEADER HORSFALL)

SERIES THREE:

TITLE:	DATE RECORDED:	DATE FIRST BROADCAST:	AUDIENCE:	ADDITIONAL CAST:
MAN OF ACTION	28/4/75	16/3/76	0.8 MILLION	JOHN LAURIE, IAN LAVENDER, ARNOLD RIDLEY, LARRY MARTYN, BILL PERTWEE, JULIAN ORCHARD (MR UPTON - THE TOWN CLERK), JONATHAN CECIL (MR NORRIS),

				FRASER KERR (CAPTAIN SWAN/THE INSPECTOR)
THE HONOURABLE MAN	28/4/75	23/3/76	0.7 MILLION	JOHN LAURIE, IAN LAVENDER, ARNOLD RIDLEY, LARRY MARTYN, BILL PERTWEE, JULIAN ORCHARD, FRASER KERR (THE VISITING RUSSIAN)
THE GODIVA AFFAIR	5/5/75	30/3/76	0.7 MILLION	JOHN LAURIE, IAN LAVENDER, ARNOLD RIDLEY, LARRY MARTYN, BILL PERTWEE, JULIAN ORCHARD, MOLLIE SUGDEN
KEEP YOUNG AND BEAUTIFUL	12/5/75	6/4/76	0.7 MILLION	JOHN LAURIE, IAN LAVENDER, ARNOLD RIDLEY, LARRY MARTYN, MICHAEL BURLINGTON (THE WIG MAKER)
ABSENT FRIENDS	6/5/75	13/4/76	0.7 MILLION	JOHN LAURIE, IAN LAVENDER, ARNOLD RIDLEY, LARRY MARTYN, BILL PERTWEE,

				PEARL HACKNEY, MICHAEL BRENNAN (TOM/GEORGE PEARSON), STUART SHERWIN (POLICEMAN)
ROUND AND ROUND WENT THE GREAT BIG WHEEL	7/5/75	20/4/76	0.6 MILLION	JOHN LAURIE, IAN LAVENDER, ARNOLD RIDLEY, LARRY MARTYN, BILL PERTWEE, JOHN BARRON (COLONEL PIERCE), MICHAEL KNOWLES (CAPTAIN STEWART)
THE GREAT WHITE HUNTER (RADIO EQUIVALENT OF 'MAN HUNT')	30/5/75	27/4/76	0.6 MILLION	JOHN LAURIE, IAN LAVENDER, ARNOLD RIDLEY, LARRY MARTYN, PEARL HACKNEY, ELIZABETH MORGAN (HOUSEWIFE), FRASER KERR
THE DEADLY ATTACHMENT	30/4/75	4/5/76	0.5 MILLION	JOHN LAURIE, IAN LAVENDER, ARNOLD RIDLEY, LARRY MARTYN, FRANK WILLIAMS, PHILIP MADOC

				(CAPTAIN MULLER), FRASER KERR (COLONEL WINTERS)
THINGS THAT GO BUMP IN THE NIGHT	7/5/75	15/6/76	0.7 MILLION	JOHN LAURIE, IAN LAVENDER, ARNOLD RIDLEY, LARRY MARTYN, JOHN BARRON (CAPTAIN CADBURY)
MY BRITISH BUDDY	6/5/75	18/5/76	0.7 MILLION	JOHN LAURIE, IAN LAVENDER, ARNOLD RIDLEY, LARRY MARTYN, BILL PERTWEE, JACK WATSON (COLONEL SCHULTZ), PEARL HACKNEY, MOLLIE SUGDEN, WENDY RICHARD, MICHAEL MIDDLETON (THE AMERICAN SERGEANT)
BIG GUNS	5/5/75	25/5/76	0.8 MILLION	JOHN LAURIE, IAN LAVENDER, ARNOLD RIDLEY, LARRY MARTYN, JULIAN ORCHARD, MICHAEL MIDDLETON

				(THE PICKFORDS MAN)
THE BIG PARADE	2/5/75	1/6/76	0.8 MILLION	JOHN LAURIE, IAN LAVENDER, ARNOLD RIDLEY, LARRY MARTYN, BILL PERTWEE, EDWARD SINCLAIR, PEARL HACKNEY
ASLEEP IN THE DEEP	9/5/75	8/6/76	0.8 MILLION	JOHN LAURIE, IAN LAVENDER, ARNOLD RIDLEY, LARRY MARTYN, BILL PERTWEE
WE KNOW OUR ONIONS	8/5/75	15/6/76	0.7 MILLION	JOHN LAURIE, IAN LAVENDER, ARNOLD RIDLEY, LARRY MARTYN, BILL PERTWEE, ALAN TILVERN (CAPTAIN RAMSAY), MICHAEL MIDDLETON (SERGEANT BAXTER)
THE ROYAL TRAIN	29/4/75	22/6/76	0.7 MILLION	JOHN LAURIE, IAN LAVENDER, ARNOLD RIDLEY, BILL PERTWEE, FRANK WILLIAMS, STUART SHERWIN

				(THE STATION MASTER), FRASER KERR (THE TRAIN DRIVER), MICHAEL MIDDLETON (THE DRIVER'S MATE)
A QUESTION OF REFERENCE (RADIO EQUIVALENT OF 'THE DESPERATE DRIVE OF CORPORAL JONES')	12/5/75	29/6/76	0.5 MILLION	JOHN LAURIE, IAN LAVENDER, ARNOLD RIDLEY, LARRY MARTYN, PETER WILLIAMS (THE COLONEL), MICHAEL BURLINGTON (THE SIGNALLER)
HIGH FINANCE	27/6/75	6/7/76	0.7 MILLION	JOHN LAURIE, IAN LAVENDER, ARNOLD RIDLEY, LARRY MARTYN, BILL PERTWEE, PEARL HACKNEY, FRANK WILLIAMS
THE RECRUIT	1/5/75	13/7/76	0.6 MILLION	JOHN LAURIE, IAN LAVENDER, ARNOLD RIDLEY, LARRY MARTYN, BILL PERTWEE, FRANK WILLIAMS, EDWARD SINCLAIR, ELIZABETH

				MORGAN (THE NURSE AND THE SMALL BOY)
A JUMBO-SIZED PROBLEM (RADIO EQUIVALENT OF 'EVERYBODY'S TRUCKING')	18/6/75	20/7/76	0.7 MILLION	JOHN LAURIE, IAN LAVENDER, ARNOLD RIDLEY, LARRY MARTYN, BILL PERTWEE
THE CRICKET MATCH	1/5/75	227/7/76	0.5 MILLION	JOHN LAURIE, IAN LAVENDER, ARNOLD RIDLEY, LARRY MARTYN, BILL PERTWEE, FRANK WILLIAMS, EDWARD SINCLAIR, ANTHONY SMEE (G C EGAN)
TIME ON MY HANDS	29/4/75	3/8/76	0.9 MILLION	JOHN LAURIE, IAN LAVENDER, ARNOLD RIDLEY, LARRY MARTYN, BILL PERTWEE, FRANK WILLIAMS, ERIK CHITTY (MR PARSONS), FRASER KERR (GERMAN PILOT)
TURKEY DINNER	2/5/75	10/8/76	0.7 MILLION	JOHN LAURIE, IAN LAVENDER, ARNOLD RIDLEY, LARRY MARTYN, BILL

				PERTWEE, FRANK WILLIAMS, PEARL HACKNEY, HAROLD BENNETT (MR BLEWITT)
THE CAPTAIN'S CAR	9/5/75	24/8/76	0.9 MILLION	JOHN LAURIE, IAN LAVENDER, ARNOLD RIDLEY, LARRY MARTYN, BILL PERTWEE, BETTY MARSDEN (LADY MALTBY), GERARD GREEN (COLONEL)
THE TWO AND A HALF FEATHERS	8/5/75	24/8/76	0.9 MILLION	JOHN LAURIE, IAN LAVENDER, ARNOLD RIDLEY, LARRY MARTYN, BILL PERTWEE, MICHAEL BATES (PRIVATE CLARKE), AVRIL ANGERS (EDNA)
IS THERE HONEY STILL FOR TEA?	11/7/75	31/8/76	0.8 MILLION	JOHN LAURIE, IAN LAVENDER, ARNOLD RIDLEY, JOAN COOPER (CISSY GODFREY), FRASER KERR (SIR CHARLES RENFREW-

				MCALLISTER/ THE COLONEL)
TEN SECONDS FROM NOW (RADIO EQUIVALENT OF 'BROADCAST TO THE EMPIRE')	18/6/75	7/9/76	0.9 MILLION	JOHN LAURIE, IAN LAVENDER, ARNOLD RIDLEY, LARRY MARTYN, FRANK THORNTON (BBC PRODUCER), ROGER GARTLAND (BERT - THE BBC ENGINEER)

APPENDIX II - IT STICKS OUT HALF A MILE

With *'Dad's Army'* officially over, Harold Snoad had believed that the characters still had potential for another burst of life. After sitting down with Michael Knowles, his partner for the adaptations of the TV series to radio, the pair drew up 15 episodes of a new programme set some years after the end of the Second World War and the disbandment of the Home Guard. After obtaining the blessings of both Jimmy Perry and David Croft, the BBC commissioned the series. The writers floated the idea amongst the actors of the original series, which drew favourable views and Arthur Lowe suggested that he liked the idea and that it was strong enough to make it on television. Snoad did try to get the spin-off commissioned for the small screen but the BBC felt its true home would be on the airwaves. As a try-out, a pilot was commissioned in 1981. It was Snoad and Knowles' intention to only include Mainwaring and Wilson from the original premise and the episode was recorded in July of that year. Sadly, any hopes of the series taking off were severely hampered by the death of Arthur Lowe the following year. The pilot was shelved and was consequently lost for a period of time within the BBC's dilapidated archives. However a copy it was eventually discovered in the hands of

Snoad himself and given its first broadcast on a BBC Radio 7 compilation called *'Some of Our Archives were Missing'* in May 2004.

The BBC decided to commission 13 episodes, including a second pilot, this time including 'Dad's Army' stalwarts Ian Lavender and Bill Pertwee as regulars and featuring Janet Davies as Mrs Pike in a cameo appearance later in the series. For years, the BBC had only retained the master tapes to the two pilots and the second and fifth episodes of the series as it was discovered that the corporation was still purging its audio archives as late as the end of the 1980's. With so much material missing, it was deemed that these episodes were gone forever.

Luckily, by the turn of the millennium, the BBC had acknowledged the gaps in its archives and set up a scheme called 'Treasure Hunt' which set to find missing material that was missing believed wiped. By the early 2000s, the entire series was located from off-air recordings made by fans of the series who had kept them since their transmissions. Despite some recording lacking in quality, broadcast-standard recordings were also recovered meaning 'It Sticks Out Half a Mile' is now complete in the archives once again and has enjoyed repeated numerable outings on BBC Radio 4.

STARRING:

John Le Mesurier as Arthur Wilson
Ian Lavender as Frank Pike (second pilot onwards)
Bill Pertwee as (Bert Hodges)
Vivienne Martin as Miss Perkins (second episode onwards)

PRODUCTION CREDITS:

Written by Harold Snoad and Michael Knowles
Produced by Jonathan James Moore (first pilot) and Martin Fisher (second pilot and series)

TITLE:	DATE RECORDED:	DATE FIRST BROADCAST:	ADDITIONAL CAST:
FIRST PILOT	19/7/81	29/05/04	ARTHUR LOWE (GEORGE MAINWARING), JOSEPHINE TEWSON (MISS BAINES), DOUGIE BROWN (STEPHEN RAWLINGS), TIMOTHY WESTON (GUTHRIE), ANTHONY SHARP (CHARLES HUNTER), SIDNEY BRONTY (PERCY SHORT), HAYDEN WOOD (THE MAN)
SECOND PILOT	11/9/82	13/11/83	ROBIN PARKINSON (MR HUNTER), EDWARD BURNHAM (MR SHORT), GORDON PETERS (MR RAWLINGS), SPENCER BANKS

			(COUNCIL EMPLOYEE)
EPISODE TWO	19/2/83	20/11/83	GLYNN EDWARDS (FRED GUTHRIE), MICHAEL BILTON (MR JOHNSON)
EPISODE THREE	23/2/83	27/11/83	GLYNN EDWARDS (FRED GUTHRIE), BARRY GOSNEY (MR WATKINS), JAMES BRYCE (THE BANK CASHIER AND THE LIBRARIAN), STUART SHERWIN (ELECTRICITY SHOWROOM ASSISTANT)
EPISODE FOUR	23/2/83	4/12/83	NO ADDITIONAL ACTORS
EPISODE FIVE	19/2/83	11/12/83	CAROL HAWKINS (AVRIL), JANET DAVIES (MRS PIKE), GORDON SALKILD (TELEPHONE ENGINEER)
EPISODE SIX	26/2/83	18/12/83	GLYNN EDWARDS, MICHAEL KNOWLES (ERNEST WOOLCOT), HILDA BRAID

			(OLIVE BRIGGS)
EPISODE SEVEN	5/3/83	1/1/84	GLYNN EDWARDS, MICHAEL KNOWLES, HILDA BRAID, MICHAEL BILTON (THE ELDERLY MAN), MADI HEDD (THE WOMAN), JILL LIDSTONE (THE YOUNG LADY)
EPISODE EIGHT	8/3/83	8/1/84	PAUL RUSSELL (DEREK)
EPISODE NINE	5/3/83	15/1/84	MICHAEL KNOWLES, HILDA BRAID, GORDON CLYDE (WILOUGHBY SMALLPIECE), MIRANDA FORBES (THE WAITRESS)
EPISODE TEN	26/2/83	21/8/84	GLYNN EDWARDS, STELLA TANNER (MYRTE SPIVY), GORDON CLYDE (MR FISHER), CAROLE HARRISON (THE BUILDERS RECEPTIONIST), KATHERINE PARR (THE IRISH NUN)
EPISODE ELEVEN	8/3/83	4/9/84	REGINALD MARSH (SIR

			WENSLEY SMITHERS), GORDON CLYDE (CIVIL SERVANTS 1 AND 5), JON GLOVER (CIVIL SERVANTS 2 AND 4), MICHAEL BILTON (MR THORNEDYKE AND CIVIL SERVANT 3)
EPISODE TWELVE	15/3/83	18/9/84	CHIRSTOPHER BIGGINS (DUDLEY WATKINS), ROBIN PARKINSON (MR HUNTER)
EPISODE THIRTEEN	15/3/83	9/10/84	GLYNN EDWARDS, BETTY MARSDEN (MADAME ZARA)

With the death of John Le Mesurier, the show after just fourteen episodes was over. But Snoad and Knowles believed that the series format had legs and decided to take their creation to a visual format on television. The remake, entitled *'Walking the Planks'* was filmed without the 'Dad's Army' characters and starred Michael Elpick as Ron Archer, Richard Wilson as Richard Talbot, Vivienne Martin as Miss Baxter and Gary Raynsford as Trevor Archer. The show was transmitted on BBC1 on Friday 2nd August 1985 but despite the pilot drawing a bigger audience than some of the later episodes of its parent show at 11 million viewers, the programme was not picked up. Eventually, the pair took the programme to Yorkshire Television and under the renamed banner *'High and Dry'*, seven untitled episodes were made and broadcast with some of the actors being recast. The main cast now included Bernard Cribbins as Ron Archer as Richard Wilson and Vivienne Martin returned as Richard Talbot and Miss Baxter respectively, Angus Barnett as Trevor Archer, Arthur English as Fred Whattle and Diana Coupland as Mrs Briggs. Slotted in the prime-time of 8.30pm and broadcast from 7th January to 18th February 1987, the studio-bound sets and failed realisation of exterior scenes in the absence of location filming spelled the end of the show and a second series was not commissioned.

APPENDIX III - THE STAGE SHOW

Upon the show's debut at the Billingham Forum Theatre, the production found glowing reviews in the form of Kevin Easton from 'The Hartlepool Mail.' He wrote on 9th September 1975 that the show was a 'British-Hollywood musical'1 and that 'The special bond of affection between the cast and audience helped each item spark along.'2

The show was also the subject of an amateur-dramatic company called the Thetford Music and Drama Society whose adaptation was the first one performed by an amateur group. It enjoyed a nine-night run in 1981 that took in six nights at Thetford's Carneige Room and three at the Theatre Royal, Bury St Edmunds. Directed by Fred Calvert, the show began on 11th May with proceeds from the ticket sales going to two local charities.

PRODUCTION CREDITS:

Written by Jimmy Perry and David Croft

Directed by David Croft and Jimmy Perry

Staged by Roger Redfarn

Designed by Terry Parsons

Musical Director - Ed Coleman

Choreography by Sheila O'Neill

Lighting by Robert Ornbo

Costumes by Mary Husband

Sound by David Collison

Orchestrations by Don Savage, Dennis Wilson and Ed Coleman

Vocal Arrangements by Ed Coleman

Musical Associate to Jimmy Perry and David Croft - Jo Stewart

Company Manager - Peter Bevis (Billingham, The Shaftesbury, Manchester, Nottingham and Bradford), Tony Cundell

Stage Manager - Max Chowen

Deputy Stage Manager - Teena Steel (Billingham, The Shaftesbury, Manchester, Nottingham and Bradford), Trevor Ritchie.

Assistant Stage Managers - Ruth Halliday, Kevin Hubbard, Vivien Pearman and Gina Batt

Technical Assistant Stage Manager - Stephen Ward (who also operated as Sound Operator)

Assistant to Mary Husband - Ron Lucas

Assistant Wardrobe Mistress - Helen Pritchard

Wardrobe Master - David Morgan

Assistant - Roy Lovegrove

Sound Operator - Roy Lovegrove

Assistant to Robert Ornbo - Spike Gaden

Press Representative - Reg Williams

Lighting and sound equipment by Theatre Projects Services

Costumes by Bermans Nathans

Wigs by Summonwigs

Watches by Timex Corporation

Binoculars by Dixons Photographic Ltd

Paper Bags by Progressive Supplies (Paper) Ltd

Sharpening Steel by Scanlon Bros, London

Spectacles by C W Dixie Ltd

Prop Costumes by Malcolm Waldock

Head-dresses by Pat Dawson and Mark Embledon

South American costumes executed by Natasha Kornitoff

Fur coats by Richard Catermole

Chesney Allen hats and suits by Moss Bros and Carnaby Cavern Tights by Elbeo

Miner's helmet and lamp supplied by The National Coal Board

Poster transparencies by courtesy of Trustees of the Imperial War Museum

Shirts executed by Katy Stevens

Pens by W A Shaeffer, Pen Company

Furniture by Old Times Furniture Co Ltd

Presented by Bernard Delfont and Richard M Mills for Bernard Delfont Organisation Ltd and Duncan C Weldon and Louis I Michaels for Triumph Theatre Productions Ltd.

CAST:

Arthur Lowe as Captain Mainwaring and Mr Lovejoy (The Shaftesbury onwards)

John Le Mesurier as Sergeant Wilson

Clive Dunn as Lance Corporal Jones (except Blackpool, Bournemouth, Newcastle, Surrey, Brighton and Bath where Jack Haig played the part)

Arthur Ridley as Private Godfrey

Ian Lavender as Private Pike and Enoch (The Shaftesbury onwards)

Hamish Roughead as Private Frazer (Billingham and The Shaftesbury)

Michael Bevis as Private Staines (Manchester onwards)

Jeffrey Holland as Private Walker (except Billingham and The Shaftesbury where played by John Bardon, who also played Dave)

Graham Hamilton as Private Meadow (Billingham and The Shaftesbury only)

Eric Longworth as Private Woods and the Town Clerk (Billingham and The Shaftesbury only)

Norman MacLeod as Private Maple (Billingham and The Shaftesbury only)

Bill Pertwee as Chief ARP Warden Hodges and General Von Seltz and Max Miller (The Shaftesbury onwards)

Frank Williams as Rev Timothy Farthing

Edward Sinclair as Mr Yeatman

Janet Davies as Mrs Pike (Billingham and The Shaftesbury only, played elsewhere by Bernice Adams)

Joan Cooper as Mrs Holdane Hart (WVS) and Godfrey's sister.

Pamela Cundell as Mrs Fox (Billingham and The Shaftesbury only, played elsewhere by Peggy Ashby) and British Restaurant Lady

Jeffrey Holland as German Inventor

Michael Bevis as BBC Announcer and Ramsbottom (The Shaftesbury onwards)

Ronnie Grainge as Newspaper boy

David Wheldon Williams as Hermann Goering

Graham Hamilton as Raymond (Billingham only)

Jeffrey Holland as Jim

Bernice Adams as Carmen Caramba

Michael Bevis is General Gordon (Billingham only, played elsewhere by John Conroy)

Norman MacLeod as General Wolsey (Billingham and The Shaftesbury only, played elsewhere by Bill Pearson)

Barrie Stevens, Ronnie Grainge and Kevin Hubbard as Dervishes (Billingham only)

Peggy Ann Jones as Britannia (Billingham only)

Graham Hamilton as Soldier (Billingham only) and Man on the Beach (Billingham and The Shaftesbury only, played elsewhere by Bill Pearson)

Eric Longworth as Happidrome Announcer (The Shaftesbury) Bill Pearson (elsewhere)

Joan Cooper and Pamela Cundell as Gert and Daisy (The Shaftesbury only)

Arthur Lowe as Robb Wilton (The Shaftesbury onwards)

Arthur Lowe and John Le Mesurier as Flanagan and Allen (The Shaftesbury onwards)

Bernice Adams, Debbie Blackett and June Shand (The Shaftesbury onwards) Elizabeth Suggars and Marianne Parnell (elsewhere) as Girls on the Beach

The Home Front Company, who appeared throughout the production were: Bernice Adams, Michael Bevis, Debbie Blackett, Ronnie Grainge, Graham Hamilton, Jeffrey Holland, Vivien Pearman, Peggy Ann Jones, Eric Longworth, Norman MacLeod, Kevin Hubbard, June Shand, Michele Summers, Barrie Stevens, Jan Todd, David Wheldon Williams, Alan Woodhouse, Peggy Ashby, Gina Batt, John Conroy, Marsha Harris, Marianne Parnell, Bill Pearson, Pauline Stork, Elizabeth Suggars.

Eric Longworth, Michael Bevis and Norman MacLeod stood in for Arthur Lowe, John Le Mesurier and Clive Dunn respectively.

UK TOUR DATES:

Venue	City	Start	Finish
Forum Theatre	Billingham	Thursday 4th September 1975	Saturday 20th September 1975
The Shaftesbury Theatre	London	Thursday 2nd October 1975	21st February 1976
Opera House	Manchester	Tuesday 23 March 1976	Saturday 10 April 1976
Theatre Royal	Nottingham	Monday 12 April 1976	Saturday 1 May, 1976

Bradford Alhambra	Bradford	Monday 3 May, 1976	Saturday 15 May, 1976
Hippodrome	Birmingham	Monday 17 May, 1976	Saturday 22 May, 1976
Pavilion Theatre	Bournemouth	Monday 24 May 1976	Saturday 5 June 1976
Winter Gardens	Blackpool	Monday 7 June 1976	Saturday 19 June 1976
Theatre Royal	Newcastle	Monday 22 June 1976	Saturday 3 July 1976
Richmond Theatre	Richmond upon Thames	Monday 12 July 1976	Saturday 24 July 1976
Theatre Royal	Brighton	Monday 26 July 1976	Saturday 21 August 1976
Theatre Royal	Bath	Monday 23 August 1976	Saturday 4 September 1976

The show's running order was as follows:
Act One

Scene 1 Who do you think you are kidding Mr Hitler?
Scene 2 Put that Light Out!
Scene 3 Carry On on the Home Front British Restaurant (replaced 'When can I have a banana again?' after Forum Theatre try-out)

Scene 4 Command Post

Scene 5 Private Pike's Dream (replaced Carry On on the Home Front, Butcher's shop and British Restaurant scenes from Forum Theatre try-out)

Scene 6 Cliff top: Lance Corporal Jones stands guard (called 'Cliff Top' and 'Don't Panic' in Forum Theatre try-out)

Scene 7 Lords of the Air (entitled Battle of Britain in Forum Theatre try-out)

Scene 8 Choir practice

Interval

Act Two

Scene 9 The song that we would rather forget

Scene 10 Unarmed combat

Scene 11 Tinpan alley Goes to War (named just Tinpan alley in the Forum Theatre try-out)

Scene 12 Morris Dance (Replaced a scene called 'Too Late Rumour' from the Forum Theatre Try-out)

Scene 13 A Nightingale sang in Berkley Square

Scene 14 Radio personalities of the 1940 (originally 1941 instead of 1940 in Forum Theatre Try-out)

Scene 15 The beach

Scene 16 Finale

THE AMERICAN PILOT - THE REAR GUARD

ORIGINALLY TRANSMITTED 10TH AUGUST 1976 (BROADCAST ONCE ON THE ABC NETWORK IN AMERICA)

PLOT:

1942, The Long Island Civil Defence unit are put in charge of guarding a German U-Boat crew following their discovery by a local fisherman called Frank Sanicola upon his return from a fishing trip. Led by Captain Nick Rosatti and his brash Sergeant Raskin, the Captain of the U-Boat and his five-man crew make life difficult for their captors as the regular army are situated 85 miles away, meaning they have to hold up in the church hall overnight. After a short while, the tables turn and Rosatti is put in a very difficult situation as the Germans take over.

CAST:

Lou Jacobi as Sergeant Max Raskin
Cliff Norton as Captain Nick Rosatti
Eddie Foy Jr. as Bert Wagner
John McCook as Don Crawford
Dennis Kort as Bobby Henderson
Arthur Peterson as Mr. Muldoon
Jim Connell as Father Fitzgerald

James McCallion as Colonel Walsh
Conrad Janis as German Captain
Ronda Copland as Marsha Wilson
Dave Morick as Frank Sanicola
Don Diamond as Foster
Claude Jones as Krupinsky

PRODUCTION TEAM:

Executive Producer: Herman Rush
Associate Producer: Dee Baker
Written and produced by Arthur Julian
Music by The Willow Sisters
Art Director: Edward Stephenson
Costumes: Ed Smith
Assistant to the producer: Lorraine Sevre Kenney
Casting: Marsha Kleinman and Pat Harris
Associate director: Anthony Chickey
Post Production: Associate Director: Hal Collins
Unit Manager: Robert M. Furiga
Engineering Supervisor: Gerry Bobian
Studio Supervisor: Darrell Gentry
Technical Director: Jim Doll
Lighting Director: Jack Denton
Senior Video: Bud Hendricks
Audio: Art Du Pont
Stage Managers: Jerry Blumenthal and James Woodworth
Production Administrator: Ron Von Schimmelmann
Production Co-ordinator: Bryant Henry
Production Supervisor: Conrad Holzgang
Based on *Dad's Army*, created by Jimmy Perry and David Croft, a BBC production

Videotaped at ABC Television Centre, Hollywood, California
Herman Rush Associates in association with Wolper Productions.

MEMORABLE MOMENT:

Not so much a memorable moment for this version but more for the comparison with its original - the scene in which the German Captain argues with Rosatti over the outcome of the war and young Bobby Henderson sings a song ridiculing the Fuhrer, leading to THAT classic line, except this time it's lacking in the same conviction and punch that the original possessed. Funny, really, that's quite an apt way to describe the whole, flipping thirty minutes!

LINE:

Raskin: At ease men (The U-boat crew take their hands down) Not you, you Nazis!
Rosatti: They can take their hands down, Raskin.
Raskin: I knew an Italian would be soft on the Germans.
Rosatti: I was born in Bayor, New Jersey. I ain't no Italian, I am an American.
Raskin: You can take the boy out of the olive oil but you can't take the olive oil out of the boy!

TRIVIA:

The pilot's failure led to the original videotape that the episode was recorded on to be wiped by ABC not too long after the show had it's one and only airing. Long forgotten (and for good reason in my eyes) and thought to have been lost forever, the likelihood of the pilot ever seeing the light of day again was futile - until missing episode hunter David Homewood made a breakthrough in 1999 when he received a letter from actor Cliff Norton, who had tracked down a domestic recording of the show. Homewood telephoned Jimmy Perry upon the discovery who was thrilled by the news and a copy was made and handed to the Dad's Army Appreciation Society New Zealand and is now also kept by the DAAS of Great Britain after it was converted from NTSC to PAL standard.

WATCH OUT FOR:

- **The pilot begins with a prologue, which reads: 'Much has been written about those gallant soldiers of World War Two who met and defeated the enemy. But there were those who stayed behind to defend our shores. They were the men of the Civil Defence to whom this show is dedicated.'**
- **Amongst the many comparisons between this and the original show, the sailors are given salami sandwiches instead of fish and chips as food.**

- On this occasion, the grenade is planted down the Captain's trousers - as opposed to Corporal Jones in the British version.

REVIEW:

Terrible, just...terrible.

MARK OUT OF TEN: 1/10

The Back Row and Production Team Roll-Call

The Back Row Performers (In the order of appearances with number in brackets):

Colin Bean (76)
Desmond Cullum-Jones (63)
George Hancock (60)
Freddie Wiles (57)
Freddie White (51)
Hugh Cecil (50)
Leslie Moyes (49)
Michael Moore (45)
Vic Taylor (37)
Hugh Hastings and Evan Ross (34)
Roger Bourne (28)
Frank Godfrey (23)
Jimmy Mac (22)
Richard Jaques (17)
David Seaworth, Richard Kitteridge and Alec Coleman (11)
William Gossling and Vernon Drake (7)
Peter Whitaker, Martin Dunn and Chris Franks (5)
Ken Wade (3)
Emmett Hennessy and Arthur McGuire (2)

Freddie Payne, Derek Chaffer and Lindsay Hooper (1)

Scripts by: Jimmy Perry and David Croft
Signature Tune: Words by Jimmy Perry. Music by Jimmy Perry and Derek Taverner. Sung by Bud Flanagan.
Closing Theme: Band of the Coldstream Guards conducted by their Director of Music, Captain Trevor L Sharpe, M.B.E, L.R.A.M, A.R.C.M., p.s.m.
Costumes by: George Ward (series 1 and 4); Odette Barrow (series 3); Michael Burdle (series 3); Barbara Kronig (series 4); Judy Allen (episode 40); Susan Wheal (series 5-7); Mary Husband (series 8 and 9, episodes 73 and 74).
Make-Up: Sandra Exelby (series 1); Cecile Hay-Arthur (series 3); Cynthia Goodwin (series 4 and 5); Penny Bell (episode 40); Anna Chesterman (series 5 and 6); Ann Alles (series 6); Sylvia Thornton (series 7 to 9, episode 73 and 74).
Visual Effects: Peter Day (series 3 to 6 and 8); John Friedlander (series 4); Ron Oates (series 4); Len Hutton (episode 40); Tony Harding (series 5); Jim Ward (series 7); Martin Gutteridge (series 9).

Lighting by: George Summers (series 1, 2 and 4); Howard King (series 3 to 9, episodes 40, 73 and 74).

Studio Sound by: James Cole (series 1 and 2); Michael McCarthy (series 3 to 8, episode 74); John Holmes (series 3 and 4); John Delany (series 5); Alan Machin (series 8, episode 73); Laurie Taylor (series 9).

Film Cameraman: James Balfour (series 3, 5 and 6); Stewart A. Farnell (series 4 and 5); Len Newson (series 7); Peter Chapman (series 8 and 9).

Film Sound by: Les Collins (series 4 and 5, episode 40); Ron Blight (series 5); John Gatland (series 6 and 7); Bill Chesneau (series 8); Graham Bedwell (series 9).

Film Editor: Bob Rymer (series 3, 5, 6 and episode 40); Bill Harris (series 4 to 7); John Stothart (series 8); John Dunstan (series 9).

Production Assistants: Bob Spiers (series 7); Jo Austin (series 8, episode 73 and 74); Gordon Elsbury (series 9).

Designer: Alan Hunter-Craig (series 1); Paul Joel (series 1 to 6, episode 40); Oliver Baylon (series 2); Ray London (series 3); Richard Hunt (series 3); Bryan Ellis (series 7); Robert Berk (series 8, episode 73), Geoff Powell (series 9); Tim Gleeson (series 9).

Directors: Harold Snoad, Bob Spiers and David Croft (various episodes)

Producer: David Croft

ABOUT THE AUTHOR:

Hayden Gribble was born in Cambridge in June 1989. He has always loved writing and released his debut novel, The Man In The Corner, as an eBook in 2013 before it went paperback the following year.

Since then, Hayden has managed to top the Amazon best seller list on three occasions, although the Booker Prize still seems some way off.

The Stratos Conundrum is Hayden's eighth book and the fourth in the Captain Random saga.

Away from writing, Hayden loves reading, walking, sports, music, film and TV.

He has also been a regular member of the Diddly Dum Podcast, a show about Doctor Who, since February 2015.

He lives with his wife and son in Suffolk.

You can find out more about Hayden and Captain Random at www.haydengribbleauthor.com

Index

<u>Cast Factfile</u>

1. Michael Mills, quoted by David Croft in conversation with Graham McCann, Dad's Army: The Story of a Classic Television Show, p54, ISBN 1-84-115-309-5
2. Jimmy Perry, conversation with Graham McCann, Dad's Army: The Story of a Classic Television Show, p56, ISBN 1-84-115-309-5
3. Jimmy Perry, conversation with Graham McCann, Dad's Army: The Story of a Classic Television Show, p57, ISBN 1-84-115-309-5
4. Michael Mills, quoted by David Croft in conversation with Graham McCann, Dad's Army: The Story of a Classic Television Show, p57, ISBN 1-84-115-309-5
5. Jimmy Perry on John Le Mesurier, Dad's Army: A Celebration, p 45
6. David Jason, in correspondence with Graham McCann, 1st June 2000, Dad's Army: The Story of a Classic Television Show, p59, ISBN 1-84-115-309-5
7. David Croft, Dad's Army: A Celebration, p 73
8. David Croft, interview with Graham McCann, Dad's Army: The Story of a Classic Television Show, p61, ISBN 1-84-115-309-5
9. Jimmy Perry, Dad's Army: A Celebration, p 73
10. David Croft, interview with Graham McCann, Dad's Army: The Story of a Classic Television Show, p62, ISBN 1-84-115-309-5
11. David Croft, Dad's Army: A Celebration, p 157

12. David Croft, interview with Graham McCann, Dad's Army: The Story of a Classic Television Show, p60, ISBN 1-84-115-309-5
13. David Croft, Dad's Army: A Celebration, p 107
14. David Croft, Dad's Army: A Celebration, p 114
15. Bill Pertwee, Dad's Army: A Celebration, p 160-162
16. Frank Williams on Edward Sinclair, interview with Graham McCann 4th October 2000, Dad's Army: The Story of a Classic Television Show, p112, ISBN 1-84-115-309-5
17. Gladys Sinclair, Dad's Army: A Celebration, p 172
18. Frank Williams, interview with Graham McCann 4th October 2000, Dad's Army: The Story of a Classic Television Show, p112, ISBN 1-84-115-309-5
19. Jimmy Perry on Frank Williams, Dad's Army: A Celebration, p 177

<u>Series One</u>

The Man and the Hour

1. Jimmy Perry, in conversation with Graham McCann, Dad's Army: The Story of a Classic Television Show, p 74, ISBN 1-84-115-309-5

Museum Piece

2. Caroline Dowdeswell, Dad's Army: A Celebration, p 48

Command Decision

3. Ian Lavender, in conversation with Graham McCann, Dad's Army: The Story of a Classic Television Show, p 73, ISBN 1-84-115-309-5
4. Hugh Hastings, Dad's Army: A Celebration, p50

The Enemy Within the Gates

5. Ian Lavender, in conversation with Graham McCann, Dad's Army: The Story of a Classic Television Show, p ?, ISBN 1-84-115-309-5

The Showing up of Corporal Jones

6. Ian Lavender, Dad's Army: A Celebration, p 51

Shooting Pains

7. Thérèse McMurray, Dad's Army: A Celebration, p 50
8. BBC WAC: Dad's Army file T12/880/1: memorandum from Kevin Smith to David Croft, 16 September 1968

Series Two

Operation Kilt

1. Jimmy Perry, Dad's Army: A Celebration, p53

The Battle of Godfrey's Cottage

2. Jimmy Perry, Dad's Army – The Lost Episodes, p 36

Sgt. Wilson's Little Secret

3. Jimmy Perry, quoting head of Comedy at the BBC, Michael Mills, Dad's Army – The Lost Episodes, p86
4. Jimmy Perry and David Croft, Dad's Army – The Lost Episodes, p105

A Stripe For Frazer

5. John Laurie, quoted by Bill Pertwee, Dad's Army: The Making of a Television, p. 22.

Series Three

The Armoured Might of Lance Corporal Jones

1. Pamela Cundell, Dad's Army: A Celebration, p58

The Lion Has 'Phones

2. Richard Jacques, Dad's Army: A Celebration, p65

The Bullet Is Not For Firing

3. Frank Williams, Dad's Army: A Celebration, p61

Something Nasty in the Vault

4. Joan Le Mesurier, Dad's Army: A Celebration, p62

Big Guns

5. Arthur Lowe, as quoted by Jimmy Perry, Dad's Army: The Best of British Comedy, Richard Webber, p105

The Day the Balloon Went Up

6. Frank Williams, Dad's Army: The Best of British Comedy, Richard Webber, p22

War Dance

7. David Croft, Dad's Army: The Best of British Comedy, Richard Webber, p57
8. Ian Lavender, Dad's Army: The Best of British Comedy, Richard Webber, p53

Branded

9. Jimmy Perry, Dad's Army: The Best of British Comedy, Richard Webber, p29
10. David Croft, Dad's Army: The Best of British Comedy, Richard Webber, p29

Man Hunt

11. Robert Aldous, Dad's Army: A Celebration, p68

No Spring for Frazer

12. Hugh Cecil, Dad's Army: A Celebration, p69

Sons of the Sea

13. John Leeson, Dad's Army: A Celebration, p69

Series Four

The Big Parade

1. Ian Lavender, Dad's Army: A Celebration, p80

Don't Forget the Diver

2. Don Estelle, Dad's Army: A Celebration, p82

Boots, Boots, Boots

3. Ian Lavender, Dad's Army: The Best of British Comedy, Richard Webber ,p63

Sgt - Save My Boy!

4. Jimmy Perry, Dad's Army: The Best of British Comedy, Richard Webber ,p23

Don't Fence Me In

5. Edward Evans, Dad's Army: A Celebration, p83

Absent Friends

6. David Croft, The Complete A-Z of Dad's Army, Richard Webber with Jimmy Perry and David Croft, p162

Put that Light Out!

7. Harold Snoad, The Complete A-Z of Dad's Army, Richard Webber with Jimmy Perry and David Croft, p167

Mum's Army

8. David Croft, Dad's Army: The Best of British Comedy, Richard Webber ,p53

The Test

9. Accident and Industrial Disease Report Form quoting the accident involving Arthur Lowe on 20/10/70, The Complete A-Z of Dad's Army, Richard Webber with Jimmy Perry and David Croft, p12

10. Ian Lavender, Dad's Army: A Celebration, p89

A Wilson (Manager?)

11. Caroline Dowdeswell, Dad's Army: A Celebration, p50

Uninvited Guests

12. Rose Hill, Dad's Army: A Celebration, p90

Fallen Idol

13. Don Estelle, Dad's Army: A Celebration, p90

1971 Christmas Special

1. Peter Chapman, The Complete A-Z of Dad's Army, Richard Webber with Jimmy Perry and David Croft, p40

Series Five

Asleep in the Deep

1. Paul Joel, Dad's Army: A Celebration, p93

Keep Young and Beautiful

2. Ms Cornewall-Walker, Dad's Army: A Celebration, p94

A Soldier's Farewell

3. Joy Allen, Dad's Army: A Celebration, p94

Getting the Bird

4. Pamela Cundell, Dad's Army: A Celebration, p96

The Desperate Drive of Corporal Jones

5. David Croft, Dad's Army: The Best of British Comedy, Richard Webber ,p78

If the Cap Fits...

6. Evan Ross, Dad's Army: A Celebration, p87
7. Ian Lavender, Dad's Army: A Celebration, p74

The King was in his Counting House

8. David Croft, Dad's Army: The Best of British Comedy, Richard Webber ,p13

All is Safely Gathered In
9. Brenda Cowling, Dad's Army: A Celebration, p98
Where Did You Last See Your Money?
10. Tony Hughes, Dad's Army: A Celebration, p99
Brain versus Brawn
11. Jimmy Perry, Dad's Army: A Celebration, p163
A Brush with the Law
12. David Croft, Dad's Army: A Celebration, p173
Round and Round Went the Great Big Wheel
13. David Croft, Dad's Army: The Best of British Comedy, Richard Webber ,p93
Time on My Hands
14. David Croft, Dad's Army: A Celebration, p101

Series Six

The Deadly Attachment
1. Ian Lavender, Dad's Army: A Celebration, p116
My British Buddy
2. Desmond Callum-Jones, The Complete A-Z of Dad's Army, Richard Webber with Jimmy Perry and David Croft, p164
The Royal Train
3. Frank Williams, Dad's Army: The Best of British Comedy, Richard Webber ,p101
The Honourable Man
4. Stephen Lowe, Dad's Army: A Celebration, p120
Things That Go Bump in the Night
5. Jo Austin, The Complete A-Z of Dad's Army, Richard Webber with Jimmy Perry and David Croft, p21
The Recruit
6. Kay Beck, Dad's Army: A Celebration, p154

7. Jo Austin, The Complete A-Z of Dad's Army, Richard Webber with Jimmy Perry and David Croft, p21

Series Seven
Everybody's Trucking
1. Felix Bowness, Dad's Army: A Celebration, p123
A Man of Action
2. Robert Mill, Dad's Army: A Celebration, p124
Gorilla Warfare
3. Ian Lavender, in conversation with Graham McCann, Dad's Army: The Story of a Classic Television Show, p 195, ISBN 1-84-115-309-5
The Godiva Affair
4. Eric Longworth, Dad's Army: A Celebration, p127
The Captain's Car
5. Mavis Pugh, Dad's Army: A Celebration, p128
Turkey Dinner
6. Hugh Cecil, The Complete A-Z of Dad's Army, Richard Webber with Jimmy Perry and David Croft, p164
Series Eight
Ring Dem Bells
1. David Croft, in conversation with Graham McCann, 23rd May 2000, Dad's Army: The Story of a Classic Television Show, p 196, ISBN 1-84-115-309-5
2. Jimmy Perry, in conversation with Graham McCann, 27th August 2000, Dad's Army: The Story of a Classic Television Show, p 197, ISBN 1-84-115-309-5
3. Ian Lavender, Dad's Army: A Celebration, p131
When You've Got to Go
4. Freddie Earlle, Dad's Army: A Celebration, p131
Is There Still Honey For Tea?

5. Jo Austin, The Complete A-Z of Dad's Army, Richard Webber with Jimmy Perry and David Croft, p21

Come In, Your Time Is Up

6. Jo Austin, The Complete A-Z of Dad's Army, Richard Webber with Jimmy Perry and David Croft, p21

7. Peter Day, Dad's Army: A Celebration, p135

High Finance

8. Hilda Fenemore, Dad's Army: A Celebration, p137

The Face on the Poster

9. BBC Audience Report Extracts, The Complete A-Z of Dad's Army, Richard Webber with Jimmy Perry and David Croft, p19

The Christmas Specials

1. Ian Lavender, in conversation with Graham McCann, 29th May 2000, Dad's Army: The Story of a Classic Television Show, p 197, ISBN 1-84-115-309-5

2. Bill Cotton, The BBC as an Entertainer, p 49

Series Nine

Wake-Up Walmington

1. Joan Le Mesurier, Lady Don't Fall Backwards, p184-185

2. David Croft, in conversation with Graham McCann, 23rd May 2000, Dad's Army: The Story of a Classic Television Show, p206, ISBN 1-84-115-309-5

The Making of Private Pike

3. Jean Gilpin, The Complete A-Z of Dad's Army, Richard Webber with Jimmy Perry and David Croft, p133

Knights of Madness

4. Bill Pertwee, Dad's Army: A Celebration, p162
The Miser's Hoard
5. Colin Bean, Dad's Army: A Celebration, p144
Number Engaged
6. Ian Lavender, Dad's Army: A Celebration, p145
Never Too Old
7. Pamela Cundell, Dad's Army: A Celebration, p146
8. Susie Belbin, The Complete A-Z of Dad's Army, Richard Webber with Jimmy Perry and David Croft, p28
9. BBC Audience Report Extracts, The Complete A-Z of Dad's Army, Richard Webber with Jimmy Perry and David Croft, p19

The Movie
1. David Croft, Dad's Army: A Celebration, p168
2. Andrew Gardiner, Dad's Army: A Celebration, p168
3. Film review in the Daily Express, dated 15th March 1971 according to The Complete A-Z of Dad's Army, Richard Webber with Jimmy Perry and David Croft, p71
4. Alexander Walker, film review in the Evening Standard, dated 17th March 1971 according to The Complete A-Z of Dad's Army, Richard Webber with Jimmy Perry and David Croft, p71
5. Jimmy Perry, The Complete A-Z of Dad's Army, Richard Webber with Jimmy Perry and David Croft, p73

The Radio Series
1. Harold Snoad, Dad's Army: A Celebration, p181
2. Ian Lavender, Dad's Army: A Celebration, p182

The Stage Show

1 and 2. Kevin Easton, writing in the 9th September 1975 of The Hartlepool Mail, quoted in The Complete A-Z of Dad's Army, Richard Webber with Jimmy Perry and David Croft, p203

Whatever Happened to the missing episodes of Dad's Army?

1. David Croft, June 2001, the BBC Archive Treasure Hunt website
http://www.bbc.co.uk/cult/treasurehunt/finds/dadsarmy.shtml

Also Available:

The Lurking ISBN: 978-1999865955

Rob is a hopeless loser in the game of life. With work, his relationship with his long suffering girlfriend Claire, with everything in general. Tonight he will change for the better, make a fresh start by taking it to the next step and propose to her.

But fate has other intentions.

After an accident that leaves him stranded, Rob takes shelter in an abandoned aircraft hangar and soon discovers that he is not alone. There is something lurk- ing in the darkness, taunting him, haunting his every movement.

Soon trapped in a living nightmare, Rob must learn the terrible truth of his tormentor and escape its clutches before it is too late...

Available from all good bookshops.

Captain Random and the Rainbow Chasers

ISBN: 978-1999865962

The Zedron Flux is the most powerful energy source in the known cosmos. In the right hands, it has the power to end all suffering. In the wrong hands, it could bring an end to all things. After a narrow escape from an army of ancient gods, Random, Anji, Jake and Skate-board crash land on the beautiful planet of Spectronia, a paradise of colour and home to a peaceful race ruled by the elegant Solenia and her Valkyries. Upon recovering they ally themselves with a band of explorers led by Lon, who is hell bent on finding the Flux after it was taken from his grasp by a rival archaeologist. But nothing for the crew of the Venus II is ever simple. As the quest continues, danger is not far away and, as the Flux gets closer and closer, Random is left with a terri-ble choice that will have major consequences, not just for him and his friends, but for the entire universe...

Available from all good bookshops.

Captain Random and the Eater of Souls

ISBN: 978-1999865931

Following their explosive battle with the Sandman, and struggling to come to terms with life out in space, the crew of the Venus II decide to throw themselves into a spot of retail therapy on the friendly planet of Genocia.

But almost as soon as they arrive, they realise that this new world is not all that it seems. Outside the splendour and vast wealth of the Grand Chamber lies a neglected wasteland where terror lurks within the poisonous gloom whilst deep within the bowels of the planet lies a terrible secret.

At the very heart of it all is the ruthless leader Consula, whose designs for supremacy mean ultimate devastation to all of those who oppose her. But the greed and corruption of the government is nothing compared to what lurks in the shadows for Random and his friends. Separated and fighting for their lives, Random, Anji, Jake and Skateboard must work quickly to save the lives of the prisoners stuck in the mines deep below the surface, where death is very close by...

What is the Soul Destroyer? What part does it play in Consula's diabolical plan? Will Anji ever see her friends again? One thing is for sure. The Eater of Souls is hungry...

Captain Random vs the Sandman

ISBN: 978-1999865924

Rodas. The scorned planet of Ursa-17. Ravaged by centuries of war between two factions, the villainous Sapphire Regime and the ruthless Crimson Empire. The reason behind the conflict of red and blue? The people of Rodas were unable to make the colour purple.
Until one day, when two rebels, one from either side, combine to create the ultimate warrior. A being who could put an end to the battle of ages and bring peace to the volatile planet of Rodas once and for all.

There is one tiny drawback. The warrior is a boy.

***** Fantastic book, enjoyed every part of it!
Highly recommend it for Dr Who/Red Dwarf/Rick and Morty fans.

***** Hayden Gribble's writing is witty and clever with an essence of Douglas Adams in there too. Would thoroughly recommend for anyone with an adventurous spirit.

***** I really enjoyed it. I can well imagine Kids getting swept along with the interstellar, action packed adventure and chuckling along with all the funny scenarios and characters and wanting to know just what happens.

Available from all good bookshops.

Child Out of Time: Growing Up With Doctor Who in the Wilderness Years

ISBN: 978-1999865900

For 26 years, DOCTOR WHO was a British institution, capturing the imaginations of generations of children. But then, in 1989, it was cancelled. The Doctor and his on-screen adventures were no more. There was no longer a hero, a champion for the outcasts who struggled to fit in. It was as though he had walked into his TARDIS and set his controls for dematerialisation, never to return: a whole generation lost to the powers of Science Fiction's greatest creation. It was in this Doctor-less world that I grew up. This is the story of how one little boy would try to find the Doctor in any way, shape or form and the obstacles he faced in doing so. This is the story of growing up without Doctor Who in the Wilderness Years...and how I lived through it.

***** An engaging and enjoyable insight into a fan discovering Doctor Who during the wilderness years

***** A very passionate account of one fans discovery of the greatest science fiction of all time.

**** Perfect for fans of the Doctor in any of his or her forms.

Available from all good bookshops.

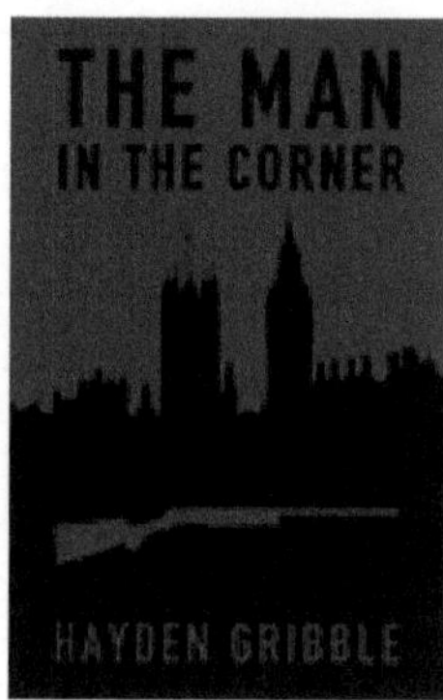

The Man In The Corner

ISBN: 978-1500549862

A mysterious assassin wants out of his life as a cold and ruthless killer but must face one last assignment before he flicks the escape switch. As he closes in on the biggest criminal mind in the country, he is reminded of what he left behind and how getting closer to the light at the end of the tunnel might also reunite him with a person from his long and distant past. Who is the Big Chief? Why must he be brought down and will it be the end, not just for himself and his superior, but also to the only link to the life he has lost.

***** An exciting book! Whilst focusing on the dark story of an unnamed man, you find yourself sucked into a city of criminals. The chapters contain their own stories which really draw you in and make you want to read more. Great read! The only negative is that it was over too fast.

***** Brilliant read. Did not want to put the book down.

*** This book is a great little read about the path to redemption; not too long, in fact in some places I found myself wishing it might go on a little longer. It's got a sort of style all its own.

Available from all good bookshops.

Milton Keynes UK
Ingram Content Group UK Ltd.
UKHW020624100424
440866UK00013B/256